Engaging Modernity

WOMEN IN AFRICA AND THE DIASPORA

Series Editors

STANLIE JAMES
AILI MARI TRIPP

Engaging Modernity

Muslim Women and the Politics of Agency in Postcolonial Niger

Ousseina D. Alidou

The University of Wisconsin Press

The University of Wisconsin Press
1930 Monroe Street, 3rd Floor
Madison, Wisconsin 53711-2059
uwpress.wisc.edu

3 Henrietta Street
London WC2E 8LU, England
eurospanbookstore.com

Printed in the United States of America

Library of Congress Cataloging-in-Publication Data
Alidou, Ousseina.
Engaging modernity: Muslim women and the politics of
agency in postcolonial Niger / Ousseina D. Alidou.
p. cm.—(Women in Africa and the diaspora)
Includes bibliographical references and index.
ISBN 0-299-21210-6 (cloth: alk. paper)
1. Muslim women—Niger. 2. Muslim women—Education—Niger.
3. Women in politics—Niger. 4. Women in Islam—Niger.
5. Women and war—Niger. 6. Women—Niger—Social conditions—21st century.
7. Sex role—Niger. I. Title. II. Series.
HQ1812.A45 2005
305.48′697′0966909049—dc22 2005005434

ISBN 978-0-299-21214-8 (pbk.: alk. paper)

This book was published with the support of Rutgers,
the State University of New Jersey.

For my two mothers:

My late, beloved Grandmother,
HAJIYA KANI BOUKARI SIDIBÉ
(May her soul rest in peace)

and
SOEUR MICHELINE GODBOUT
(Notre Dame du Perpétual Secours, Saint Damien, Québec)

With Love and Gratitude

Contents

Part 1: Women, Education, and Epistemological Traditions

Part 2: Women, Folklore, and Performative Identities

Illustrations

Tables

Acknowledgments

I completed writing this book in a period of tense and polarized global politics in which any reference to Islam or Muslims raised wary eyebrows, sadly even in academic circles. Yet it is precisely in this geopolitical climate that a study such as this, which seeks to bring out the complexities of the Islamic experience, has become crucial. Though focused on one country, the Republic of Niger has long been intimately connected with broader political trends in the rest of the Muslim world. And the recent false accusation that it supplied uranium to Iraq propelled it to new levels of global prominence. Thus, my work and the title of the book stand as they are at this historical juncture without being embedded within a negative global politics that makes religious belligerence its field of action. The fields of linguistics and social theory used in this study—to deconstruct the relationship between gender (oral or material) discourse(s) and power as tied to the lived experiences of contemporary Muslim women of the city in Niamey—provide an excellent framework to meet the academic challenge posed by the "new" political dispensation, especially as it relates to the lives of women.

This work would not have been possible without the support and intellectual generosity of a number of people. Prominent among these are the many Nigerien women—too many, in fact, to mention by name—who participated in this research by allowing me to be part of their lives during the research process and by agreeing to let me subject their stories, intertwined with my own, to the interpretive exercise based on my scholastic training in the humanities and social sciences. My sincerest gratitude to each one of them for their contributions. Challenging me in my own academic assumptions, they led me to engage reflexively with my own location as a Nigerien woman (like themselves) who has benefited and continues to benefit from the intellectual and material privileges accorded to me by my academic profession.

The fieldwork itself gained immensely from the investigative skills of my research assistant, Bashar Mahamane. His enthusiasm about the topic of the research and his unfailing support throughout the years of the fieldwork were indispensable to the success of the project. Furthermore, his background as a high school graduate of Franco-Arab *medersa,* and of Abdou Moumouni University Law School and his training in film studies were a formidable resource for the fieldwork. To him I owe a monumental debt of gratitude. I am also indebted to Fatouma Alidou who assisted me in numerous occasions to decipher certain texts and translate shifts in meaning of the language of the new Islamist women I interviewed, for her availability to provide information about new women's mosque groups and their philosophical orientations and for her untiring willingness to establish contacts for me in these circles. Similarly, I would like to thank Sheikh Alafia Teke for linking me to the network of organizations and individuals who have played a pivotal role in the promotion of Arabic and Islamic studies and business.

By 1997, I had begun to discuss my project with some of my most esteemed colleagues and friends who kept reminding me that I must present the full ethnographic analysis of the situation of Muslim women in the era of the imposition of Structural Adjustment Programs (SAPs) and the struggle for democratization in a coherent book. One of these cherished colleagues and critics is my partner, Alamin Mazrui, with whom I share not only a background in linguistics, but also a similar background as a Western-educated Muslim of Africa. Though our cultural and professional areas of research converge and diverge, his unfailing constructive critique of my work has been a tremendous intellectual inspiration. Thus, if I may borrow his mother-tongue, Kiswahili: "Nashukuru sana mpenzi wangu." I am also indebted to my fellow linguist and twin-sister Hassana Alidou whose comments assisted me in revising earlier versions of chapter 2, which focuses on women and education in Niger.

I used to frown at the phrase "sisterhood is global" given the reality of the sisterly hegemony within global sisterhood, especially in North-South relations. The literature addressing this issue is abundant. Many times, familial, local and global sisters in social movements walk into relationships with a sense of "caution." However, my friendship with Professor Silvia Federici of Hofstra University which began in 1994 has been one of the most fulfilling sisterly experiences in my adult life. I have the deepest gratitude to her for the love, and openness that led me to a deeper appreciation of the various manifestations of global women's sociopolitical movements across time and space. In many ways, Silvia's belief in me and her inspiring men torship gave me the strength to work diligently to complete this book. She kept reminding me that I must not only tell her the stories of grassroot Muslim women's social activism against militarism and SAPs in Niger, but must write and finish the book as soon as possible. I thank her for the intellectual nourishment and for making her place a home for me at any time. Silvia read all the parts of the manuscript and provided insightful comments that helped me to reshape the final version. I am also grateful to Professor George Caffentzis whose calmness and generosity sustained me during moments of self-doubt. I owe him a profound gratitude for the moral support. George also created opportunities at his Southern Maine University campus and at other venues for me to present my work beyond my familiar Africanist circles. The comparative perspectives treated in these venues that he helped organize on other Islamic cultures or communities struggling against old and new hegemonic local and international structures have been an eye opener for me in my analysis of how the struggles of the Muslim women I cover in this book fit within this global picture.

More than any specialist in the field, perhaps, Professor Beverly Mack of Kansas University made the most thorough reading of an earlier version of this manuscript. As a literary specialist with expertise on the interplay between verbal arts, literacy and gender in Muslim societies of the Sahel, her comments were most valuable in clarifying many areas of my work. My deepest appreciation for her contributions. Many thanks also go to Professor Clifford Alden Hill of Columbia University for his abiding disposition to discuss my work in light of the intricacies of literacy acquisition and functions in Muslim Africa and Asia, and more particularly in Nigerien cultures. Our discussions on literacy theories provided me with ways of addressing the complexities of the streams of oralities and literacies in Nigerien societies and the methodological predicament with which linguists and other social scientists are faced when they attempt to integrate cultural meaning and social functions in an ethnographic account. I am also thankful to his wife, novelist Professor Kathleen Hill, for her warm hospitality during my visit to their home in New York and for her memorable visit to my African literature class at Rutgers University. *Na gode.*

Chapter 6 of the book was initially inspired by a workshop on "Women and War in Africa" held in Dakar, Senegal, in 1998. The forum played a key role in broadening my interest in Nigerien women's identities beyond situations of relative peace. In this regard, I owe special thanks to Professor Meredith Turshen of Rutgers University for inviting me to the workshop and for reading and commenting on an earlier version of my essay on women and war in Niger. The encouragement and constructive comments of Professor Robert Charlick of Cleveland State University and his willingness to share his expertise on Niger's political culture from independence to the present have also been very helpful for the development of this particular chapter on women and war in Niger. In addition, he and his wife Julie were a wonderful host family to me throughout my stay in Cleveland. To both of them I say, *Na gode.*

Also linked to the history of the same chapter 6 is Professor Kathy Rakowsky of the Ohio State University who created the first academic space for me in that institution to present my initial findings and welcomed me to the circle of academic women and social activists on campus working with Women in International Development (OSU-WID). A few years later at Rutgers University, Professor Barbara Cooper invited me to present a version of this chapter on "Women and War in Niger" in her graduate seminar on African Studies. She and her graduate students provided a wonderful opportunity for critical engagement with the piece and posed sharp questions that were very useful in assisting me to address certain aspects of my analysis that needed further clarification.

It was at a WID lecture at Ohio State University that I first met Professor Margaret Mills who presented a talk on the state of education and literacy among Afghan women a few years before the United States' war in Afghanistan against the Taliban. She took great interest in my work on Muslim women in Niger and welcomed me to discuss it with her, a memorable opportunity that I have cherished since. In the process, she shared with me her own work on Cinderella in the South-Asian Muslim world that motivated me a great deal in writing chapter 4, a version of which appeared in 2002 in volume 54 (3) of *Comparative Literature*. It was also at Ohio State University that I met Dr. Ruthmarie Mitsch, the managing editor of *Research in African Literatures,* who provided tremendous editorial input in the final stages of the manuscript. I am very thankful to her. My gratitude goes to Dr. Stephanie Shaw from Ohio State University History Department for extending her friendship and unfailing mentorship to me throughout the years, especially at critical times of deep uncertainty.

The resurgent interest in the study of Islam and Islamic cultures in the United States and other western countries has stimulated many conferences on Islam in Africa in several U.S. universities. Invitation to these conferences provided me with opportunities to present earlier versions of various components of this book and to receive insightful comments that assisted me tremendously in their revisions. In this regard, I am particularly indebted to the following senior scholars: Professor Ali Mazrui and his team at the Institute of Global Cultural Studies at Binghamton University for inviting me to present my earlier work on "Women and the Politics of Islamic Identities" at a conference on Islam in Africa that metamorphosed into chapter 4; Professor Ann Dunbar and Professor Lesch who were members of my panel at the same conference and whose insightful comments on my presentation showed me ways of improving it; Professor Babarba C. Lewis for extending an invitation to me to present at the 2003 Islam in Africa conference she convened at Rutgers University and Professor Carolyn Brown for her insistence that I present not only at the conference's K–12 teachers' workshop on the place of Arabic and Islam in Sub-Saharan Africa, but also that I take this opportunity to present my work on Muslim women in Niger—that conference also gave me the opportunity to meet great colleagues in the U.S. and elsewhere working on similar subjects in various parts of Africa whose constructive comments and suggestions have been beneficial in the rewriting of the earlier versions of chapter 2 and chapter 4; and Professor Margot Badran of the Institute of Islamic Thought in Africa (ISITA) at Northwestern University for inviting me to the symposium on "Gender and Islam in Africa" where I presented an earlier version of chapter 2, which deals with Muslim women's social biography and marginality. My deep appreciation to Professor Badran also for her willingness to read other material covered in chapter 3 on women and education, and for her availability to discuss my work as well as for her encouragement.

Professor Renee Larrier of Rutgers University has been an unfailing mentor with regard to my academic progress in research and scholarship. Her work on the poetics and politics of Black women's words and arts in the francophone world has been quite influential in broadening my views on how to approach Nigerien Muslim women's (oral and material) discourses. I cannot thank her enough for her support. My special thanks to her and her students also for inviting me to her class in the French Department at Rutgers University to present parts of what came to constitute chapter 3 on women and performance in Niger. The rewriting of chapter 3 has also benefited from the insightful comments of Professor Ann Biersteker, Professor Sandra Sanneh, and their graduate students at their seminar in African Studies at Yale University where I shared with them some of my thoughts on women, performance, and politics in Niger. I thank them all.

It is a special blessing to feel welcomed at one's own institution and I am very grateful for the wonderful colleagues who have made my stay at Rutgers University such a rewarding experience. But most of all I would like to acknowledge the invaluable social and academic friendship of Professors Abena Busia, Richard Schroeder, Carolyn A. Brown, Richard Serrano, Allen Howard, Walton Johnson, Akinlabi Akinlabi, Dorothy Hodgson, Phillip Rothwell, and Cesar Braggo Pinto. Both Professors Abena Busia and Carolyn Brown provided a comfortable intellectual space for me and made their houses available to me at all time. I am deeply grateful to them. My special thanks to my friends Ingrid Peterson and Aziz Jeng for their friendship and encouragement during the writing this book in New Brunswick.

I could not have handled the juggling between teaching and the administration of the African languages and literature program while writing this book without the encouragement of supportive chairs of my department, Dr. Leonard Bethel and Dr. Kim Butler, and the spiritual friendship of two most gracious administrative staff members of the Department of Africana Studies, Ms. Barbara Mitchell and Ms. Janice Gray. My most gracious gratitude also goes to Dean Barry Qualls, Dean Douglas Blair, Dean Ed Rhodes, and Executive Dean Holly Smith for their tremendous support of my teaching and scholarship and for granting me timely sabbatical leave to complete the writing of this book.

The preparation of this work has also benefited from a visiting faculty fellowship in Germany from the Department of Cultural Studies at the University of Lüneburg and a visiting scholar's fellowship from the Department of Linguistics and African Studies at the University of Hamburg. I wish to thank all the colleagues in Germany who created the environment and time for me to discuss my work with them and for their insightful comments. I wish to particularly thank Ms. Julia Patrut, Dr. Alexandre Patrut, and Dr. Ulrich Loeke at the University of Lüneburg, and Professor Joe McIntyre, Professor Gehardt Luwig, Professor Ulmann, and Louis Henry Seukwa and his wife Kirsten Encke at the University of Hamburg, who were wonderful colleagues and friends. Other friends who also extended their hospitality to me during my stay in Germany included Senfo Tonkam, Tareq and Rabi Diallo. I thank them all.

Ultimately, this book is dedicated to my two mothers, my beloved belated grandmother Hajiya Kani Sidibé, a devoted Muslim woman, and Sister Micheline Godbout, a Catholic nun of Notre Dame du Perpétual Secours order of Saint Damien, Québec (Canada), who mothered me and my siblings when a premature death took my biological mother who I have known only in pictures and dreams. I am forever grateful to them for teaching us about human decency, love, and care beyond boundaries. I also extend special gratitude to my beloved uncle, Alhaji Mahamane Wadai Sidibé, for taking up the role of fathering us with genuine love after the premature passing of my beloved father. To all my relatives in Niger, Columbus, California, Kenya, and Binghamton, I extend my deep appreciation for all their moral and material support throughout the process of writing this book. And to my big sister Pauline Mazrui, my most grateful appreciation for being there whenever I needed her.

Last but not least, to my young sisters and daughters, Nafi Cissé and Nuwayla Alamin Mazrui, and my beloved son, Halirou Cissé, thanks for being so understanding when I became so consumed by this book project and for your unconditional love. I hope reading the pages of this book will bring you to a further understanding of why obstacles and struggles could not make me give up writing this book. I also hope such endurance learnt from my mothers will bring us closer together and that after you complete reading you will see how Muslim women's agency works! I love you all.

Engaging Modernity

Introduction

Background to the Study

This book explores the interplay between Muslim women and agency in the Republic of Niger as shaped by religion, ethnicity, class, schooling, and citizenship. Drawing on biographical and sociological data, these intersections of vectors of agency are examined in four domains: political Islam, education, popular culture, and war and its aftermath. Hitherto dominated by men, these domains form areas in which Muslim women have begun to inscribe their agencies in a manner that is more visible than in any other sphere of society. The context of this study is principally urban and its temporal frame is the so-called democratization era that began in the early 1990s. A central theme is how Muslim women have seized the space opened up by the momentum of democratization to use their agency in the public and private spheres to inscribe a woman's dimension in the transformations taking place in the nation during this period. The process has sometimes involved the appropriation and recrafting of characteristics of identity traditionally associated with the male "other" and their mobilization toward particular women-centered ends.

I employ the concept of agency to refer to a wide range of conscious actions and initiatives, large and small, that Muslim women in Niger (individually or collectively) have engaged in, as a response to their conditions of subordination emanating from multiple legacies—indigenous traditions, the Western impact, and Islam. This notion of agency that guides my analysis of Muslim women's experiences throughout this book is in line with Saba Mahmood's definition of agency, which is understood *not* as a synonym "for resistance to relations of domination, but a capacity for action that historically specific relations of subordination enable and create. . . . Agency, in this form of analysis, is understood as a capacity to realize one's own interest against the weight of customs, tradition, transcendental will, or other obstacles (whether individual or collective). Thus, the humanistic desire for autonomy and self-expression constitute a substrate, the slumbering ember that can spark to flame in the form of an act of resistance when conditions permit" (Mahmood 2001, 203–6).

My contention, then, is that agency cannot be apprehended outside the realm of possibilities—material or otherwise—available to individuals or communities in the larger society. To use Mahmood's words, it takes place "when conditions permit." As a result, it can have various manifestations in both the secular and religious spaces, and may range in ideology from the conservative to the radical. Nor is it unusual, as demonstrated in this book, for agency to be exercised in overlapping boundaries of identity as defined by ethnicity, class, and political affiliations.

What we see from these different expressions of agency is an emerging, though still diffuse, understanding of what modernity means for Muslim women in Niger. Kwame Gyekye (1997) explains that the idea and substance of modernity have tended to be so inextricably linked to the history and influence of the West, that the possibility of a modernity without Westernism is often considered an absurdity. Against this Eurocentric and totalizing sense of modernity—whose historical legitimation has included enslavement, colonialism, and neocolonialism (Gilroy 1993, 46–50)—several scholars have presented empirical studies that demonstrate the vibrancy of alternative articulations of modernity across and within cultures (Ong 1997). Some of these scholars consider these alternative modernities as derivative of Western modernity (Giddens 1990; Ivy 1995), others as reactive to it (Simone 1994), and others still as modes of expressions that, even when they incorporate the global, have their own independent local lives (Abu-Lughod 1998; Ong 1990, 1992, and 1997; Appadurai 1990 and 1996: 4; Pigg 1996; Rofel 1999; Bernal 1994; and Kane 2003). Trends and developments in postcolonial African societies fall within the ambit of these varied discourses on modernity.

In spite of their theoretical differences, however, these "alternativists" are in agreement that the phenomenon of modernity itself is plural and multidirectional (Schein 1999; Appadurai 1996; Comaroff and Comaroff 1993). The experiences of Muslim women explored in this book certainly confirm these plural and nuanced conceptions of modernity. In fact, within the national space of Niger, there are several competing modernities, from the Western mode to the Islamicist brand. Furthermore, within these varieties of modernity, there is the inscription of a phenomenon that is peculiarly feminine, suggesting distinctive Muslim women's local modernities. It would be misleading, therefore, to rush to the conclusion that Islamicist modernity in Niger Republic, for example, is experienced in the same manner by Muslim men and Muslim women. And almost invariably the women have taken advantage of the malleability of "tradition" (including the religious and the secular) to craft their modernity.

The impulse that led to the writing of this book was born in 1993 when I was doing my dissertation fieldwork on a totally different area of linguistics, syllable and prosodic structures in West African languages. It evolved out of what I witnessed as the social transformations of the urban landscape of Niamey (the capital of the Republic of Niger) through various representations and activities of women in the private and public spheres—in households, at the market, at the tailor shops, at weddings, at health centers, in schools, and in administrative offices—shifts that seemed to encode great cultural and political significations.

These observations, quite naturally, led me to research the literature on Muslim women. While there is a large body of literature on the subject of Muslim women, I was dismayed by the scarcity of scholarly publications on Muslim women in regions of Africa that are "ethnically" not Arab-dominated. Study after study claiming to look at the experiences of women in the Islamic world was, in fact, confined to the Arabic and Asiatic regions. There is a scarcity of scholarly studies conducted by Muslim scholars or non-Muslim scholars of the West that focus on Muslim women of the so-called "sub-Saharan" African regions.

Muslim women scholars have, of course, contributed to this reproduction of the colonial division between Islamic societies of sub-Saharan Africa and those of the rest of the Muslim world. When they write comparatively about women's issues in Islamic societies, their analyses often fall short of including Muslim women of "sub-Saharan" Africa in spite of the common nodes of a shared historical heritage. When attempts to include sub-Saharan Africa are made at all, they tend to stop at Arabized entities like the Sudan and Mauritania. For example, a country like Niger, with more than 80 percent of its geographical space situated in the Sahara Desert and constituting a historical region of trans-Saharan trade that led to (and continues to lead to) linguistic, cultural, and ethnic convergences between populations of the Sudanic Belt (the southern fringes and south of the Sahara) and those of the so-called North Africa and the Mediterranean, must make us rethink the criteria for its classification as "sub-Saharan" Africa (Abu Manga 1986 and 1999; Adamou 2002; Hamani 1989; Hunwick and Powell 2002). The overwhelming majority of the population of the western Sudanic Belt, which includes countries such as Niger, Mali, Senegal, and Burkina Faso, is Muslim. For many centuries this region has been a source of labor migration to North Africa, thus suggesting constant interactions and mutual sociocultural, religious, economic, and political influences. Part of the explanation for this division was the color complex that developed in the Arab societies located within the African continent. In this regard, Nawal El Saadawi comments: "Our eyes and our faces were always turned towards the Mediterranean, Europe and America, our backs towards Africa, away from ourselves. When one turns one's back on one's self, one is ashamed of one's own brown or black skin and tries to hide with white make-up, how can one know oneself?" (El Saadawi 1991, 171).

An equally important explanation is political, and can be traced to the emergence of a particular brand of Arab nationalism, itself a byproduct of the European colonial legacy. This is the phenomenon that Anouar Majid has captured incisively:

> Arab nationalism . . . has invented a new global identity whose effect was to sever the Arabic-speaking peoples that include Black Africa. As a secular European concept, nationalism was introduced to the land of Islam during its phase of political decay and was part of a deliberate strategy to weaken Muslims and other colonized peoples. Through powerful propaganda mechanisms during the twentieth century, nationalism became an inextricable part of the identity of Arabic-speaking peoples. Black Muslims and the Turks, thus, became the Arabs' Other in what has been termed the "postcolonial" world, as if the scourge of forced dependency and Orientalism have magically removed the political independence, "Post-al" theories. (Majid 2000, 20)

Thus, prominent Muslim women ended up embracing an Arab nationalism that is antithetical to the Islamic concept of Muslim *Umma*, seeing the religion or the cultural face of the religion as specifically constitutive of Arab identity rather than of a wider transnational Muslim identity.

The combination of the color complex alluded to by Nawal El Saadawi and the political hegemony of Arab nationalism pointed out by Anouar Majid thus led many Muslim women writers (in North Africa, the Middle East, and Asia) to continue marginalizing black African Muslim women's experiences even though their works are comparative in perspective. This omission is committed repeatedly in spite of the demographic magnitude of black Muslims in sub-Saharan Africa—the number of Muslims in Nigeria alone, for example, surpasses that of Muslims in the largest Arab nation, Egypt—and in spite of the continuing transnationalism between the two regions of Africa and between sub-Saharan Africa and the rest of the Muslim world. For me, then, this marginalization of the black Muslim woman became an added motive for doing this research.

There are, of course, important and pioneering works on African Muslim women in the specific Sahelien country of my focus, even though these are extremely few. These have included, for example, Fatouma Agnès Diarra's *Femmes africaines en devenir: Les femmes Zarma du Niger,* which represents a pioneering work on Zarma women (1971); Barbara Cooper's *Marriage in Maradi: Gender and Culture in a Hausa Society in Niger, 1900–1989* (1997), which provides exciting historical insights into the experiences of Hausa women of the eastern region with regard to the institution of Muslim marriage; and Adeline Masquelier's *Prayer Has Spoiled Everything: Possession, Power, and Identity in an Islamic Town of Niger (Body, Commodity, Text)* (2001), which offers another powerful account of *Bori* (spirit possession) among another Hausa subgrouping called the Mauri (or Maouri or Mawri) of Dogondoutchi in southern Niger. A prominent and common thread of these fascinating studies is that they are all ethnic-bound, exploring the experiences of women within specific ethnic groups. Studies that have been transethnic and transnational, on the other hand, have often focused on a single dimension of women's lives. Hadiza Djibo's *La participation des femmes africaines à la vie politique: Les exemples du Sénégal et du Niger* (2001) is a thorough analysis of the similarities and differences in women's struggles to achieve strong voices and full participation in national politics in Senegal and Niger, while Abdou Hamani's *Les femmes et la politique au Niger* (2000) offers another interesting account of women's involvement in politics in Niger. In the field of oral literature and performance, Aissata Sidikou's *Recreating Words, Reshaping Worlds: The Verbal Art of Women from Niger, Mali and Senegal* (2001) is a brilliant comparative study of female *griottes* in the three Sahelian countries that share a great deal of common cultural heritage in spite of other areas of divergence. Amsou Maiga's *Analyse de la situation actuelle de la femme au Niger* (2001) is perhaps unique in that it is both multiethnic and multithematic, even though it is clearly intended to be a policy-oriented report. All these studies, to varying degrees, examine the impacts of Islam in shaping women's identities, even for the non-Muslim women in these predominantly Muslim countries and societies.

This study departs from these earlier works in two fundamental ways. First, its focus is transethnic and takes into account such important variables as class and political ideological background. Second, it is multidimensional, linking women's experiences in several domains at the same time. This intersectional approach (which looks at the subject of study across several domains and variables) is intended to minimize, if not avoid altogether, fragmenting Nigerien women's experiences. This approach also best explains the data I collected during my ethnographic fieldwork between 1994 and 2002.

Beyond Ethnicity: *Brassage Sahélien*

One of the factors that inspired me toward a transethnic approach is the fact of *brassage,* that is, ethnic and cultural blending. As much as the census record—itself a product of European colonial conceptions of African identities—has categorized the population into seemingly discrete ethnic and religious units, it masks and distorts the reality of ethnocultural dynamics and composition of the nation (Kimba 1997). "Hausaness," for example, which is said to cover about a half of the demographic map of the country, has always been a multiple and shifting identity. Within it are elements from various ethnoregional sources and, though regarded as essentially Islamic, its religious face has been equally inclusive of Hausa of other faiths (African traditional spiritualities and Christianity, whether Catholicism or Protestanism). Numerous people of Hausa origin are, for all practical purposes, regarded and see themselves as Zarma. The Mauri are an example of such a group that can claim to be both Hausa and Zarma, or a new ethnicity (Karimou 1977; Gado 1980). The people of Ader in Tahoua Department (southeastern and central Niger), Abzin in Zinder (in eastern Niger) and Agadez Departments (northern Niger), and Ingall in Agadez manifest a similar complexity at the intersection of Tuaregness, Hausaness, Fulaniness, or Zarmaness within the Saharan-Sahelien space. Yet, there are more obvious articulations of *brassage:* the Adarawa (from Ader), claim ties to both Hausa and Tuareg—as the saying in Hausa goes, *Ba'adare duk Buzu ne* (meaning any person of Ader is a Tuareg); the Damagarawa (from Zinder) are originally Kanuri-speaking people and have linguistically and culturally assimilated to the Hausa (Dunbar 1970); and the Isawaghan (from Ingall in Agadez)—whose native language Tasawaq is clearly a creole based on Songhay and Berber (Alidou 1988; Alidou and Ekkhard 2000)—claim historical ties to the old Songhay Empire of Kankan Mousa and to Arab-Berber ancestry. The popular dance song *Tigyedima* "Drum" by Abdoul Salam[1] in which he addresses the complexity of a man and his lover's identity is a great appraisal of both the scope and dynamism of Niger's cultural and ethnic *brassage.*

It is indeed true that the notion of an ethnic group in "purist" terms has been relatively new to the relational universe of the people of Niger of old and new cities, and its articulations in the modern nation-state are often linked to the opportunistic politics of power stimulated initially by European colonial agendas and carried over, subsequently, into the postcolonial dispensation. The average Nigerien, especially in the urban and in the semi-urban spaces, embodies the many-in-one and, depending on the context, can be simultaneously Tuareg, Fulani, Hausa, Zarma, and so forth without implying a crisis or a confusion of identities. Furthermore, in most Muslim family formations where polygamy is common, complex ethnicities for a single family must be expected for individuals within the family. For example, while children could share one ethnic thread through a fatherline, the same children of the same father could diverge on ethnicity through their motherline if their father's wives are of different ethnicities. Family ethnic *brassage* is a condition resulting from the predominance of Islam across ethnic groups in Niger, the government's appointment of civil servants in parts of the country that may differ from their original "ethnic" base, and other forms of rural-urban migration.

It is significant that Niger is located in the Sudanic Belt, a region that covers the entire area from Senegal in West Africa to the Red Sea in Northeast Africa, but more important, the Sahara Desert constitutes more than 80 percent of its territory. This area has a rich history and remarkable linguistic, cultural, and ethnic patterns of interactions with populations in the southern fringes of the Sahara, commonly referred to as the Sahel, as well as those of the central and northern fringes of the Sahara which are dominated by Arab and Berber populations. Just central and south of the Sahara desert, the Sudanic Belt (Sahelian region or western Sudan and the eastern Sudanic Belt) served for thousands of years as a link between the so-called sub-Saharan Africa and the worlds of the so-called North Africa and the Mediterranean. In this long period, the region has been a source of trade, religious interaction, and labor migration to North, East, and Atlantic parts of Africa, leading to multiple formations of diaspora communities that have continued to shape its complex identity (Abu Manga 1999, 1986, and 1985; Hiskett 1984; Hunwick and O'Fahey 1995; Yamba 1995). The works of Al-Amin Abu Manga (1999) and Yamba (1995) are fascinating analyses of the Arabized Hausa-Fulani populations in contemporary Sudan Republic, a country that is considered part of the Middle East. This complexity was later compounded by French and British colonial rules and their postcolonial aftermath (Miles 1994). Although both French and British colonialisms aimed to stabilize African populations in their conquered territories, they did not succeed. In fact, populations at the border of Niger and northern

Nigeria, for example, were crossing boundaries throughout the colonial period. For example, families in the "borderland" resisted colonial attempts to split them and continue to do so to the present day through creative mechanisms to subvert the legitimacy of these colonial demarcations of territories, a legacy that defines postcolonial national boundaries and citizenships. Clearly, then, *brassage* in Niger is a child of several millennia of sociocultural, political, and economic history in this wide region.

As could be expected, women have always had a critical place and role in this continuous fluidity of boundaries of identity, at both the personal and national levels. As long-distance traders, as students of religion, as spouses at home and in distant lands, as offspring of transethnic marriages, women have always been both products and agents in the configuration of *brassage* identities on the wider canvas of Sahelien social realities. But within Niger's patriarchal order, it is women's representations and identities that have been the subject of greatest contested control in the discourses of colonial, nationalist, reformist, and neocolonial forces of domination. For example, conversion to Islam brought about the concept of seclusion of women leading to a reconceptualization of the correlation between gender and space (private and public), but also gender roles and statuses in the new Islamized societies. For nomadic populations such as the Fulani and the Tuareg, which originally practiced monogamy, their conversion to Islam promoted polygyny and sedentarization. These two processes had significant implications for the marital status of Muslim Fulani and Tuareg women. European colonization also promoted a gender ideology that had severe consequences for women. For example, colonial institutions recognized only the legitimacy of the first wife and her children to claim inheritance in the case of her husband's death.[2] The rest of the wives and their offsprings were not cited as legitimate beneficiaries of the deceased polygamous man. Moreover, the colonial authorities were permeated with a European gender ideology of "man as breadwinner" that allowed them to see only men's labor, as opposed to women's labor, as wage-earning. Thus, this colonial ideology privileged the recruitment of Muslim men in the paid labor field, while Muslim women were defined as free homemakers. However, as demonstrated throughout this book, women's responses to these hegemonic constructions of themselves have been varied and have produced multiple subjectivities, ranging from those that are in conformity with the prevailing order to those in opposition to it. And within this range, we find other totally unpredictable manifestations of these women's responses to their representation as imagined by the hegemonic "other."

These readings of women's lives in *brassage* begin with my own personal and scholarly location as an African Muslim woman from a multiethnic lineage of Sahelien Niger. My formal educational training is rooted in both

Islamic and Western (francophone and Anglo-Saxon American) epistemologies, with the latter having assumed prominence in my life, as now I work in the United States as a black immigrant linguist at a prominent American university. This background essentially influences the dynamics of my cultural locations and the types of scholarly work in which I engage.

Niger: Postcolonial Developments

The transformations revealed through Muslim women's representations in the urban landscape that constitute the subject of this study are situated within a particular sociopolitical and economic climate that characterized the period. And it is to a description of this moment in the nation's history that we must now turn.

The location of this study, that is, the Republic of Niger, is a former French colony in central West Africa that obtained its independence from France on August 3, 1960. The nation is overwhelmingly Muslim (95 percent), with the remaining population being either followers of indigenous faiths (4 percent) or representing all denominations of Christianity (1 percent). Although the state is constitutionally secular, an Islamic ethos remains a powerful force in matters of policy formulation and implementation.

Niger's population is estimated at over 10 million inhabitants (according to the 1998 census figures). Its multiethnic composition includes the Hausa (50 percent), Zarma-Songhai (22.8 percent), Fulani (Fulbe) (10.4 percent), Kanuri (8.5 percent), Tuareg (3 percent), and Tubu (0.5 percent). The rest is comprised of a small host of ethnic minorities that include the Schwa-Arabs, the Gurmance, and the Buduma. Of this total population, about 50.4 percent are women, of whom 42 percent are between the ages of fifteen and forty-two. But as indicated earlier, these categories and figures totally ignore the reality of *brassage* in the nation.

Bearing in mind the difficulty of distinguishing between language and dialect, we find that in Niger there are as many local languages as there are ethnic groups. In addition, French has continued to serve as the official language of the state since the colonial days. There is also an increasing demand for classical Arabic, partly inspired by the rise of political Islam in the country since the early 1990s (Reynolds 1997, 129). For both of these transethnic languages, that is, French and classical Arabic, there is a clear gender disparity in their acquisition rates of literacy, with women having the least access.

The Period of the 1990s

After the country became independent in 1960, it enjoyed a period of civilian rule for almost fifteen years under the presidency of Diori Hamani. This early period was followed by successive military regimes from 1990 to 1994. The decade of the 1990s, however, opened with new internal as well as international Western pressures that forced the country to opt for a democratic multiparty system of government (Robinson 1994; Ibrahim and Niandou 1996). This political development has, of course, been an unstable one, with the shadow of the military still looming large. In spite of its instability, however, democracy *à la Niger* opened up fresh avenues for women's participation and choices in often unpredictable ways, some of which are explored in this book.

Although Niger is among the poorest countries of the world, it enjoyed periods of economic prosperity and social stability from the early 1970s to the mid-1980s due to the world market demand for its uranium. The economic gains from uranium mining were able to sustain a satisfactory public welfare system through state subsidization of public health, education, road infrastructure, and agriculture. But the state also used these resources to build up a strong repressive police and military force aimed at crushing dissident voices against the military regime.

That temporary economic stability also contributed to the consolidation of patriarchal power on both the religious and secular fronts. This developed through the creation of more job opportunities for men, enabling them to fulfill their sociocultural obligations as providers and heads of households. It is noteworthy that the ideology of men as breadwinners is a legacy of European gender ideology about work with wage outside the home that was appropriated by African educated male national policymakers in the independence and postindependence dispensation. While for Muslim societies in Niger, the man is required to feed, clothe, and shelter his wife according to customary Islamic family law, the same law does not prohibit the wife from earning money inside or outside the home. Men from the rural areas who were affected by declining farming due to drought or encroachment of uranium mining found jobs in urban centers. Former male farmers became laborers in road construction, trained laborers in mining companies, and domestic cooks and gardeners for European expatriates and national executives of mining companies. Many of these jobs came with social security and retirement benefits. Numerous technical schools—L'Ecole des Mines de l'Air (EMAIR) in Agadez and L'Ecole des Mines (EMIG)—intended to cater to the world market demand for uranium produced the national male graduates to serve this need (Meunier 2000, 133–54).

It is nonetheless true that the labor demands of the uranium economy also had the effect of creating training and job opportunities for women, though to a much lesser extent than for men. Furthermore, there was a noticeable increase in female enrollment in formal schools during the uranium boom era, even though the state did very little to implement the law on compulsory universal education for all children from the age of seven. Neither did it attempt to deter prevailing practices of forced premature marriage of girls, one of the leading obstacles to female education in Niger Republic (République of Niger 1995, 31; Hamani 2000).

By the mid-1980s, the collapse of the uranium market, followed by the IMF's Structural Adjustment Programs (SAPs), and shortly after by the devaluation of the currency of francophone Africa, the CFA, plunged the country into a devastating economic depression with severe sociopolitical and other consequences (Gervais 1997). Some of the negative consequences included the educational crisis characterized by student and teacher strikes followed by government repression and school closures over the years, juvenile delinquency, prostitution, and high unemployment rates that sometimes led to a high degree of the break-up of families.

As men began to lose their jobs, their cultural sense of masculinity—as male breadwinners—was also damaged. The unavailability of the male wage, fundamental for sustaining a patriarchal conception of the family, along with women's active struggles to create a material basis for themselves and their families, created a new societal crisis that led men and women alike to seek new ways to negotiate both gender and power relations not only within the private domains but also in the public spheres.

The convergence of globalization—which for women in Niger is synonymous with SAPs and their manifestations in the cultural and economic fabric of society—and political Islamicist movements precipitated by the 1990s democratization process led to the entrenchment of a gendered national development framework that excluded women from the centers of policy design and implementation altogether (Djibo 2001). As men continued to lose the economic means and opportunities that serve to define them as providers, as husbands and fathers, they embraced more and more misogynist conceptions of the "proper Muslim woman"—a religious housewife—based on a type of Islam that, in its cultural articulation, gives them a sense of masculinity and privilege to continue to define women in society. It is precisely with regard to this entrapment of Muslim women resulting from the legacies of patriarchal Westernism and Islamism that Fatouma Mounkaila comments: "Some Islamic propagandists and the French colonial regime have both proposed false cultural patterns: The Islamic dream of model woman, the forged image of an inactive Muslim woman in the panorama of Arabian Nights. But the European model is as false, since it is based on the wife of the colonial administrator, discharged of any occupation in the colonies, relieved of housework by a team of house boys, and whose sole concern is to cater for her own body and receive friends who are as idle as she" (Mounkaila 1995, 25).

Muslim women, however, responded and continue to respond to globalization's assault on the welfare of society at large and on women more specifically, and to patriarchy's attempt to control the symbolic meaning of Islam, in many diverse ways. These Muslim women's ways have often involved using the very tools that were expected to guarantee their subjugation to patriarchal, local, and global ideologies. In other words, Muslim women in Niger began to present multiple challenges to this masculinist stand by (re)defining their identities, sometimes in conformity with the status quo, sometimes against the expectations of the status quo, and at other times by crafting totally independent subversive identities in order to establish a sustainable material basis for themselves and the families they support as married or unmarried "real heads of households."

Enactment of Identity in the Urban Landscape

It is in this climate of tensions and seeming contradictions of the 1990s in Niamey that we witness the transformation of women's representations. First, there were the visible transformations of Muslim women's bodily appearances in the public sphere. These transformations were and continue to be noticeable in the new trends of Muslim women's dress fashions, ranging from the extreme of the Islamic veiling in *cador* (complete covering of the head and face), the *hijab* (covering of the head but not the face), and long dresses imported from the Arab and other Asian Islamic countries such as Dubai, Oman, Saudi Arabia, Malaysia, and Pakistan, to the other extreme inspired by Western-derived fashions, complete with colorful hair extension or wigs.

As I began to inquire about the meaning of these new women's dress discourses, I also discovered that there is an entire idiom that correlates with each representation and its essence. In popular understanding, most of those attracted to Western fashion are the young women who are referred to as *les chandelles* or *les souris d'hôtel* (the hotel mice) believed to include teenage students from middle to high school. Some of these were leading (and continue to lead) a life of prostitution targeting Western male expatriates. This phenomenon affects young females across ethnic and class background in the capital city of Niamey.

On the other hand, the *hijab* women ranged from the Islamist women by religious conviction to the *gabdi* women, "self-managed" (unmarried) women who may or may not be involved in prostitution while still living with the extended family—unlike the "traditional" prostitutes who live in private brothels. Like the Western-driven fashion, the new Islamic inspired *hijab* fashion also cuts across ethnic and class lines.

Furthermore, there were the rich *dames* or *madames* who represented the upper- and middle-class French- or English-educated women or who traveled to the Western metropolises such as Paris, Hamburg, New York, or Greensboro (called Little Niamey, I found out). These were easily identified by their expensive, Western-fashion designer jewelry (shiny earrings, necklaces), cosmetics (Fashion Fair, Revlon lipsticks, Estée Lauder fragrance), shoes and matching handbags.

The rich Muslim women also included the *Hajiyas* (meaning "pilgrims"), a title acquired regardless of whether or not they have gone to pilgrimage. In fact, the title is based on their lifestyles: their preference for expensive tie-dye *boubous* that must be long enough to sweep the dust to prove they can afford the dry-cleaning services and constant change of dress; their shiny necks, wrists, and four fingers all covered in gold jewelry; and their bodies exuding the scent of the most expensive burnt incenses (*turaren wuta* in Hausa or *duguu* in Zarma) mixed with other imported fragrances.

But the urban landscape of Niamey was also visibly transformed by the phenomenon of the barely dressed women beggars, *almajirrai* (singular *almajira*), who moved in exodus from rural areas devastated by famine and drought and settled with their numerous malnourished infants, at major traffic light intersections, to the discomfort of the local and foreign bourgeoisie who were quick to roll up their car windows to prevent the intrusion of the hands that reminded them of the poverty of the place and the problematics of their own comfort. These poorly dressed Muslim women beggars and their children could also be seen at public functions where the invited guests were busy calling for the guards to chase away these intruders who disturbed the happy, festive ambiance by fighting over leftover food. As the guests summoned the security guards to protect them, one could hear in the Hausa language, "*Ku ga maras kumnya can . . . 'yen yunwa . . . ku ji su*" (Have you seen these shameless . . . the hungry ones . . . look at them). For the Zarma speakers, their disdain for the poor was similarly expressed: "*Wa gunan day . . . harayze . . . Wa koy fun boray gaa*" (Look at them . . . hungry ones . . . stay away from people). This reaction against the poor was vented through the presumed understanding of shame in publicly exhibiting one's desire for food in both Hausa and Zarma cultures. However, I read the discomfort of the urban upper and middle class as a reflection of dwindling empathy with the poor, especially with those rural citizens forced into a life of urban squatting.

Up to the mid-1980s, the well-to-do Muslims, especially Muslim women, welcomed beggars to share the family meals. When a Muslim homemaker used to overhear a beggar chanting for alms, she used to pray that the beggar would stop by her house to take the leftover food. If the beggar did not stop by her house, a child was sent out to go and look for the beggar. This empathy with the beggar was framed within an Islamic notion of *sadaka* (giving alms), which brings more blessings to the giver and to some beloved deceased person on whose behalf the offering was made.

However, the tradition of *sadaka* began to be altered, initially by the state in the early 1980s as the regime of the now deceased General Seyni Kountché began to feel the pressure of massive rural exodus from drought- and famine-affected areas such as Ouallam and the northern nomadic zones (Agadez and Tahoua). One of the laws established by the state at this time prohibited urban families from sheltering "foreigners/ strangers" for "reasons of state security" and required that any visitor to the family who was not kin be reported to the ministry of interior. The latter would then make arrangements for the deportation of the individual to his/her hometown or "native" village.

Since *sadaka* in the form of sheltering nonkin members in need had now been criminalized by the state, the urban well to do, trying to spare themselves the brutal harassment of an autocratic military regime, opted to obey a law that had instituted a culture of disengagement between urban citizens and their disenfranchised rural compatriots (Alidou and Alidou 1988). As the economic austerity drew the entire nation into the turmoil of the 1990s, the urban populations, now also affected to varying degrees by the escalating economic disparities between classes, embraced the ideology of "apartheid" initiated by the state as a mechanism to protect the limited resources at their disposal and to mask their own insecurities and struggles in this uncertain, rapidly changing economic, political, and cultural climate.

In the meantime, the news bulletins of the country's television and radio stations were often followed by announcements of *soirées culturelles* (cultural nights) organized by various associations of middle and high school students. These *soirées culturelles*, held in the midst of strikes and school shutdowns, focused on drama, ballets, dance, and, even more prominently, fashion show performances. The main audiences were the students themselves, some of their teachers, local male friends, and Westerners (most of whom were working in "development" NGOs, as seen from the license plates of their cars or were tourist residents at the hotels). The main entertainment space was situated on the main route on which the hotels are located. The route stretches from the old Hotel Rivoli at the center of the city through Hotel Terminus and curves down to the night club *Ize Gani* "Spoiled Child," at the bank of the Niger River. This area became the new nightly refuge of teenage male and female students who resorted to prostitution with the aim of finding money to feed themselves and often to support their unemployed parents who could barely fulfill their roles as providers, or to achieve their educational aspirations by being taken as sex partners to Western countries. Thus, the Rivoli-*Ize Gani* axis, an old quarter of traditional prostitution in Niamey, was overtaken in the 1990s by teenage students-turned-prostitutes partly as a result of the collapse of the formal educational system, the state's failure to find alternative responses to the aspirations of the youth, and the assault of economic globalization on the already weakened social fabric.

From *Makaranta/Madarasa* Literacy to the Quest for Material Basis of Empowerment

Another important transformation of the landscape in Niamey is in the educational domain. With the democratization of the political space, combined with the crisis of the mainstream French schools precipitated by conditions put forward by the World Bank and International Monetary Fund, Niger has experienced a resurgence of political Islam, which asserts its reality through the promotion of Islamic literacy, especially for women and girls. I conducted additional research on the neighborhood *madarasa* (or *makaranta*), that is, Qur'anic schools, sponsored by women and often led by women Qur'anic teachers that have visibly proliferated in the city of Niamey, in order to assess their sociopolitical and economic significance for women in the nation.[3] I also collected survey data on Islamic schools throughout the country from the Ministry of Education and conducted open-ended interviews with the executive administrators and teachers in the Islamic schools to solicit their views on the state of Islamic and secular education in Niger and its interplay with gender. This led me to visit Islamic schools designed for male students, such as the Madarasa Abu Bakr Al Sidiq of Kollo, and the *madarasa* catering to female students, such as the one run by Kadija in Quartier Wadata and that of Malama A'ishatu located near the main mosque built by Libya. My fieldwork in urban centers such as Niamey and Maradi as well as in rural towns of Kollo (a town near Niamey) and Dak'oro (in the northeast) focused on exploring the educational disparities for women in the two settings and their implications.

The *madarasa* has become a space that Nigerien women in urban centers are appropriating not only to advance their understanding of Islam for religious purposes, but more importantly to create a new female space for generating economic revenue and female solidarity. While in some cases, such as the school run by Malama A'ishatu, the school is confined within a family household, in numerous other cases, it is not.

The facilities of the *madarasa* may also include abandoned public schools located within neighborhoods that women's groups reappropriate or private properties rented by women for their female-based Qur'anic literacy classes. But after the lectures, the *madarasa,* the legitimized public

Islamic space for women, becomes a place of consultation *(shawara)* for social or political issues and for coming together for other female activities, such as trading in women's products like homemade incense, baby and female clothes, shoes, and other items. These extra-Qu'ranic activities serve as both social and economic investments, and are organized around the *ziyara* (a home visit with religious intent involving collective reading and recitation of the Qur'an) or *foyandi* (a more secular term in the Zarma language), biweekly or monthly friendship gatherings where women attend to each other's material needs. These may include collecting gifts for an expectant mother or for a bride-to-be, providing food, drinks, and money to a bereaved friend and her family, and providing emotional support to one another.

Because of the religious orientation of the *madarasa*, most Muslim men who would normally object to their wives and daughters attending female gatherings end up granting them permission to go to the schools. Some women are given rides by their husbands or given money for taxi fare to attend these *madarasa*.

The actual lecture programs for all the female *madarasa* I attended are scheduled from 8:00 a.m. to 10:00 a.m. so as to allow participants, most of whom are homemakers, to have plenty of time to fulfill their duties of catering to the family. The women who are employed in the public or private sectors attend *madarasa* on Saturday and Sunday mornings from 9:00 a.m. to noon. Saturday and Sunday sessions create the conditions for both Muslim women homemakers and those who are civil servants to interact and exchange elements of common interest or negotiate participation in activities such as *foyandi* and merry-go-round contributions.

It is important also to point out that the *madarasa* is a safe meeting place for married as well as unmarried and divorced women, who are often subject of societal prejudice. This prejudice against unmarried and divorced women often constrains women's solidarity, especially in cases where marriage implies a complete break with one's former life, including abandonment of old friends for new ties with unwelcoming patriarchal female in-laws.

The so-called *gabdi* (unmarried and self-managed) women who live with their parents, unlike the overt prostitutes who lead an independent life outside the family compound, also use the *madarasa* for (re)creating a new image of themselves by subverting the patriarchal view of the "good Muslim woman" and for legitimizing their interaction with married Muslim women. Through their participation in *madarasa* activities as well as their appropriation of all the symbolic expressions of the new code of religiosity, the *gabdi* thus continue to lead a life of social and economic fulfillment that very often married life cannot offer.

A number of unmarried Muslim women who attend these *madarasa* told me they own *makis* resulting from the money they generated through their participation in their *madarasa foyandi*. The *maki* resemble fast food places: the women set up shelters where they sell food and drinks (often including alcohol), most commonly to their male clientele, as men are the usual patrons of these public eating places.

It is not only in the *madarasa (makaranta)* and the *maki* that Nigerien Muslim women combine the sociopolitical, the religious, and the economic. Some derive their income from *télécentre* (akin to multimedia cafés providing internet, phone, and printing services). For others, the national economic media have become a new source of income. The democratization of the 1990s fostered not only the proliferation of a number of private radio and TV stations with competing ideological orientation, it also created job opportunities for women who are gifted communicators to run programs that most often focus on women's issues, at times with a progressive perspective. Most of these programs are aired in local languages, creating the possibility of reaching a more grassroots audience. The high degree of autonomy in voicing their personal opinions across a broad spectrum of ideological inclinations clearly represents a sharp contrast with the experience of Muslim women in northern Nigerian media discussed by Imam (1991, 244–52). Some of the women have also taken advantage of the democratization of the media and telecommunication centers toward this general goal. As they seek to present a vision of themselves, often in contrast to what others have simplistically shaped for them, they derive income from their TV and radio programs and, in some cases, their ownership of certain *télécentres*.

For Muslim women in contemporary Niger, these places of knowledge production in Islam, in commerce, and in creative engagement such as song production also represent spaces where women converge to develop women's strategies for improving their own material conditions. In the household, the *madarasa*, the *masallaci* (mosque), the *maki*, and at ceremonies (marriage, wedding, funerals, political party campaigns), one observes a realignment of the space of men and women along with a negotiation of power and gender relations in a nation severely affected by the competing forces of economic globalization, democratization, and Islamisms.

Given the above local and global contexts of the national culture, it seems that Muslim women's identities do not respond to a monolithic and static understanding of identity that draws on only one facet of their lives to account for the sum of the interwoven complexities of their experiences. Rather, these identities that have had an impact on how they perceive and speak about themselves have been constantly altered by historical forces—the incorporation of Islamic values into their old spiritual values, European colonialism, and now globalization and its unfolding consequences. All these factors generate a dynamic of shifts resulting in personal and collective transformations at various levels. For example, although it is true that Islam, like most monotheistic religions, is patriarchal, it has been the site of a collective reconceptualization of identity for the majority of the non-French-educated urban women seeking some literacy skills with cultural relevance. The result has been a women's class-based struggle in which the privileged status of French-educated women is now being challenged by the emergence of the new Islamic-oriented women's activist initiatives.

If this new Islamist women's activism is read only as a dimension of Islamic male fundamentalism, however, then the argument has failed to register the exclusionism of secularist orthodoxy in the postcolonial era. What is needed rather is to explore the duality—of religious fundamentalism and secular orthodoxy—and its implications for Muslim women as a national constituency in a state that is male-dominated and clearly unsympathetic to the priorities set by secularist women's organizations on women's rights, as the debate on the Family Code (see chapter 5) clearly reveals. In addition, the same exploration must inquire whether or not the "Islamisms of women" are the same as the "Islamisms of men"? Could and do women appropriate or transform religion or religious symbolism according to a woman's viewpoint? Already there exists a substantial body of Muslim women's autobiographies from Africa and elsewhere in the Islamic world and Muslim immigrant world that provide an exciting and critical understanding of women's experiences of Islam. These include, for example, the works of Zaynab Al-Ghazali's *Ayyam min Hayati* (Days from My Life, 1977/1986) and *Nazarat fi Kitab Allah* (Views on the Book of God, 1994), Fatima Mernissi's *Dreams of Trespass: Tales of a Harem Girlhood* (1994), Nawal El Saadawi's *Daughter of Isis* (1999), Leila Ahmed's *Border Passage: From Cairo to America—A Woman's Journey* (1999), Sattareh Farman-Farmaian's *Daughters of Persia: A Woman's Journey from her Father's Harem through the Islamic Revolution* (1992), and Fay Afaf Kanafani's *Nadia, Captive of Hope: Memoir of an Arab* Woman (1999), to cite a few.

But orthodoxy is not only an issue of substance. It is also one of approach. In this regard, a question arises as to whether a national women's coalition can emerge in this democratic era addressing equity across class, ethnic, political, and religious ideological boundaries without imposing an orthodoxy in mode of participation. The essence of this question is best captured by Abena Busia:

> Despite the fact that we *all* have sisters, we behave as if building sisterly relations is easy and automatic work, rather than the lifetime process of

> commitment that it is. We want always to have a sense of alliance that is also always filled with a sense of ease and well-being. And if anything happens to disrupt the faith in that equanimity, we are undone, and the "revolution" stops. It is one of the hardest things to accept that to work towards a common goal, we are not obliged to choose each other as dance partners, though that is always comforting. But to work together, what it takes is a deep, enduring respect based on an acceptance of our mutual humanities. But that compassion can only come if we but show charity to each other, and doing that requires a facing of history. (Busia 2003, 258)

In the final analysis, it is important to bear in mind the convergence of processes with respect to women's identities: French colonialism and its consequences, economic globalization, political pluralism, which in the Nigerien case contends with the militarization of society—these processes witnessed transformation in women's identities from the housewife to breadwinner; from recipient of masculine religious meanings to "religious agent"; from mere voter to public politician. Nigerien women in their daily struggles are paving the way to power (even if they have not yet achieved great power) that they can use creatively to transform power relations within the family and in public institutions.

The Place of Biography

About half of the body of this text is based on biographical investigation. Here the complexity in the interplay between Muslim women and agency along such variables as ethnicity, class, religion, and education is explored through the life narratives of three women—Malama A'ishatu, Habsu Garba, and Agaisha. Together they demonstrate the potential for women to claim for themselves powerful public places of great visibility in the national arena through their creative use of language and literacy.

Much of the data for this study relied heavily on the qualitative strategy of participant observation. I spent many summer months from 1994 to 2001 in the location of my research, participating in various events and activities, interacting with a wide spectrum of women and men engaged in various acts of identity performance—through literacy, performing arts, and political events. In the process, I also conducted a series of open-ended interviews with specific individuals, both to unearth their own life histories and to develop a more comprehensive reading of the subject of my research. Complementing this qualitative data is quantitative information drawn from documents available at the Ministry of Education and from secondary sources, including studies by other scholars.

I use the term biography here in its social sense. Within the narrative I interweave the voices of the individual women in their multiple layers as well as that of myself as a linguist and cultural critic. At the same time I relate the histories of these women to the wider sociopolitical and cultural contexts that have shaped the dynamics of their identities. My sense of biography, then, is similar to F. Dale Eickelman's use of the term social biography in his study of Haj 'Abd ar-Rahman Mansuri of Morocco: "I use the term social biography rather than life history to emphasize that this narrative does not purport to be a vehicle to allow a Berber *qadi*—to speak for himself. His voice is present throughout the text, but so is mine. . . . This account incorporates multiple voices, especially that of the ethnographer. An awareness of multiple voices is, I think, essential to understanding the nature of the anthropological encounter today" (Eickelman 1985, 15). The social biographical approach also involves a certain degree of intellectual negotiation between the positions and goals of the researcher and those of the "researched." As Eickelman elaborates: "In some recent ethnographies the self-reflexivity of the ethnographer, concern about the power relation of the ethnographic encounter, almost preclude further ethnographic analysis. I think that ethnography involves a balance between the two extremes. As the *qadi* and I worked together, we both became aware of our differences in understanding how events could be narrated and interpreted, of what was said and what was left out. These differences became part of the record of interpretation. Through my questions and his, we became mutually aware and appreciative of our respective intellectual projects" (16). This methodological approach is evident in all the biographical sections of this book.

My place in the research where the site is my homeland, my birthplace with which I still maintain strong ties, is best apprehended by Sonja Lanehart's statement that speaks to the question of "self" in the pursuit of scientific objectivity for researchers who engage in the study of their own cultures. As she puts it with regard to her own book on black women's perspectives on language and literacy:

> In reading this book you will see a blueprint for what I think we all need to do at some point in our lives. We need to study ourselves, get a good look at ourselves, in order to unmask who we are within ourselves and in the context of our interactions with those who help to make us who we are. I know some could say that I am too close to the subject to see it objectively. They might be right if there were such a thing as objectivity. Who we are and how we come to be are influenced by how we do what we do and why we see what we think we see. We cannot separate ourselves from our socio-cultural and socio-historical contexts. Though this approach—collecting data about myself, performing the same tasks as the other participants, and analyzing and reporting on my own data—may be unique in this type of study and not without its critics, I think both you and I see the participants and my analysis of them without pretense. We are our mothers' daughters, warts and all. (Lanehart 2002, 10–11)

In the process, I seek neither to romanticize the struggles of Muslim women of Niger through nativist essentialism, nor to impose a reading of their lives through analytical models with agendas that obfuscate their realities. Rather, my objective is to capture the multifarious ways in which the women who are subjects of my study have responded to the patriarchal spaces of their lives at the conjuncture of forces of economic globalization, democratization, and Islamist movements.

Though the three Nigerien women who form a large part of this study are products of *brassage sahélien,* there are significant differences in their profiles. First, there is an intergenerational gap of over thirty years between Malama A'ishatu, on the one hand, and Habsu Garba and Agaisha, on the other. Second, the three represent three educational paradigms: Malama A'ishatu was tutored exclusively in the Qur'anic Islamic tradition; Habsu Garba combines aspects of both secular French and Arab/Islamic formal schooling; and Agaisha was initiated into the indigenous Tuareg literacy, Tifinagh, and French secular education. As a result of these differences, the three women represent different constituencies and experiences of Muslim women in postcolonial Niger.

Malama A'ishatu Hamani Zarmakoy Dancandu

In the summer of 1996, I traveled to Niger to begin my research on literacy among women in Niger. Given that by this time I had already transcribed several religious poems recited by Malama A'ishatu Hamani Zarmakoy Dancandu during radio or TV religious programs, I decided to begin my investigation with her.

When I met Malama A'ishatu at her residence, a few streets away from the main mosque, in Quartier Madina in Niamey, she told me she was in her late seventies. At the age of two, her father was assigned by the French colonial authority to an administrative post in Magaria, a Hausa-speaking town in the Department of Zinder in eastern Niger. Thus, her entire family on her father's side was uprooted culturally and linguistically from Zarmaland, where she was born. Raised in Magaria, Malama A'ishatu became increasingly more competent in the Hausa language than in the Zarma language that she spoke but used less frequently, especially in discussing Islam. This is so because her initial schooling and educational development took place in Hausaland with Hausa-speaking teachers and colleagues in eastern Niger as well as in Northern Nigeria where she resided temporarily with one of her husbands who was a Qur'anic teacher.

Malama A'ishatu teaches in a *makaranta,* a home-based Qur'anic school mainly for girls and women. She teaches about twenty girls and women every morning from 8:00 a.m. to 10:00 a.m., except on Thursdays and Fridays. This teaching schedule is planned to accommodate her students who are homemakers as well as their daughters who assist them in house management.

On Thursdays, Malama A'ishatu spends her time at the TV station where she offers Islamic religious commentaries in addition to reciting religious poetry that is broadcast nationally. On Fridays, she is active at the main mosque as well as at the headquarters of the Islamic Association located next to the mosque in Quartier Madina.

During my fieldwork, I regularly attended her Qur'anic school and became close to the female members of her family who are also her students and who often assist Malama A'ishatu in teaching. My participation in the *makaranta* activities facilitated my interaction with her and the students. This situation also created an environment that was conducive to negotiating possibilities for interviewing the women about the various aspects of their lives that led them to Malama A'ishatu and her *makaranta*.

The fact that Malama A'ishatu uses the Hausa language in all her professional engagements led the majority of her audience to regard her as a Hausa woman. However, a trip to her native village of Dancandu in the summer of 1996, prior to our first encounter, offered the opportunity to discover her status as a princess, born of a princely father in Zarmaland. This "discovery" challenged our previous understanding of Malama A'ishatu's ethnic background as simply Hausa, as some of her colleagues at the national TV station believed.

Malama A'ishatu never attended French formal school, but was a beneficiary of literacy emanating from Qur'anic tradition in Magaria. I investigated her life history as a Muslim woman engaged with Islamic education and in relation to the popularity of her Islamic sermons on national TV and radio and to the poetry she recites. Both her sermons and poetry are now available in the market as part of the stock of audio and videocassettes of religious materials by Islamic women preachers.

Habsu Garba

Habsu Garba, the second main subject of my study, was born to a Hausa mother of Maradi and a Zarma father from Dosso. She attended the secular French mainstream school as well as the Islamic *madarasa* where both Arabic and French are used as media and subjects of instruction, with greater weight placed on Arabic language and Islamic content. Habsu is currently in her mid-forties and is well known in the Republic of Niger as one of the leading urban female singer-dancers and entertainers of political leaders. She is the artistic icon of the ruling political party, Mouvement National pour la Société de Développement (MNSD-Nassara). In addition, Habsu Garba hosts a radio talk show and holds a clerical post at the City Hall in the Bureau of Arts and Culture.

The data on Habsu Garba's life story were gathered in several settings. I attended her daily afternoon rehearsals at Samaria Lacouroussou Hall.

Samaria Lacouroussou Hall was a neighborhood cultural center that served as a mass mobilization arena—especially for the youth—during the successive military regimes from 1974 to 1989. It served also as a concert and rehearsal hall for artists functioning as the regime's rhetorical voices. During the democratization era, Samaria Lacouroussou Hall continued to serve as a space for various artists and sociopolitical groups, though these were not necessarily affiliated with the regime in power. The other venues where I attended Habsu Garba's performances were at the Palais de Congrès and her political party gatherings. I also attended some of the gatherings at night vending places for *brochettes (Kebab)* and *pommes frites* (French fries) in Lacouroussou and other places in Niamey where some of the gay members of her dance group socialize. I found this interaction crucial for developing an understanding of the gay subculture to which the male dancers belong in addition to their membership to Habsu Garba's dance group called Group Annashuwa.

I also visited her at the radio station where she cohosts her popular radio talk show, *May no taalogo?* (Who is at fault? in Zarma), *Riga Ba Wuya?* (A shirt without a neck, in Hausa), *A qui la faute?* (Whose fault is it? in French). I also visited Habsu Garba at the city hall in Niamey. At both the radio station and at the city hall, where she worked as a clerk, my visit was about exploring Habsu Garba in other professional settings where the topic was not the performing arts.

Given that Habsu was my contemporary and we have so many common friends, and that her husband happened to be one of my very close friends in my teenage years, my home in Quartier Faycal became another setting for engagement not only with Habsu Garba, but also with her husband and other talk-show cohosts and coactresses.

Agaisha

Agaisha is a mutually agreed-upon pseudonym of my third subject. This "anonymity" is dictated by the sensitive nature of the research area, that is, women's reading and writing their identities in the context of national armed conflict as in the case of the so-called Tuareg Rebellion in the Republic of Niger. I encountered Agaisha in Niamey in 1998 at the home of one of the women political activists where we convened to discuss matters related to a common invitation to a women's conference in Dakar (Senegal) on the theme of women and war in Africa. This encounter among Agaisha, who came from Agadez, the region that served as the main battlefield; our host who is based in Niamey; and myself, a Nigerien immigrant scholar living in the USA, provided an opportunity to discuss our perspectives as Nigerien women on the conference theme, leading to a discovery of our polyphonic views on the conflict. The three of us explored our points of commonality and difference as citizens of the same country resulting from our individual positions rooted in our class backgrounds, educational experiences, and ethnoregional politics and ideological inclinations. As we spent more time talking about the impact of this national conflict on women within a women-centered frame of reference, we began to build more trust and confidence on the possibility of forging a women's coalition against war that could transcend boundaries set by identity politics. It is within this context that I asked Agaisha if she would agree to participate as a subject in my ongoing research on women, language, and literacy in Niger. She agreed to participate and allowed me to utilize our interviews on the armed conflict in my analysis of the use of orality and literacy by Tuareg women and other women of the nation during wartime.

Agaisha was born to a Tuareg mother and a "mixed" Zarma and Ba'adare father. Through her mother, she acquired the Tamajaq language, while her maternal grandmother initiated her to Tifinagh literacy. By age seven, Agaisha had enrolled in the mainstream French school. She worked several years as a typist at the mayor's office in Agadez City. As one of the few educated "native" women who saw themselves trapped by both sides of the conflict by virtue of their gender, Agaisha transformed her position of entrapment into that of sociopolitical agency by lending her voice to international radio stations such as the British Broadcasting Corporation (BBC) and Radio France International (RFI), serving as the voice of Tuareg women's liberation. My interviews with her were conducted in Niamey during our two encounters in 1998 and 2002 and during the four days we spent together in 1998 at the conference on Women and War in Africa held in Dakar.

Through an examination of Agaisha's life, I demonstrate that the space of armed conflict, with all the horrors it produces in the destruction of the social fabric of the society affected could be, ironically, a terrain for some individuals, especially women, to discover new possibilities for self-empowerment in the new social order. Agaisha's emergence from the position of a typist to a national political leader holding an executive post in the nation is clearly demonstrative of a shift from a position of "victim" to that of a subject who asserts her agency.

Outline of the Book

These multiple experiences and responses of women studied in this book can be thematically divided into three clusters, each almost evenly divided, in their approach to the subject matter, between chapters that are biographically based and those that are founded on broader sociopolitical interrogation. The first part, comprised of two chapters, examines the interplay between women, literacy, and epistemological traditions. Chapter 1, "When

Kuble (Seclusion) Literacy Invades the Electronic Space: Malama A'ishatu Hamani Zarmakoy Dancandu and the Politics of Knowledge," looks at how global imbalances of power that define Western hegemonic relations with non-Western cultures have also positioned Western epistemology at the pedestal of world scholastic and intellectual traditions. Consequently, this power equation has led to the marginalization of non-Western epistemologies, especially those of African indigenous knowledge traditions. The chapter concludes with an examination of how this wider process of epistemological marginalization of Africa has had a particularly adverse impact on women operating within indigenous knowledge systems in Africa.

In chapter 2, "Women and the Political Economy of Education," I explore the impact of Africa's multiple heritage (indigenous, Islamic, and Western) on women's access to literacy and formal education in the postcolonial dispensation. By combining statistical as well as qualitative data, it demonstrates how centrifugal and centripetal forces of globalization have contributed to crises of education in the country with major implications for women. Under these circumstances women seize their agencies to craft new educational spaces (both literally and metaphorically), drawing anew from the Afro-Islamic legacy within a recrafted modernity. In particular, the chapter poses the following questions: Is women's access to literacy always liberating? If not, what are the factors that constrain the rise of a liberatory consciousness? If yes, how are we to assess that transformative power in a given society? What do women do or not do with the literacy streams accorded to them by the combination of these multiple traditions—Islamic, *Ajami* (an indigenized version of the Arabic script used in writing local languages), French—operating in the culture?

Part 2, combining chapters 3 and 4, looks at performance and folklore as terrains for the expression of new identities among women. Chapter 3, "Politics, Popular Culture, and Women Performing Artists: A Biographical Inquiry in a Franco-Islamic Context," looks more intimately into the life of an individual performer, Hajiya Habsu Garba, through her own eyes. Selected parts of my series of conversations with her are subjected to a critical discourse analysis as a strategy for deconstructing the multiple layers of her life history.

Chapter 4, "Cinderella Goes to the Sahel," is, in a sense, part of the unfolding of Habsu Garba's life. The fairytale discussed here was one that she narrated on national radio. I argue in this chapter that Habsu's decision to select this particular version of the tale from among other existing ones is itself further evidence of the workings of a subversive counterdiscourse in the arena of female resistance through the performing arts.

The chapter looks at how Islam has influenced a recent narration of the story of the orphan who marries the Prince of Masar—a tale of the wicked stepmother popularly known as "Cinderella" in the West. This takes place in the context of growing participation by women in Niger in redefining Islam, culminating in the recreation of the tale in a way that inscribes the woman as an active agent and not merely a passive receiver and transmitter of culture.

Political contestation can be either overt or covert. Part 3 of the book examines the more overt side of women's political contestation in times of ideological conflict and even of actual militarization of conflict. This part too is divided into two chapters. Chapter 5, "Islamisms, the Media, and Women's Public Discursive Practices," is set in the 1990s, which opened with a major struggle for the political future of the nation with various social movements seeking to inscribe themselves as equal political partners in the national space. Within this context, the chapter tries to demonstrate how the dynamics and counterdynamics of this struggle inspired the women of Niger to interrogate their historical locations in the nation. This self-reflection, the chapter shows, eventually led to efforts by the women to organize themselves in new ways and, partly through the use of electronic media, to situate themselves as agents in the Islamic discursive space. This interplay between women's claim to self-definition, the state, Islamic authorities, and the media has challenged the nation to revisit its deeply embedded relationships of patriarchy and other forces of hegemony and their implications on women.

It was not only women, however, who sought to redefine their place in the national space in the wake of the new political struggles. It was also ethnoregional entities that had hitherto felt marginalized. In Niger, this "ethnic" face of the politics of difference arising from the centrifugal pull of the democratization momentum expressed itself most forcefully in the so-called Tuareg Rebellion that began in the late 1980s (Dayak 1992; Salifou 1993; Kimba 1997). In spite of its presumed "ethnic" nature, however, this armed conflict and its aftermath had a direct bearing on the lives of women both within the so-called Tuareg region and the nation at large. Chapter 6, "Through the Eyes of Agaisha: Womanhood, Gender Politics, and Tuareg Armed Rebellion," analyzes these effects of the war on women and their contribution to a redefinition of womanhood at both the local and national levels in the context of the politics of pluralism and the nascent multipartism in the shadow of impending military coups.

Finally, in the conclusion, I summarize the findings and the main theoretical arguments of previous chapters: that the "Nigerien woman" is ultimately a complex product of a new *brassage*, an embodiment of old blending and modern hybridity that are variously inscribed in their identities. This unique attribute of Nigerien society, at an historical and cultural conjuncture between the local and the global, allows women to be in a multiplicity of cultural locations simultaneously. These locations afford women a variety of strategies for self-affirmation or self-effacement that they select at different times for different reasons in furtherance of different goals—personal, familial, professional, national, and beyond. These modes of action are themselves products of dialogic interactions with the self and ultimately produce women's agencies that are heterogeneous and complex.

Part I

Women, Education, and Epistemological Traditions

Chapter 1

When *Kuble* (Seclusion) Literacy Invades the Electronic Space

Malama A'ishatu Hamani Zarmakoy Dancandu and the Politics of Knowledge

Introduction

In this chapter I examine two legacies associated with Islam in the popular imagination throughout the Sahelian region—*kuble (kulle)*, also referred to as *purdha* in some Muslim societies, and Arabic-derived literacies—and how they have defined the lives of the women who came to embrace Islam.[1] In Niger, the practice of *kuble* has both an extreme and a moderate manifestation. In the extreme instance, found mainly among the Hausa, Fulani, and Hausa assimilated communities, the womenfolk are subject to total seclusion within the domestic space. This phenomenon is particularly prominent among the families of *Sufi marabouts,* aristocrats, and merchants. The more moderate version of *kuble* is one that allows women some measure of mobility outside the domestic space, but only by permission of the male head of the household. This latter form of *kuble* is found throughout urban Niger, usually across boundaries of ethnicity.

There is an important class dimension to the various expressions of *kuble*. As indicated above, the more seclusive practice is found among the families of chiefs and emirs, merchants, and *marabouts* who constitute the aristocracy and the rich among the "traditional" communities. Among the urban middle class, on the other hand, it is the less seclusive form of *kuble* that is most prevalent. In the lives of the poor, both in urban and rural spaces, however, there is no room for either form of the *kuble*. The severity of the material conditions of families at this lower end of the social hierarchy demands that men, women, children, and the elderly are all actively engaged in seeking a livelihood unencumbered by the cultural limitations of seclusive laws, be they religious or secular.

The tradition of Arabic-based literacy can take the form of reading/writing either directly in the Arabic language or in the indigenized version of the Arabic script called *Ajami*. In recent times, these forms of literacies, but especially the Arabic one, and both dimensions of the *kuble* practices among the aristocracy, the rich, and the middle class, have become an expression of material well-being as well as cultural Islamic modernity.

Though both legacies have been used by men to keep Muslim women in "their place"—a condition that was later reinforced by the patriarchal policies of French colonial rule—the chapter demonstrates that the women themselves have not always been passive recipients of all the ideological values attached to this dual heritage. At specific historical junctures, some of the women have made use of new openings of the political and cultural space, as in the democratization era of the 1990s, to transform the received traditions of literacy and *kuble* and inscribe women's religious voices in the public arena, in their wide range of expressions—from strong allegiance to conservatism to more liberal interpretations of the meaning of Islam in their lives.

Malama A'ishatu Hamani Zarmakoy Dancandu is a Muslim woman in her seventies who rose to national prominence in Niger as a result of her Islamic radio and television programs. Malama A'ishatu was the first child of the chief of the Zarma-speaking village of Dancandu in western Niger. At age two, she moved to Magaria in eastern Niger with the rest of her family when her father was appointed by the French authorities to serve as a "native" clerk in the colonial administration. In this new location, Malam A'ishatu made her entry into the cultural space of Hausa identity and into the world of Islamic literacy through the training she received from her Hausa Muslim teachers. As she matured, she married twice, in both cases to prominent *Malams (marabouts)* who moved from place to place within eastern Niger and all the way to northern Nigeria, making a livelihood through religious instruction, healing services, and composition and performance of Islamic poetry. These travels provided Malama with new opportunities not only to expand the scope of her Islamic knowledge, but also to enrich her cultural experiences as well as her understanding of the dynamic interplay between womanhood, ethnicity, and religious identity. Eventually, she settled in Niamey, the capital of Niger, where I met her during my research, living with her younger sister whom she had raised from infancy. There, she began her new life in her mid-sixties as a teacher in a home-based Qur'anic school for girls and women.

It was during this period that Malama A'ishatu heard a radio recitation of a religious poem, "Imfiraji" by the late Aliyu na Mangi, the famous composer of classical Hausa-Islamic poetry.[2] This is a poem she had committed to memory since her marriage to a Malam of Dan Lima, a town near Sokoto in northern Nigeria. As she explains,

> When I lived in Dan Lima [Sokoto, Nigeria], we recited the poem with my co-wives and the other neighbors. I did not know it at the beginning. So I decided to call a younger brother of our husband who happened to own the book with the original poem. I asked him to teach it to me because any type of studying requires *'usuli* [the authentic or original text] from which to learn. So he instructed me.

What is significant here is not only Malama A'ishatu's description of how she came to be versed in Aliyu na Mangi's famous poem, but also the importance she attaches to the power of memory on the basis of the composition in its original form. For her, as Beverly Mack (2004) has also observed, orality and literacy are not dichotomous entities, but processes that constantly feed on each other. And what emerges quite clearly is her lack of appreciation of learning that is based purely on secondary sources.

With this background knowledge of the original poem, then, Malama A'ishatu was convinced that the poem "Imfiraji," as she heard it several years later on the national radio in Niger Republic, had been misrendered. She thus took it upon herself to approach Sheikh Alfa Ismael, the chairperson of the Islamic Association of Niger, to express her opinion on the subject. To convey her point she produced a copy of the original text of the poem that she possessed in her rich collection of Islamic material from Hausaland and beyond. This quest for truth and knowledge as an aspect of intellectual Islam therefore led Malama A'ishatu to transgress the boundaries of *kuble* and address the highest religious male authority in the country in order to correct the rendition of a popular religious poem. Extremely impressed by Malama A'ishatu's demonstrated knowledge of Islamic poetry, in particular, and Qur'anic scholarship, in general, the Sheikh and his association proposed to the national television and radio that she be appointed to host a program catering to Muslim women. Thus began Malama A'ishatu's shift from the confines of *kuble* to the public arena of national electronic media.

What follows in the rest of this chapter is an analysis of the interaction between the personal, the public, and the epistemological in the complex life of Malama A'ishatu Hamani Zarmakoy Dancandu based on a series of personal interviews that I had the opportunity and privilege to conduct with her in Niamey during my various field trips to the country from summer 1996 to winter 2001.

Gendered Spaces: Between Indigenous Tradition and French Colonialism

From her early years of childhood, Malama A'ishatu was trapped between the forces of tradition, on the one hand, and French colonialism, on the other. This was particularly evident in the area of education. She was born into a tradition that privileged boys' education over girls', and men over women in the access to Islamic literacy and scholarship. It was not uncommon for girls and women to be restricted to a limited body of Islamic texts sufficient only for the performance of mandatory rituals like the *salat* (prayers). This, of course, is not to deny the fact that some Sahelian women of aristocratic background did have the opportunity to pursue Islamic learning to relatively advanced levels. The experiences of women like Nana Asma'u (1793–1865), the daughter of the legendary Sheikh Usman Dan Fodiyo, and her female siblings are striking cases in point (Boyd 1989; Boyd and Mack 1997; and Mack and Boyd 2000). In general, however, for the majority of Sahelian Muslim women, access to Islamic learning was circumscribed to a very narrow and often ritualistic space of Islam. Most local Qur'anic schools, known locally as the *makaranta,* therefore, tended to be exclusively male, especially at the higher levels of instruction.

At the same time, the French colonial government had just introduced their own schools intended partly to promote its cultural and linguistic policies of assimilation and partly to produce subaltern clerical support for its local administration. This French colonial system was bent on delegitimizing the Afro-Islamic schools that were then in vogue and were responsible for training the educational elite of this Muslim polity. Equally important, the French educational system, influenced by the European tradition of female domesticity, proceeded to marginalize girls and restrict their access to French-based education. This colonial pattern in the education of girls in Niger is similar to those documented by Barbara Callaway and Lucy Creevey with regard to Senegal and Mali (1994, 61).

It is against this backdrop that, as a child, Malama A'ishatu witnessed boys in her neighborhood attending the *makaranta* while her own male siblings, being children of a "native" colonial clerk, were enrolled in the newly established French colonial school. As a girl-child, her role had been crafted for her as one of providing domestic support for the women of the household in their (re)productive roles. But early completion of the daily domestic chores left Malama A'ishatu idle and lonely, in a world of adult female homemakers. In the meantime, she kept overhearing the chanting of male children from the *makaranta* next door. Eventually, as she tells it, female empathy with her circumstances began to open a small window of *makaranta* literacy for her:

> When we were taken to Magaria [a town bordering Nigeria and eastern Niger], it was decided that I would not be sent to *lakkwal* [*école*, French school] even though I was the eldest child. I had to help my mothers with their chores. My younger brothers were sent to *lakkwal*. After finishing my chores, I was left to play by myself. My mother then asked my father if he would allow me to attend the *makaranta* next door. She said to him, "Take her to the *Malam* (teacher) so that she can learn what is necessary for prayers." My father agreed and I was admitted to the *makaranta*. I was the only girl in the *makaranta*. People were amazed at how quickly I acquired the *suras* [Qur'anic chapters] and how well I retained everything in my head. [Laughs]

Though intended to provide her with no more than basic training for purposes of prayers, this initial childhood experience became an important foundation for her lifelong learning within the Islamic paradigm. As she comments with respect to her parents' intention, "Yes, I did learn what was necessary for prayer. *Alhamduillah* [thank Allah]. Isn't that right [laughs]. I say I got what was necessary for prayers. But today I can also teach someone. [Laughs]" What began as an incidental occurrence precipitated by the gendered space of education within both the Afro-Islamic and French colonial educational systems turned out to be the beginning of a cherished profession that Malama A'ishatu carried over into the postcolonial period.

There is no doubt that the prevailing ideology of the time was hegemonic, articulated in gendered policies that circumscribed the condition of participation in the production and consumption of knowledge and promoted patriarchal biases accompanying those processes. Malama A'ishatu was by no means above the ideological contradictions of her time and place. Her espousal of patriarchal thinking is particularly evident in her comments about the role of the husband in a woman's access to knowledge:

> It is required for husbands to instruct their wives. If a man is not a learned one or not literate, he must look for someone to instruct her. He must look for someone who can come instruct her privately or [otherwise] she must go to a safe place [that is, to a woman teacher, *malama*] to learn.

It is important, however, to realize that it is also within these same confines of patriarchy that Malama A'ishatu found a place within Islam to inscribe a relatively progressive position for women by insisting on their right to knowledge even if it is men who end up choosing for them the specific path of access to that knowledge.

In this work of advocacy for women's education, Malama A'ishatu invokes the tradition of the prophet Muhammad, who is reported to have said: "The search for knowledge is mandatory for all Muslims, male and female alike." She explains:

> Well, Isn't it during the old day of *ijtihad* [the quest for truth] that the prophet endeavored to call for knowledge and the end of *jahilci* [that is, *jahiliyya,* the period of ignorance]? In fact, his talk on the importance of *Ilimi* [knowledge, education] was a recurrent one. And he did not say that women should not seek it. In fact, it is to women that the prophet bestowed the greatest responsibility for acquiring knowledge. . . . Knowledge, therefore, is *wajibi* [compulsory] and a woman must be allowed to seek it. Isn't that right?

She reasons that the importance of women's education over that of men lies in the recognition that women, as mothers and nurturers, are the ones who give shape to the early cultural and intellectual formation of both male and female children. The transmission of Islamic and other values that are important to the early development of the "Muslim" child is part of the critical role of women in society. As Malama A'ishatu explains once again:

> When a woman is knowledgeable, her children will learn before attending school. They [the women] will make use of it [their knowledge] from the beginning. That is why a woman's knowledge is not like a man's knowledge. . . . You see my children here, no matter how young they are, I teach them the Qur'an because we are Muslims and we have to teach them this from home. That is why it is *wajibi* [compulsory] for women to seek knowledge.

Therefore, in spite of her traditional conservatism Malama A'ishatu is able to draw on aspects of Islamic doctrine as part of her campaign for the right of girls and women to education.

It is also significant that her understanding of the realm of knowledge goes beyond the religious. Here too Malama A'ishatu benefits from her understanding of Islam by drawing on one of the *hadiths* (sayings) of the prophet Muhammad exhorting Muslims "to seek knowledge even if it be in China" (a rather distant land at that time where obviously no Islamic learning existed). Thus, she came to appreciate the value of both the religious education that she herself was privileged to receive and the secular modern learning to which she had been denied access:

> As far as knowledge is concerned, it is not said that one must not learn the Western knowledge or the Islamic knowledge. Qur'anic learning is for

> knowing how to prepare for the day-after and learning to live a harmonious Islamic social life. As for the other one, Allah grants it to us so that we can assist ourselves; you help yourself and help others. Now what can daughters do for their own parents that a man can object to? The way female children assist their parents, there are men who do not do that. Haven't they sent their mothers and fathers to *Hajj*? Hasn't a daughter built a house for them? Hasn't she bought them a car? Is it what they are saying? . . . This is what is valued, isn't it? Which one of all these things hasn't a woman done? And without *lakkwal* . . . [laughs] . . . how could she have achieved this?

Elsewhere Malama A'ishatu observes:

> Now, for our sake . . . our children are educated in both *Mahammadiyya* [Qur'anic or Islamic education] and *lakkwal*. Even now there are some who attend *madarasa* and others who attend *lakkwal*. All our children attend *lakkwal*. They do both—they attend *lakkwal* and attend *Mahammadiyya*, our own children. So, could you tell someone's child not to attend? Seeking knowledge is a wonderful thing.

Malama A'ishatu thus sees modern secular education inherited from the French colonial tradition as important, especially for girls, not only in terms of the material benefits it provides for them and their families, but also for enabling parents to fulfill their religious obligations like the *Hajj* [pilgrimage to Mecca], which require material means. Thus, by fusing the material and the religious, she makes her argument for girls' and women's education both compelling and urgent.

In other words, Malama A'ishatu celebrates the educational hybridity that shapes Nigeriens as francophone Muslims through the complementarity between the Qur'anic school arising from a predominantly Islamic tradition and the formal school inherited from the French colonial legacy. This complementarity is crucial in addressing the need to be grounded spiritually, as required by Islam and, through the knowledge and skills acquired in formal school, to satisfy our individual as well communal material obligations. Her position seems to conform with the saying of the prophet Muhammad: "Work for the hereafter as if you are to die tomorrow. And work for this world as if you are going to live forever."

In Sheikh Hamidou Kane's *Ambiguous Adventure*, the question is posed about the process of acquiring knowledge in the following words: "Can one learn *this* without forgetting *that*, and is what one learns worth what one forgets?" (Kane 1963, 34). The concern of the community here was whether initiating their young to the newly introduced French colonial education might result in their estrangement from the knowledge they had acquired in their traditional Afro-Islamic training. Obviously, Malama A'ishatu suffers from no such anxiety. She sees the possibility of combining the old and the

Malama A'ishatu at her home based Qur'anic school for women and girls.

One of Malama A'ishatu's students.

new toward the construction of a new francophone Afro-Islamic modernity that hinges, of necessity, on the integration of the womenfolk.

Equally important in Malama A'ishatu's observations is the connection between women's education and women's role in the economic well-being of the family. In the "traditional" patriarchal set-up it is the man (as husband, as father, as son) who is defined as the primary breadwinner and provider. With the intrusion of French colonialism and its aftermath, and its effects on the preexisting moral order of the society and its refashioning of the areas of skills needed for employment in the modern sector, the responsibility of providing for the family has increasingly been assumed by the daughters and women of the household. It is true, of course, that the growing economic hardships in society now require that both men and women contribute to the family income. Yet, ironically, it is precisely at this juncture that more and more men are failing to fulfill the requirements of their traditionally ascribed roles as providers while nominally assuming that status.

There was a time when marriage was considered a form of material security for the Muslim woman. But with the increasing rate of divorce and increasing failures by husbands to sustain their families economically—due to a variety of reasons, such as polygamy, absenteeism, alcoholism, prolonged migration, and unemployment—women see themselves as having no alternative but to struggle to become income-generators for themselves and for the welfare of their families. Under these uncertain circumstances of marriage, it has become normal (especially in urban areas) for mothers to counsel their daughters to invest more rigorously in education and ensure the acquisition of skills necessary to sustain themselves and their children in the event of failed marriages. The result of this conjunction of forces, then, is what appears to be the steady rise in the proportion of women-headed households in Niger both in rural and urban areas.

These new realities, then, have reinforced Malama A'ishatu's efforts to advocate for the need to provide girls and women with maximum opportunities for schooling, both secular and religious. In this regard, Malama has sometimes locked horns with Muslim men who have opposed, either openly or in more subtle ways, the provision of secular Western education for their girls, which they believe would turn them into "bad" women. These beliefs she has often exposed as hypocritical. Observing how the young themselves have to come to appreciate the benefit of secular education, she comments in relation to the songs and poems aired in her radio and television programs:

> Well, you see, today's children see it for themselves and they articulate this understanding by themselves. Moreover, if their parents are sitting and listening, they too hear the message "For Allah's sake, send your children to school regardless of their number" in those songs. And you see, this is not

too much (a message), you see. From this, children will understand and know that illiteracy is not good. However, *lakkwal* is not a sin. This is what some say. But those in *wannan zamani* [these times] who tell us that *lakkwal* is not good have their children attending *lakkwal*. This is the truth . . .

The opposition to Western secular education for girls was particularly pronounced during the initial phase of the colonial period. It has acquired a new momentum with the resurgence of Islamic conservatism and some of its adherents who take a public stand against Muslim women's education in the secular realm. Much of their reasoning is based on an idea of Islamic morality that, as Malama A'ishatu argues, is not necessarily consistent with the religion's doctrine. At the same time, however, some of these men are quick to exploit every opportunity to enroll their own female children in modern schools, both locally and internationally. It is this double-standard, privileging men and undervaluing women's education, that Malama A'ishatu criticizes as both hypocritical and detrimental to a "modernist" vision of Islamic society that incorporates women as agents in nation-building. This modernism is the essence of Malama A'ishatu's allusion to *wannan zamani* (these times) displaying a consciousness of tradition as malleable, one that constantly reconfigures itself to adapt to new circumstances and demands, notwithstanding the conceptual purism that its patriarchal guardians and ideologues seek to ascribe to it.

Poetry, Piety, and Identity

Poetry has long been an important didactic tool of religious expression in Afro-Islamic societies throughout the continent, as Mack has amply illustrated (2004). It was almost natural therefore that Malama A'ishatu would seek to make poetry a tool of her advocacy work, especially when she was called upon to launch her radio and television Islamic programs for Muslim women. With her efforts focused on the theme of education *(tarbiya)*, she made her students' recitation of the poem "Ilimi" (knowledge/education/science/intelligence) the signature opening of all her media programs.[3] The full eighty-two verses of the poem are reproduced below to show the power of their memory and how much students are expected to commit to learning on a regular basis. The goal of this exercise in memorization is to cultivate a high level of concentration and focus, essential to successful learning in whatever field:

Mun gode Allah mun yaba ma ma'aiki	We're grateful to Allah and we worship his messenger
Za ni jawabina ga 'yem *makaranta*	This is my advice to the students of Qur'anic school

Mun gode Allah mun yaba ma ma'aiki Za ni jawabina ga 'yem *makaranta*	(chorus)
Za ni jawabi wun iyayen yara	This will be my advice to children's parents
(chorus)	
Don Allah mai yaro shi sa *makaranta*	For Allah's sake whoever has a child send him to school
(chorus)	
Don sai da *ilimi* duniya ke ƙaruwa	Because it is with knowledge that the world progresses
(chorus)	
In babu *ilimi* ya ake a wadata?	If there is no knowledge how can we have comfort?
(chorus)	
Shi *ilimi* daɗinshi ba shi masantuwa	The goodness of knowledge is that it does not vanish
(chorus)	
Yara ku sa himma zuwa *makaranta*	Children focus your energy into attending school
(chorus)	
Abin da ke sawa a samu *karatu*	What can allow one to gain knowledge (or to acquire literacy)
(chorus)	
Su shidda ne farko zuwa *makaranta*	There are six. First to attend school
(chorus)	
Sanad da ka y [ka yi] fa hankali ga lura	Enlightenment, diligence, and observation
(chorus)	
Ga ladabi gum malamim *makaranta*	And good behavior toward the school teacher
(chorus)	
Sanan ḍa daurewa da yi ba fashi	Then patience and endurance
(chorus)	
Yaro shi bar fashin zuwa *makaranta*	The child must not give up going to school
(chorus)	
Sanad da samun malami mai hali	Then identifying and getting a teacher with character
(chorus)	
Mai iya tarbiya ga 'yem *makaranta*	One who knows how to educate pupils
(chorus)	

Abin da ke sawa a samu *karatu*	What allows one to gain knowledge
(chorus)	
Su shidda ne farko zuwa *makaranta*	There are six. First to attend school
(chorus)	
Abin da ke sawa mutum shi wadata	What allows one to be fulfilled
(chorus)	
A duniya farkonshi yim *makaranta*	In the world (life), first is schooling
(chorus)	
Abin da ke sawa mutum shi talauta	what can make a person poor
(chorus)	
A duniya farko rashin *makaranta*	In the world, first is the lack of schooling
(chorus)	
In ka yi *ilimi* ka tsaya ka gane	If you gain knowledge and you are critical
(chorus)	
Ba yanda za a y [a yi] duniya ta talauta	There is no way for the world to be poor
(chorus)	
Shi *ilimi* na maida yaro babba	Knowledge can transform a child into an adult
(chorus)	
Shi maida bawa ɗa saboda gabta	It can transform a slave into a noble son because of enlightenment
(chorus)	
Ni dai ina fata iyayen yara	I do pray that the children's parents
(chorus)	
Su gane amfanin zuwa *makaranta*	Would understand the importance of attending school
(chorus)	
Sun sannya' ya'yensu su yi ta *karatu*	They ought to enroll their children in school
(chorus)	
Komi yawan' ya'yenka ka sa *makaranta*	Whatever the number of your children do send them to school
(chorus)	
Shi *ilimi* farkonshi ga shi da daɗi	Knowledge is first of all sweet
(chorus)	
ɗaci ga rai [(ga re shi)] ɗacinshi ya wuce gauta	It is bitter and its bitterness is beyond the taste
(chorus)	
Amma fa in ya samu ga shi da daɗi	However, once acquired it is sweet (tasty)
(chorus)	

Daɗi ga rai daɗinshi ya wuce tsinta	It is tasty and its sweetness is beyond unexpected treasure
(chorus)	
Shi *ilimi* tamƙar uwa da uba ne	Knowledge grants sustainability for one's mother and father
(chorus)	
Mai *ilimi* shi bai zama da talauta	A person with knowledge is never poor
(chorus)	
Shi *ilimi* ka ƙara duɓe basira	Knowledge is what increases wisdom
(chorus)	
Shi kau da jahilci shi kau da makanta	It chases away ignorance and it chases away blindness
(chorus)	
Yara ina jan hankalinku ku gane	Children, I am calling on your attention to understand
(chorus)	
Ba ku da aikin yi kamar *makaranta*	You don't have a better task than school
(chorus)	
Shi *ilimi* daɗinshi in ya samu	The sweetness of Knowledge once gained
(chorus)	
Komi wuyad da ka sha ta ba ka ganinta	Whatever hardship you undergo, you will learn from it
(chorus)	
Daure da yawan shanta ya zama doli	Endure the hardship, for acquiring it has become a must
(chorus)	
In dai karatu za ka yi ka sha ta	If you are to study, you will absorb it
(chorus)	
Allah Ta'ala duniya shi ya yi ta	Allah the Almighty is the one who created the world
(chorus)	
Komi kake son duniya ka bar ta	However much you love the world, you will leave it
(chorus)	
Allah Ta'ala in ya ba ka *karatu*	Allah the Almighty if he granted you knowledge
(chorus)	
To in da more ka more zamanta	Well, if there is rejoicing, you will rejoice
(chorus)	
Nina ga halin duniya halinta	I see the way of the world

(chorus)	
Kuna cikin daɗi ku ce kun ɓata	As you enjoy its sweetness it spoils
(chorus)	
To shi ya sa tilas mutun shi yi *ilimi*	So, this is why a person ought to search for Knowledge
(chorus)	
Don shi kaɗai ke maganin cutatta	Because it is the only remedy to illness
(chorus)	
Yara ku sa himma ga neman *ilimi*	Children, put your effort to the quest for Knowledge
(chorus)	
A bar kasala nan da nan an huta	Do not be playful and decide to rest
(chorus)	
In ko ana nemanshi a yi ta biyayya	And then if one must seek it one must do it with obedience
(chorus)	
Gum Malammai shi ne mabuɗi nata	Toward the teachers who hold the key to it
(chorus)	
Ita *makaranta* ba ta son mai fitina	School does not want someone who is troublesome
(chorus)	
Mai rena kowa nan da nan an ɓata	An arrogant who can easily mess up with everybody
(chorus)	
Ita *makaranta* cin kashinta ga yaro	School does challenge a child
(chorus)	
Babu kamar fashin zuwa *makaranta*	There is no such thing as missing school
(chorus)	
Ita *makaranta* ba'a sonta da ƙiwya	One does not go to school with laziness
(chorus)	
Kuma ba'a son wauta cikin sha'aninta	Moreover, one does not want silliness in its undertaking
(chorus)	
Yaro ana son tunda safe ya tashi	One needs a child to wake up early in the morning
(chorus)	
Cikin nisha'i za shi je *makaranta*	Full of inspiration, he heads to school
(chorus)	
Ya dena wasa mai yawa kan hanya	He must stop playing a lot on the way to school

(chorus)	
Shi maida himma tai [(ta shi)] wajen *makaranta*	He must focus his energy toward school
(chorus)	
Yaro ana son zuciyarsa ta saba	One would like the child to engage full heartedly
(chorus)	
Ko za shi yawo wajen *makaranta*	Even if all his outings be to school
(chorus)	
Yara ana son hannuwansu su saba	One would like the hands of children to become used to
(chorus)	
Da yin *rubutu* kun ji 'yen *makaranta*	Writing. Do you hear students!
(chorus)	
Su yi ta tunanen yanda za su yi *ilimi*	They must keep on thinking about how to gain Knowledge
(chorus)	
Ku maida himma kun ji 'yen *makaranta*	You must focus your energy. Do you hear students!
(chorus)	
Ku dena ƙosawa ku dena kasala	You must stop being rigid, you must stop fooling around
(chorus)	
Rago abin ƙi ne wajen *makaranta*	The lazy one is not desired in school
(chorus)	
Wuyar karatu mai yawanci ku sani	The difficulty of studying is to know the most
(chorus)	
In babu himma ƴa ake a rabauta	If one does not put an effort how could one gain?
(chorus)	
In dai ana son duniya da kiyama	If we wish the world and the afterlife
(chorus)	
Su samu tilas ne a je *makaranta*	To be reached, we ought to attend school
(chorus)	
Babbar muƙami ba kamar mai *ilimi*	There is no greater stature than that of the knowledgeable
(chorus)	
In ya yi aiki yanda duk ya kamata	If one works hard as it is required
(chorus)	
In ka yi *ilimi* mai yawa ya samu	And you gain a lot of knowledge

(chorus)

In babu aiki sai a fara *makaranta*	If there is no other activity then one must start to teach (or study)

(chorus)

The word *makaranta* (school) appears twenty-four times in the main poem and eighty times in the chorus verses, making a total of one hundred and four occurrences. *Ilimi* (knowledge) and *Karatu* (reading/studying), on the other hand, turn up for a total of sixteen and four times, respectively. In this poem, repetition, a common strategy of the oral tradition, has been used for emphasis to demonstrate the importance of school and the acquisition of knowledge through education. Furthermore, the verses that say *Shi ilimi tamkar uwa da uba ne* (Knowledge grants sustainability for one's mother and father) and *In dai ana son duniya da kiyama* (If we wish the world and the afterlife) imply the valuing of *ilimi* (knowledge) that is religious, intellectual, and material.

For Malama A'ishatu, then, the power of poetry lies not only in its aesthetic appeal, but also in its didactic and functional value. Through the poem "Ilimi" she seeks to conscientize the particular audience of her programs, a constituency characterized mostly by both religious and secular illiteracy. As a social commentator, public educator, and religious authority figure, Malama A'ishatu uses her new role and power to speak on the crucial importance of literacy in the life of the community.

While Malama A'ishatu speaks of a variety of written poetic compositions that she uses in her programs and of her gift in committing them to memory, she points to the place and role of Hausa language as a transethnic language through which Qur'anic learning, teaching, and artistic performances are mediated. The Hausa language has come to define her personal and public identity in spite of the fact that she was born in the village of Dancandu. In this process, the Hausa language has become a lingua franca even for the immigrant families from neighboring countries, such as Mali, Burkina Faso, and Benin, who have settled in the urban centers of Niamey where Qur'anic education is taking place:

> As for the songs, they are so many in all sorts. I love songs. . . . Everywhere I hear songs . . . some of the songs I don't even know where their papers are. But I did retain them in my head. The songs I sing are in Hausa and this is why people say I am Hausa ethnically. So, this is how I lived my life in Dan Lima, Kano, and now here. And this is what I teach the children, but they are all fluent speakers of Hausa language and they are learning. All the female children can speak Hausa. Those who are literate and those who are not are all part of it.

By stating, "the songs I sing are in Hausa language and this is why people say I am Hausa ethnically," Malama draws attention to the complexity of her "hybrid" linguistic and cultural identity. As indicated earlier, Malama was born during the French colonial era, the biological daughter of the royal Zarma family of Dancandu, a village located in southwestern Niger, a few kilometers away from the capital city, Niamey. Her father had been assigned to a "native" post in the administration, which took him and the family to Magaria, a Hausa-speaking town in the eastern region of the Department of Zinder at the northern Nigeria border. Here her family resided and shaped a new bilingual and biregional identity. Thus, it was within this historical and social context that Malama A'ishatu acquired her linguistic and cultural identity as a Muslim "Zarma-Hausa."

Furthermore, Malama's training in Qur'anic schools in both the Arabic and Hausa languages by Islamic Hausa teachers and her subsequent marriages to Hausa men of Niger and Nigeria have drawn her more deeply into "Hausaness." These influences have also created confusion in the minds of people with a narrow understanding of the process(es) that shift and shape complex individual sociocultural identities.

Malama further establishes a link between the linguistic shift from Zarma language as the family language to Hausa language as a new family language and a medium of instruction in Qur'anic school in transethnic and transnational urban milieus. Increasingly, Hausa came to define her intellectual life, as a religious teacher, poet, and television and radio religious commentator. Furthermore, because of the linguistic complexity of her current multiethnic and multilinguistic location, she has come to use the transethnic Hausa language as a medium of instruction. As Malama points out, "So this is how I lived my life in Dan Liman, Kano, and now here. And this is what I teach the children [students]. Some of them can speak [Hausa]. Those who are literate and those who are not are all part of it. . . . This is what we do." By pointing out during the course of our interactions that some of her students are children of Marka and Bambara from Mali, Malama is stressing the fact that the Hausa language relates even to the children of immigrants who live in Niger for whom the issue is beyond that of "national" identity or ethnic affiliation; they are neither citizens of Niger Republic nor do they belong to any of the groups supposedly defining the "original" ethnic make-up of the country.

This question of language and identity also concerns Malama A'ishatu with regard to the more current issues affecting the welfare of the nation in the wake of political democratization and the reemergence of multiparty politics. Malama A'ishatu challenges the ethnicization of politics that has become overt among the Westernized middle-class who make opportunistic appeals to ethnocentric regionalism. Their political orientation is reflected in their request that she run her programs on public radio and television in the Zarma language to assert her "Zarma roots." In response to such subjective postcolonial politics, Malama retorted, switching from Hausa to Zarma:

> One day I went to visit a teacher at *Garbaa-do* and he told me, "For Allah's sake A'ishatu, speak in the Zarma language for my *komi* [from French *commis,* "clerical officer," a term used to refer to Westernized elite] so they can hear that you are a Zarma person." So I said this is a problem. . . . I then decided to greet him and his company in Zarma by a saying, "Did you sleep well? In peace? . . . [laughs and switches to Hausa] I said [in Zarma], "Did you sleep well?" They replied in Zarma, "In peace. So you are Zarma?" I replied in Zarma, "I am a Hausa." [In Zarma] "Please, leave me alone with this business of Zarma-Zarma." [In Hausa] "My people the Zarma are too proud, my people. . . . In the past, they forbade me to do what I am doing now. They didn't want me to do it. . . . But now that they derive pride in seeing me in national Muslim programs, they want me to run the program in Zarma. . . . [laughs]. . . . Now, people see everything through ethnic pride. . . . This is ignorance. We are all Muslims at the mosque, and in my family some are married and have children with non-Zarma, like my sister with whom I now live. . . . Do you hear me . . . ?

In this regard Malama A'ishatu belongs to the same school of thought as some of the leading Islamists who see the relationship between Islamicity and ethnicity as mutually exclusive and even conflictual, and the resort to ethnicity in modern day politics as belonging to the world of *jahilci,* as understood by F. Dale Eickelman and James Piscatori: "The idea that Islam and ethnicity are antithetical and antagonistic also appears in the thinking of Islamist such as Egypt's Sayyid Qutb, who consigns ethnicity, tribalism and nationalism to the category of the *Jahiliyya.* In using this term, which originally refers to the pre-Islamic "age of ignorance" he powerfully criticizes the validity of particularistic ties" (Eickelman and Piscatori 1996, 100).

On the question of poetry, piety, and identity, then, unlike the traditional *griottes* (female praise-singers) whose relationship to song or verbal art performance in general is located in the realm of orality and is most commonly a skill inherited through ancestral blood tradition, Malama A'ishatu's relationship to religious songs (most commonly identified as religious poetry in Hausa language when written) reveals an interplay between literacy and Islamic identity. As she says, "Everywhere I hear songs . . . some of the songs I don't even know where their papers are. But I did retain them in my head." Hence, unlike the *griotte,* Malama's love for songs is not rooted in ancestral tradition. It emanates rather from her personal artistic attraction to songs and to her initiation to Islamic poetry recitation, as her reference to some of the lost papers of her collection suggests. At best Malama A'ishatu Hamani Zarmakoy Dancandu is a "griotte of Islam."

Transitional "Digraphia": From Hausa *Ajami* to Arabic Script

For Malama A'ishatu the issue of Hausa language is not only important with regard to questions of identity and practicality of communication; it is also central in the methodology for her Qur'anic literacy work, which I here describe as "transitional digraphia." Applied linguistics offers the idea of transitional bilingualism in which one language, usually the native one, is used as a bridge to the acquisition of another, usually a second or foreign language. By the same token, I am using the term transitional digraphia to refer to an educational process where a script tied to the students' native language is used transitionally to help them acquire a script and literacy skills of a second or foreign language. In the context of this research, the more local script is *Ajami,* which, though itself an adaptation of the Arabic script for writing the Hausa language, has become more indigenous to the students. The "foreign" script, on the other hand, is associated with Arabic, which the students may acquire later in life (either in a limited way for religious purposes or more comprehensively for some more communication needs).

Malama's educational efforts and methodology raise the broader issue of an epistemological contrast between societies and cultures. It is now widely known that global imbalances of power, which define Western hegemonic relations with non-Western cultures, have been successful in positioning Western epistemology at the foothold of world scholastic and intellectual traditions. This power equation has contributed, to a great extent, to the marginalization of other indigenous/native modes of knowledge and their undervaluation vis-à-vis the Western norms or standards. The hierarchization of the different forms of epistemologies in accordance with their cultural origins signals the unequal relations between Western-trained scholars (whether of Western or non-Western origin) and other non-Western trained scholars and intellectuals whose scholarship and intellectual products are grounded in more independent, "organic/native" discursive paradigms.

Most often the interactions between Western-trained scholars and their non-Western colleagues are determined by: (1) what Chandra Mohanty defines as "the global hegemony of western scholarship" in the production, distribution, and consumption of information and ideas (1991, 55); and (2) the exploitation of the power inherent in the privileged location of the Western trained intellectuals, legitimizing theirs as the only authorized voice to validate and then interpret the knowledge of their non-Westernized colleagues. The pursuit of scientific objectivity required within the Western framework imposes distance that hinders collaborative intellectual negotiation of meaning from all parties over the subject of inquiry on equal terms.

For example, numerous studies dealing with education or literacy in Islamic cultures in Africa present the following kinds of comments that portray Islamic education in a rather negative light:

> Islamic education is largely *Thomistic* in approach; spiritual and literary authority, rather than intellectual curiosity, are emphasized. At higher levels theology and law are the basic disciplines, and the emphasis is on preserving the truth, which rests on revelation and interpretation. Thus, for Muslim leaders the sole purpose of education is to learn Islam's doctrine. . . . [C]hildren enter Quranic school between the ages of four and six and immediately set about learning the Quran, beginning with the first chapter and proceeding straight through. *Learning* is by rote rather than through discussion and discovery. Fixed sections of the Quran are recited by the teacher and repeated by the students until the texts are learnt by heart. . . . *Islamic education* is noncompetitive, and examinations are foreign to it. The students' educational proficiency is determined by the status of the teacher, not by individual performance. There are no examinations or specific requirements to be met and no teaching materials to bridge the gap between the instructor's knowledge and the wide world. (Callaway and Creevey 1994, 61)

Several problems accrue to such views that have been repeated over and over again over the years. Among these are (1) They overlook the fact that learning by rote and memorization happens mainly at an early stage in order to initiate the beginner student to the principle of *tajwid*—the art of reciting the Qur'an in accordance with established rules of pronunciation and intonation. (2) They fail to emphasize that since Qur'anic Arabic is a foreign language for most Muslims, Thomistic learning is important for developing the mental capacity for retention, a concept whose relevance in cognitive development is in keeping with Western epistemology itself. (3) They disregard that dimension of Islamic learning that is based on the doctrine of *fiqh,* which is related to the quest for Islamic truth through the exercise of intellectualism and scholarship involving the study of Islamic history, contexts of various *hadiths,* and testing the validity or supremacy of a given interpretation over a multiplicity of interpretations.[4]

The picture provided by most studies of the Hausa framed within Western epistemological paradigm of an Islamic education that discourages critical thinking is in marked contrast to the one provided by Malama A'ishatu. During my interviews with her, Malama articulated a well-rationalized curriculum design for her students. She understood when to use rote-learning and memorization, and for what purpose; she knew when to introduce writing in *Ajami* and when to transfer this skill to the writing and learning of Arabic; she was very conscious of when to promote critical skills and which Islamic texts to choose for that purpose; and she understood the importance of fostering a competitive spirit, not with other fellow students, but with the *self.* Consider the following words of Malama A'ishatu: "When they [the students] reach *Alamtara kaifa* I introduce them to the slate [writing]. Or when they reach *Sabbi* in reading the Qur'an, I introduce them to the consonants and vowels whether it be the Arabic ones or the Hausa ones. You know there are the Hausa consonants and the vowel markers, for example when you write the subscript (-) under the consonant marker, you have the syllable *bi;* you keep moving till the end. And if it is the Arabic ones that we will do, it goes *a, ba, ta, sa ja. . . .* But ours [*Ajami*] is much easier for the minds of the child to grasp. Once she or he understands it then one introduces the Arabic one. . . . But usually this comes around the fifth *izb.*"[5]

What Malama's comment suggests is a great understanding of the cognitive implications of learning a new language, becoming literate simultaneously in one's mother-tongue and a foreign language (Arabic), and mediating mother-tongue literacy through a foreign alphabet and mediating the learning of this foreign language through literacy in mother-tongue. My invitation to Malama to explain her methodology as a teacher allowed her to provide a rational account of her teaching approach that demonstrates her intellectual understanding of what in the Western epistemology is located within the discipline of psycholinguistics, a concept that she herself might never use.

A comparative examination of my interview with Malama A'ishatu and quotes from Western-trained experts, then, demonstrates the total lack of collaborative engagement in the construction of an understanding of "what is actually going" on in the Qur'anic school. What we have here is the "gazing" interpreter's understanding of that "traditional system" without the indigenous/native teachers' own voices explicating the approach they are using and the rationale for their choice.

Indeed, the Qur'anic text itself is replete with verses calling on those who are reading it to engage, at the same time, in a reflective exercise about the relationship between the physical and the divine: "This conception of nature finds its appropriate place in the overall context of Islamic cosmology, which acts as a bridge connecting pure metaphysics with the physical world" Al Zeera (2001, 67). It is difficult to understand how such an epistemological paradigm that seeks to be holistic and comprehensive can be described in reductive terms as simply Thomistic.

Malama A'ishatu: Between Womanhood and Motherhood

The question of epistemologies, however, is relevant not only with regard to Malama A'ishatu's public work as a teacher, but also to a more intimate part of her personal life as a woman who did not bear a biological child in a society that puts high value on a woman's capacity to bear children. How does Malama A'ishatu relate to her condition of childlessness? Even in this very private domain—which Malama A'ishatu addressed without my prompting—she makes a clear connection between the personal and the professional dimensions of her life: "A person who can read this paper and another who can't, we are not the same. I have told you about my happiness, reading, the quest for knowledge and teaching young girls and composing songs and that I used to cry for not having children. Haven't I told you? However, since the day I completed my *Saukar Qur'ani* [Qur'anic training] . . . I knew now that even this smallest piece of paper has someone to take it . . . that bitter yearning [for childbearing] was gone from me. I forgot since that day the subject of childbearing. However, I used to in the past." In other words, like her male counterpart in the society, the woman intellectual can also claim the heritage of her scholarship. And her ability to bequeath this knowledge to posterity rises above the childbearing consideration to become the prime determinant of her identity and her value in society.

But absence of childbearing does not mean absence of mothering. As Malama A'ishatu herself reminded me in the course of our interviews, she mothered her own younger siblings until they became of marriageable age. In fact, her Qur'anic school is located in the home of one of her younger siblings that she raised as her daughter. Malama A'ishatu also assisted in mothering the children of her cowives and other relatives. And in her own mind, the boundary between teaching and mothering her students was often blurred, shown by her references to them at times as "my students" *(dalibaina, almajirraina)* and other times as "my children" *(yarana).*

Conclusion

The life of Malama A'ishatu has demonstrated how for a long time tradition and modernity colluded to marginalize her in the realm of knowledge. It is true that she had opportunities to acquire a substantial amount of Qur'anic knowledge from precolonial times into the colonial era. But the forces of Afro-Islamic patriarchy allowed her little possibility of entering the advanced spheres of Islamic knowledge or of engaging in the exchange of ideas in public, even on issues related to Muslim women.

The current status of Malama A'ishatu is that of elite *Sufi* scholar and leader. In many ways, her aristocratic birth parallels that of the legendary Nana Asma'u Dan Fodiyo of Sokoto Caliphate, the contemporary *Sufi* women leaders, *Muqqadamat,* of Kano (Nigeria), amply discussed by Alaine Huston (1997, 1999) and Balaraba Sule and Priscilla Starratt (1991, 29–49). It also parallels that of their counterparts in Senegal known as the *Mouride*

Shaykhas (Coulon 1988). Unlike all these other Muslim women leaders in the Sahelian region who were elevated to the highest religious ranks through the patronage of their male kin Malama A'ishatu did not rise to the status of a *Sufi* woman leader of the *Tijaniyya* order as a product of a patrilineal inheritance. For although Malama comes from a family of devout Muslim parents, she was, based on her account, the only female child to attend Qur'anic school while her male siblings were given the privilege to join the newly established French school. Thus, as a media figure, a teacher of a women's home-based Qur'anic school, and a transmitter of Islamic literacy to her female kin, Malama A'ishatu has built a new and significant family legacy, especially for the womenfolk. It is also noteworthy that the gender ideology that discriminated against her enrollment in French school had an unforeseen outcome: it created the conditions for Malama A'ishatu to rise to her current status of *Sufi* women's leadership.

The introduction of Western secular education under French colonialism further reinforced her marginalization, as no real effort was made in the new dispensation to provide an opportunity for the education of women. For Muslim women of her generation, the state of affairs continued well into the postcolonial dispensation. It was not until the 1990s that Malama A'ishatu became a recognized authority in her own right in the wider public arena. This, as indicated earlier, was the period in which the sociopolitical and cultural terrain was reconfigured by the democratization momentum, and the women began to seize the opportunity to exercise their agency in new ways. While it was the younger generation of women who were at the forefront of this struggle to create an alternative modernity for (Muslim) women (within the indigenous traditions, Western secularism and new Islamisms) in Niger, their efforts also opened up new spaces for women of the generations of their mothers and grandmothers, such as Malama A'isḥatu Hamani Zarmakoy Dancandu.

Chapter 2

Women and the Political Economy of Education

By educating a man, you educate an individual, but by educating a woman, you educate, within the human unit that the family represents, a whole generation which will be born and evolve under guidance and influence.

Abdou Moumouni

Introduction

The field of education and its interplay with gender is one cultural arena in Niger Republic where the convergence between Africa's indigenous traditions, Islamic heritage, and Western legacies is best at play. But while I utilize terms like "tradition," "indigenous," and "Western" in exploring this historical experience, I wholly share the view of the late Nigerien educational psychologist Idrissa Diawara: "[E]ven as we refer to the remote eras, the question of an autonomous social development must be looked at with great reserve. For the phenomena of contacts, exchanges, and borrowings are such that it would be vain to try to establish a distinct picture of cultural elements that were 'originally' created in the milieu from those evolving from the phenomenon of diffusion" (Diawara 1988, 10).

The discourse on education in Africa cannot be divorced from the development of literacies and their connection with orality. As a result, throughout this chapter, education and literacy/orality are considered as integral components with overlapping meanings. Several studies of literacy across cultures have demonstrated the oral/literate continuum in discourse as well as in modes of imparting knowledge (Heath 1983; Gee 1996; Kress 1997; Levine 1986; Mack 2004; Street 1984, 1995 and 2000; Tannen 1982 and 1994). As Jacqueline Jones Royster rightly points out in her study of literacy streams and social life changes among African American women: "Knowledge is grounded in experiences; conventions and traditions can be treated with great skepticism; notions of truth and insight are rooted in the particularities of time and place and thereby subject to revision. With such protean genre, inevitably, there is possibility—even probability—of fluidity and flexibility in the meaning-making process. In other words, there is an opportunity for oral and literate practices to merge variously" (Royster 2000, 31). Mack further shows that even those Muslim women who acquire knowledge through the written word often tend to favor oral means of imparting and (re)constructing knowledge (Mack 2004).

In this chapter, I demonstrate how each stream of education in Niger set (and continues to set) its intent and goals and how the latter determine how women have either succeeded or failed to gain access to educational opportunities in the country. In addition, I explore the interplay between women and the politics of education (including orality and literacy) in Niger. I examine the complementarity of orality to literacy as a social practice necessarily involving reading events (Gee 1996; Street 2000) and the crucial place of particular literacies as well as epistemic traditions as embedded in the given ideologies in society. The latter culturally set the criteria as to who in society will have access to which type of literacy and for what purpose(s). Thus, the gendered manifestation of literacy as social practice in society is a significant parameter to factor in any critical analysis and formulation of literacy/educational recommendations.

Furthermore, I analyze Nigerien women's own responses to educational policies as framed and implemented by dominant structures such as the state, religious bodies, ethnicity, class, and international educational funding agencies, as well as the transformative outcomes of their responses in shaping new educational reforms in the country.

In looking at education and literacy, it is crucial not to continue marginalizing those women in Nigerien societies who have contributed and continue to contribute to knowledge production from within the spaces of orality. This is particularly significant in a society like Niger where orality characterizes the life of the majority of the population regardless of gender. Beverly Mack's *Muslim Women Sing: Hausa Popular Song* (2004), which focuses on the verbal artistry of Northern Nigerian women, Thomas Hale's *Griots and Griottes* (1998), and Aissata Sidikou's *Recreating Words, Reshaping*

Worlds: The Verbal Art of Women from Niger, Mali and Senegal (2001), for example, are excellent illustrations of the wealth of orality of the women of the Sahel in general and of Niger in particular, in the realm of song and poetry. Elsewhere, along with many other literary critics, I have also demonstrated how African women's oral genres have been appropriated by male writers and scribes in the production of literature in local and European languages (Alidou 2002; Stephens 1981, and others).

The postcolonial promotion of girls' formal education in Niger Republic has fostered the development in the 1990s of a nascent Nigerien women's literary culture in the French language, a trend illustrated by the acclaimed short story by Hélène Kaziyende entitled "Le déserteur" (The deserter, 1992) and much more recently by the publication of women's novellas in national languages, as exemplified by Fatimane Moussa-Aghali's award-winning autobiographical novella written in Hausa, titled *Yarintata* (My childhood, 2000). The publication of a distinctively Nigerien literature in national languages and in French was the initiative of a bilingual (mother-tongue-French) educational program by the Ministry of Education through the sponsorship of the German development foundation Deutsche Gesellschaft für Technische Zusammenarbeit (GTZ). This is a significant development in Niger Republic, given the country's past reliance on written literature produced in Nigeria for texts in Hausa and Fulfulde and from other francophone countries or France for texts in French. This is a new and exciting area of research that is yet to be investigated.

Renée Larrier's study *Francophone Women Writers of Africa and the Caribbean* offers an even broader and more complex theoretical understanding of black women's orality in francophone Africa and the Caribbean, creating the possibility of the transmission of knowledge by women in a wide range of "oralized" domains that include literature, painting, pottery, textile design, and fashion (Larrier 2000, 14–44). Larrier's paradigm is equally applicable to the situation in Niger as my analysis of women's dress discourse in the introduction and other parts of the book demonstrates. It is equally important to examine the impact of the cultural ethos and didactic values of Nigerien societies on gender ideologies as embedded in women's oral narratives, and the consequences of these ideologies on women's identities and access to literacies/education.

The evaluation of the politics of women's literacy practices is especially urgent now that the overall educational system is in a state of chaos throughout Africa. Looking at how women are or are not being accommodated within the new educational reforms is pertinent to this study, especially in a context where the patriarchal state and international educational planning agencies often sideline developmental issues pertaining to women for other "priorities." What is even more problematic about the marginalization of women's needs in literacy/education (as well as in public health and agriculture) is how historical arguments, often couched in patriarchal interpretations of religion (Islam), are deployed by local as well as international policymakers and implementers to justify their lack of commitment to women's literacy/education. The call by the renowned Moroccan feminist sociologist Fatima Mernissi to women scholars in the Muslim world to rethink how masculinist hegemony appropriates Islamic history as a tool to justify antiwomen agendas, especially in education, is also relevant for the Nigerien context:

> Historical argument seems to be crucial to questions concerning the rights of women in Muslim theocracies. This is because all kinds of state policies to do with women, be they in the economic sphere (the right to work outside the home), or in the legal sphere (issues concerning personal status or family law), are justified and legitimized by reference to the tradition of the Prophet, that is, to historical tradition. Progressive persons of both sexes in the Muslim world know that the only weapon they can use to fight for human rights in general, and women's rights in particular, in those countries where religion is not separate from the state is to base claims on religious history. (Mernissi 1996, 92)

The recent state of gender inequalities in literacy/education programs in Niger can be traced to the colonial period. Smock makes the following observation in her introduction to women's education in the former British colonies: "The development of western education within the framework of a Victorian mentality and a dependent economy, consistently led to the exclusion of women from the educational system. . . . The European conception of females as helpless homebound creatures, inclined administrators to favor the admission of boys to the limited number of places available" (Smock 1981, 254).

Similar observations have been made about the plight of women's education in such Muslim francophone countries as Morocco (Sadiqqi 2003, 190), Algeria (Lazreg 1994, 63–64), and Niger Republic (Djibo 2001, 79–80). Marnia Lazreg rightly observes that Frenchmen, even in their own society, did not recognize the principle of equality between men and women that made them totally unwilling to consider women as either legitimate interlocutors (even if inferior) or worthy instruments in the construction of the new colonial order (Lazreg 1994, 63). Consequently, the female colonized African subjects received little consideration in the colonial project of the so-called French civilization mission, in which education in the French language was assumed to uplift the colonized from their "state of savagery."

Given the two facets of the nature of French domination—hegemony rooted in the emasculation of other men and hegemonic patriarchy over the female colonized subjects—it was ironic that when the first private

French Catholic missionary school opened its doors in 1949 in Niamey, it only admitted male students with a French Catholic nun as headmistress. Gender ideology within the French colonial framework in Niger shows how the colonial women were (made) agents in this conquest and also how their agency did not involve a sensitivity to colonized native women. Only in 1961 did the private Catholic mission school begin to open its doors to female students in a gender-segregated set-up. This gap of twelve years between the introduction of schooling for boys, on the one hand, and for girls, on the other, is significant in what came to account for the gender gap in educational opportunities and outcomes between male and female in both the national colonial and the postcolonial dispensations.

The denial of colonial education to women affected their chances of participating as direct agents in the Western-style capitalist economies (Amadiume 1998). However, this outcome was to be expected, given that Western capitalism is framed within a patriarchal ideology that did not incorporate women as "wageable" productive labor outside the household. Thus, European colonialism not only further marginalized women from the public sphere of labor economies, but also added a new hierarchy in literacy practices in the society. In the case of Niger, the new literacy inherited from French colonization, which imposed the use of Latin script and the French language as the sole medium of instruction, severely undervalued the pre-existing forms of literacy practices in Arabic language and *Ajami* script (the indigenized version of the Arabic script) and placed them at the bottom of the literacy pyramid. As Benedicta Egbo rightly points out more generally, with African women "excluded from educational opportunities, wage labor, politics and government, colonialism increased and consolidated (at great cost) the gender-base of social chasm that may have existed, leaving women unprepared for the emerging world order which their societies were fast becoming an integral part of. At least such was the case up until the late 50s" (Egbo 2000, 3).

The factors that hindered women in their access to educational opportunities during the precolonial and colonial eras extended into the postcolonial dispensation. These have combined with new types of constraints, notwithstanding the well-meaning rhetoric of nationalist leaders and international educational funding agencies for African women's empowerment through literacy and education. The fact is, the underlying intent and goal of the various educational projects and reforms undertaken throughout Niger's recent history are rooted in hegemonic patriarchal local and international frameworks and tend to incorporate women only for instrumental purposes, not for women's own advancement.

Furthermore, numerous studies in educational philosophy have demonstrated that literacy education is not a neutral enterprise. In any culture, literacy education is conceived within an ideological framework that serves to attain defined aims (Eickelman 1985, 57–71; Heath 1983; Scribner and Cole 1988; Street 1984 and 1995; Gee et al. 1996, Levine 1986). To this extent, the multiple forms of educational, literacy, and orality practices in Niger are embedded in the ideologies of power that define the values they assign to the practices as well as to the individuals who develop the imparted skills.

Moreover, this interplay between orality/literacy/education and power must address the place of women in this dialectic, especially in the case of predominantly Muslim societies where "the women's question"—not "the men's question"—is almost taken as correlating with the identity of the entire nation, as Mernissi (1996) has pointed out. This consideration is critical to understanding women's cultural location in the nation. In this regard, Olivier Meunier's observation concerning the significance of culture and its weight on educational reforms is very important: "*Culture* as a collective identity is historically produced. It undergoes continuous change in time and space depending on the interests and functions it fulfills in the moment. This is often manifested through political conflicts in society. Thus, culture is a 'reservoir' of practices and representations which are exploited by social agents in their aim to (re)negotiate their identity. Thus, society is constantly refashioning itself in order to survive" (Meunier 1997, 14; emphasis added).

In line with Meunier's powerful remarks, I will show in the remainder of this chapter how Niger's indigenous traditions, Islamic heritage and the Western legacy have contributed to shaping women's orality/literacy and educational experiences in the country. Furthermore, I will show that Nigerien women also use their understanding of the multiple levels of patriarchal hegemony over national policies and resources to (re)create orality/literacy and educational possibilities for themselves in a way that often subverts the status quo.

Women, Orality, and Literacies in Precolonial Niger

Before the inception of Islam in the Sahelian cultural landscape currently known as Niger Republic in the so-called francophone West Africa, orality played a central role in the lives of people and characterized the majority of the cultures of the peoples who inhabit the area. The only exceptions were the Tuareg and Schwa-Arabs, who had literate traditions: Tifinagh in the Tamajaq language for the Tuareg and Arabic script for the Schwa-Arabs. While among the Tuareg both men and women can read and write Tifinagh, Tuareg women are more closely associated with the literate use of Tifinagh literacy for the production of classical poetry in Tamajaq language (Foucauld 1920; Nicolaisen and Nicolaisen 1998; Klute 2002 pers. comm.) and other purposes such as letter writing.

The oral landscape began to face new challenges with its encounter with Islam. The advent of Islam around the ninth to thirteenth centuries led to the adoption of the Arabic language and Islamic literacy, initially for the purpose of reading religious texts and producing religious discourse. Later, writing in Arabic became an established literacy and literary tradition. Moreover, writing in Arabic also served as a precursor to *Ajami* literacy in local languages (in Kanuri, Fulfulde, Hausa, and Zarma-Songhay) (Chtatou 1992; Hunwick and O'Fahey 1995).

The consolidation of Islam in precolonial Nigerien societies, however, also brought a new ideological ethos that had important gender implications. At the spiritual level, conversion to Islam also put heavy pressure on new converts who practiced (and continue to practice to the present day) indigenous forms of spirituality (known as *Folley* or *Holley* among the Zarma-Songhay and *Bori* among the Hausa) to abandon the ritualistic practices associated with these pre-Islamic religions. Consequently, other types of traditional knowledge, such as songs, dances, and music of spirit communion based on pre-Islamic cosmogony that involved much female participation began to be repressed. However, in most cases Sahelian women who did not have access to Islamic literacy and other forms of knowledge held on to traditional spirituality by incorporating into it some Islamic idioms,[1] as local Islam also borrowed (and continues to assimilate idioms) from indigenous African spirituality (Diarra 1971, 151–54 and 192–212; Bovin 1983; Echard 1991, 211 and 215; Cooper 1998, 21–37; Masquelier 2001; and others). Eleanor Abdella Doumato makes similar observations about how the exclusion of women from "sacred spaces" of Islam in Saudi Arabia and the Gulf States has inadvertently created a context for the women to redefine Islam and its relationship to pre-Islamic spirituality. This process, in turn, has led to the ascription of new meanings and functions in religion, blurring the boundaries between Islamic and non-Islamic spirituality (Doumato 2000).

Between its doctrinal position and popular practice, Islam gradually transformed and deepened structures and relations of patriarchy. With the interpretation of Islamic doctrines having become predominantly masculinist, the legacy naturally favored that those most tutored in Islam be male and in an institutional environment—the elementary *makarantar Allo* (slate school) for children and adolescents and the more advanced *makarantar ilimi* for (young) adults who follow this lifelong educational trajectory—where Arabic and *Ajami* literacy was imparted.[2] It was natural, therefore, that under this system women would be disadvantaged and the bulk of literature in print arising from it would be male-dominated and male-oriented.

Some women who grew up in the household of the *'ulema* (religious teachers/leaders), however, managed to acquire literacy skills in both Arabic and their native languages as was the case of the womenfolk related to the Islamic Fulani leader Sheikh Usman Dan Fodiyo (Boyd 1989; Boyd and Mack 1997; Mack and Boyd 2000). Although much of the literature dealing with the impact of Sheikh Usman Dan Fodiyo's dynasty focuses on northern Nigeria, most of the southeastern and northern part of Niger shared and continues to share historical and contemporary continuities with the cultures and societies of northern Nigeria. For example, the training of Sheikh Usman Dan Fodiyo by *'ulemas* in Agadez (in northern Niger), the knowledge of Tamajaq (a language of Niger) acquired by his legendary daughter Nana Asma'u (who was also a renowned scribe, poet, teacher, and scholar), and the contacts they both had with scholars who resided in areas located in Niger are well-documented facts (Mack and Boyd 2000, 12–13).

Many women from the ruling class who were learned Islamic teachers made their contribution to the campaign to spread the religion and forge an Islamic identity by providing home-based religious teaching to women from the newly converted communities. The acquisition of a rudimentary reading knowledge of the Qur'an was part of this religious training. But the capacity for literacy in these circumstances was not sufficiently developed for purposes of creative writing or recording of women's other areas of knowledge. The exceptions were the aristocratic women from the caliphate household who produced classical religious literature (Boyd and Mack 1989 and 2001).

Hostile to other expressions of African spirituality such as *Bori* (in Hausa) or *Folley* (in Songhay-Zarma), the Islamic conversion campaign set a new hierarchy of knowledge, validating Islamic epistemology over indigenous pre-Islamic ways of knowing and of using that knowledge. Here *elite* Islamic women, such as Nana Asma'u Dan Fodiyo and her siblings, played a crucial role in educating newly converted Hausa women from Gobir (which extends to present-day Niger Republic), especially those who resorted to *Bori* for cures. In fact, Nana Asma'u became a model teacher in this transnational region. In the view of Malama A'ishatu: "Nana Asma'u is our prime role model in Islam, from Kebbi [Sokoto, Nigeria] to Magaria [Niger] to Koni [Niger] to Argungun [Niger]. . . . She even assembled women. She made a name among historical Muslim women like other Islamic women who are saints. Even the male *'ulemas* celebrate her. Haven't you ever heard of her poem *Mahammada* on television and radio used on Thursdays and Fridays. Remember, it is usually her praise poem of the prophet Muhammad (Peace be upon him) that is used to announce important events or the death of famous people, like when Rais [President] Seyni Kountché died" (interview with the author, July 20, 1996).

Malama A'ishatu's reading is supported by the research work of Moumouni (2002) and stands in contrast to the view that Hausa women in Niger did not benefit from the legacy of Usman Dan Fodiyo and his daughters

(Cooper 1998, 35). In reality, men and women in Nigeria and Niger have continued to interact frequently and maintain strong ties in spite of the artificial colonial divisions between "Anglophone" and "francophone" spheres. As a result, when the democratization of the 1990s was in full swing, Islamicist women in Niger drew freely from that common Islamic heritage in the Sahel.

Islamic knowledge acquired by new converts gradually came to be integrated into traditional African spirituality, healing songs, and medicinal remedies. The dialectics of the interplay between women, class, religion, and knowledge production in the earlier period of Islamic expansion in the Sahel became evident, for example, in Nana Asma'u's encouragement of the new women converts to turn to memorization and recitation of "curative" Qur'anic verses and chapters (Boyd 2001, 7–22).

Women's Other Educational Skills in the Precolonial Era

Analyzing the interplay between skill acquisition and gender in precolonial Niger, Abdou Moumouni argues that precolonial African education must be assessed in the context of its responses to the economic, social, and political conditions of societies. He adds that education was framed within an agrarian and feudal system. Within such a system, knowledge and technology were essentially empirical and acquired through actual experience, and the transmission of facts and training in a vocation were most commonly inherited by individuals in a socially stratified system and were localized at the village level.

Additionally, Moumouni points out that the precolonial educational system was characterized by three main stages: (1) The initial stage relates to childbearing and rearing until about age eight when teaching and educating is exclusively women-centered regardless of the sex of the child. (2) The adolescent stage refers to the stage of child (girl or boy) training for participation in productive activities. Teaching and educating were gendered and took place in gendered spaces, in the household for the girls (cooking, sweeping, baby-sitting), and, for boys, outside the house, especially on the farm or with the herds. Thus, mothers are responsible for initiating the daughter(s) to an understanding of their sex roles as framed by their societal values while fathers take care of their sons' socialization to the values associated with their gender roles. (3) The third stage is the one Moumouni refers to as the stage of logical apprenticeship where the adolescent (girl or boy) is initiated to the cultural rites informing his/her adult identity (Moumouni 1968, 24–29).

Moumouni's contribution to our understanding of education in precolonial African societies is indeed insightful, and he must be credited for pointing out its gendered structure. However, he fails to interrogate the hierarchical structure within indigenous African cultures and the issue of women within a caste system engaged in the subjugation and exploitation of slave women's labor. This is especially problematic given that his main goal, as he stated in his book, is to offer alternative strategies for "decolonizing" African education. Decolonization is not only needed from the point of view of Africa's relationship with the educational legacy of European colonialism, but also must encompass inherited indigenous educational practices that are discriminatory and that were carried over into the colonial and the postcolonial dispensations. The latter pertain to the gendered approach to knowledge linked to power relations between high caste and low caste (most often slaves) in precolonial societies and to the ways these relations continue to affect access to knowledge in the various cultures and across and within genders.

Among the Tuareg, for example, high-caste (noble) women lived off the labor of their female and male slaves. In this power configuration, the type of vocational skills that a slave Tuareg woman would learn in childhood would be different from those of her high-caste (noble) female contemporary. Moreover, the knowledge acquired by the female slave child would normally benefit the female master rather than herself. The investment of labor by female children of the same society, but of different social strata, would be radically different. Thus, precolonial caste ideology had and continues to have a bearing on which women would learn what and for whose advantage. Johannes and Ida Nicolaisen paint the following picture of the interplay between women's skills and women's servitude among the Tuareg:

> Women of the "noble" tribes do not contribute their labor to the household economy. A "noble" woman does absolutely no work, except for occasionally making luxury objects of leather and woods. All important household tasks are performed by slave girls. Thus, the "noble" woman leads a life of leisure. . . . Among other Tuareg the female contribution is of the greatest importance to the domestic economy. If a woman has no male or female slaves at her disposal . . . then the management of the family goat and sheep herds are entirely in her hands, as is the milking of cows among the Southern Tuareg [Niger and Mali]. (Nicolaisen and Nicolaisen 1997, 706–7)

Moumouni's analysis of the interplay between women and education in precolonial Africa is articulated within a framework that homogenizes all African women in spite of the differences in their regional, ethnic, caste, class, and nomadic or sedentary backgrounds. His analysis does not critically examine the contrast between the educational trajectories of women in traditionally patriarchal societies (Hausa, Schwa-Arabs, Zarma, Gurmance, and Tuareg) and those of matriarchal societies (Bororo and Wogo).

What are the implications of these axes of difference and systemic change for women as educators or learners in such societies in the aftermath of Islamic and European colonization?

Many studies of West African Muslim societies stress the fact that patriarchy was strengthened by Islamization. In their study of the situation of women in Niger Republic, for example, Mary White-Kaba and Hassana Alidou made the following observation: "Women's status and freedom of choice (e.g., of her husband) are generally higher in ethnic groups with a nomadic tradition (Arabs, Fulani, Kanuri, Tuareg and Tubu). A hypothesis is that in small nomadic communities the active voluntary participation of all family members is necessary for daily survival. Women's status, e.g., in Tuareg society, is being restricted by increasing sedentarization and Islamization" (White-Kaba and Alidou 1994, 5). This social transformation brought about by Islamization had a direct bearing on women's choices and learning opportunities. Increasingly men came to appropriate and control the new literacy skills introduced by Islam. As a result, the visibility of women, as in the case of the Fulani, in public spaces such as the market where they sold their dairy products, has been erased gradually as the practice of *kuble* (seclusion) became prevalent among conservative Islamic families. Consequently, vocational differentiation evolved between Fulani women nomads who still lead an active lifestyle in the public sphere and urban Fulani women who might resort to new types of skills—Islamic literacy or trading—from within the private household.

In Hausa culture, Islam influenced the value of women's oral narratives by discouraging the performance of narratives that dwell on the *Bori* ethos. In the process, women's oral narratives involving spirits and ogres were gradually recrafted to incorporate an Islamic ethos. Furthermore, with the privileging of male literacy in Hausa culture, the male literati began to appropriate in script women's folktale genres and infused them with additional Islamic imagery (Skinner 1969 and 1977; Stephens 1981 and 1991, 221–31; Alidou 2002).

In summary, then, the inception of Islam in Nigerien societies brought about two practices—Islamic literacy and *kuble* (seclusion)—that transformed and continue to shape the cultural dialectics of women's identity and their struggle to have access to literacy and education as rights in the new patriarchal Islamized cultures. However, the few studies that are available on contemporary women in sub-Saharan Muslim societies show that within this patriarchal framework of seclusion, a great number of Muslim women have succeeded in creatively redefining their lives and relationships to society (Djibo 2001; Sidikou 2001; Hirsch 1998; Huston 1997; Cooper 1997; Callaway 1987; Callaway and Creevy 1994; and Coles and Mack 1991; Mirza and Strobel l989; and Strobel 1979).

Education and the French "Civilizing" Mission: Gender Implications

French colonization is widely known for its (in)famous policy of cultural assimilation of its invaded peoples and territories. This is the policy that is said to have distinguished French from British and German colonialism, while showing affinity with Portuguese colonialism. In both the French and Portuguese colonial experiences the colonial subjects and their territories were considered to be extensions of the metropole.

The French colonial regulations focus more directly on the French language policy because they had great confidence in their language as a transmitter of French cultural values. By implication, therefore, any subversive knowledge that the African could have acquired in the process of education in the French language was expected to be neutralized by the "potency" of French culture. French colonialism, therefore, sought its security in linguistic and cultural assimilation policies. And generally speaking, it is in French (and to some extent Portuguese) colonies that we find the clearest evidence supporting the nationalist thesis that the imposition of European languages was an important cultural aid to colonialism. Commenting on "francophone" Africa, for example, Paulin Djité explains: "French was imposed at the outset of the colonial era as an instrument of multidimensional domination. . . . Persons who did not speak French were considered barbarians, and the civilized people of France had the divine duty to educate such persons. . . . The imposition and expansion of the language was then seen as the best way to control and "assimilate" the "subjects" of the colonies" (Djité 1992, 166).

Unlike the British, who were sometimes wary of the rapid and "reckless" spread of their language, then, the French were linguistically hegemonic to the extreme. Where the British provided some room for the use and development of some African languages, for example, the French officially banned the use of African languages in education and "ruled that only French was to be used" (Djité 1992, 166).

Unlike in northern Nigeria where the British adoption of indirect policy allowed Islamic literacy in both the Arabic language and *Ajami* to survive, the opposite trend was manifested in French-dominated Islamic Africa. In order to assert its colonial project in its dominated territories, the cultural production of the educated French *assimilé* in Africa required both the exclusion of local languages and the construction of a hierarchy among the streams of literacies in the dominated cultural landscape, with literacy in the French language and Latin alphabet at the apex of education as well as administration. This led to the undervaluing of local Afro-Islamic literacies in Tifinagh and Arabic.

From this same logic followed the dismissal of local literacy practices that evolved from the adoption and adaptation of Arabic script and the privileging of Latin script. According to Mohamed Chtatou:

> This smear campaign against the Arabic language was complemented by another aiming at the replacement of the Arabic script by the Latin one in writing national and local languages on the ground that Arabic script is difficult, very complicated and cannot be used as easily as Latin in typing and printing. Moreover, unlike the latter it is not guaranteed an international status and cannot be understood widely. (Chtatou 1992, 19–20)

This linguistic imperialism undertaken by the French colonial administration therefore rejected the historical connection between Muslim people of sub-Saharan Africa with Islam, the Arabic language, Islamic literacies, and Arabic-speaking people of Africa and elsewhere. The colonial policy in Niger often restricted the use of the Arabic language and Islamic literacies (in Arabic language and *Ajami*) to the mosques and Qur'anic community schools.

The imperial intent underlying the French cultural assimilation project in education was essentially economic. This is clearly demonstrated by the selectivity of the educational process—the tiny proportion of the educated "natives," mostly male, that ultimately made it through the process and the inferior quality of the received education: "A [William Pointy 1903] diploma [designed for African schools] was never recognized in France and was a dead end educationally throughout the interwar period, with a few notable exceptions" (Snipe 1998, 28).

The colonial educational policy in Africa was framed within a social reproduction ideology that viewed the school as a means to exacerbate or perpetuate social inequalities. Schooling responded less to popular impulses for advancement and local empowerment, and more to the requirements of discipline and conformity demanded by capitalist production and the nation-state. It served to reproduce rather than transform existing structural inequalities.

In addition to its class bias, French colonial educational policy in Niger had severe gender implications. It was based first on the marginalization of women's heritage, including women's knowledge embodied in oral literature in local languages, Arabic-Islamic orality/literacy for a significant number of traditional women, and women's inherited vocational skills, especially those related to the management and protection of the environment. As Hadiza Djibo points out:

> Colonial powers having not immediately felt the urgency to use women, the fate of the latter was the least of its main concern, as consequently revealed

> by the following statistics: in 1918, only 503 girls attended the French West African schools; in 1925, 2500 [girls], and in 1940, 7140 [girls], that is, hardly a tenth of the overall school enrolled male population, a derisory number even when compared to the overall female population. Thus, this constitutes the origin of the imbalance between men and women from the point of view of their integration into a professional life. (Djibo 2001, 79; my translation from French)

There has been a colonial religious bias with its own implications for Muslim girls in Niger (Meunier 2000, 62). In much of colonial francophone West Africa, schooling for girls was initiated by Catholic missions, and girls in countries such as Niger, which did not have these missions, naturally had more limited educational opportunities. On the other hand, even where Catholic missions did exist (as in Senegal, for example), there was tremendous discrimination against girls who had not converted to Christianity. Thus, girls who continued to cling to the Islamic faith remained marginal (Djibo 2001, 79–80). This educational discrimination of girls on the basis of religion is reminiscent of the colonial situation in Morocco before World War II where the French colonial government privileged non-Muslim over Muslim girls in educational recruitment (Sadiqi 2003, 190).

When women were used at all in the labor market, they were not valued, as compensation for their labor was channeled through their husbands who were granted the status of legitimate "household breadwinners" by colonial employers. Thus, the marginalization of women in formal education that had been fostered by conservative Islam was now reinforced by the European colonial dispensation. Similar conclusions were advanced earlier by Callaway and Creevy (1994) in their study of women and education in Senegal, another African country that, like Niger, is predominantly Islamic and a former French colony:

> The Islamic and French invasion of Senegal, then, combined to undermine the status of women. By independence in 1960, women were seriously disadvantaged relative to men in their access to the benefits of society, including political office, inherited wealth, the status of paid jobs, the advantages of education, the ability to get credit. (Callaway and Creevy 1994: 27)

As a result, at the dawn of Niger's independence from French colonialism, the women of the new nation had little to show from the French educational heritage, as the record of student enrollment in 1960 shows in table 1. With their declining numbers in the higher levels, and in a system where power was increasingly tied to French language and education, women entered the postcolonial era severely disadvantaged by the combination of local and colonial forces of patriarchy.

Table 1. Female access to French education in 1960

Level	Boys	Girls	% Girls
Kindergarten	287.000	232.000	44.70
Primary school	18.719	7.790	20.94
Secondary school	1.085	274.000	20.23
Technical school	61.000	–	0.00
University level	100.000	–	0.00

Source: Hamani (2000, 130).

Women in Education in the Aftermath of Independence

Decades after the country became independent, it continued to pursue a patriarchal educational ideology that maintained Nigerien women at the margins of structures of power. From the period of colonization to 2000, there was still a significant gender disparity in the percentage of women who attended the streams of modern forms of education in the country as illustrated by tables 2 and 3 on female enrollment in primary and secondary education. By the turn of the new century, therefore, the male-to-female ratio among school students was almost two to one. It is also very clear from the above figures that the rate at which the gender gap is closing is very sluggish and may take decades before parity is established.

At the university level, women represent less than 20 percent of the overall enrollment of students at Abdou Moumouni University, the country's main university, and, worse, only 1 percent of female students successfully

Table 2. Female access to primary/elementary education in 1982–92 and 1996–98

Years	Boys	Girls	% Girls
1982–83	155.977	86.592	35.7
1983–84	–	–	–
1984–85	159.395	88.292	35.6
1985–86	174.651	96.938	35.7
1986–87	188.333	105.178	35.8
1987–88	194.255	106.700	35.5
1988–89	203.047	114.793	36.1
1989–90	235.477	133.252	36.1
1991–92	238.988	138.514	36.7
1996–97	440.522	165.306	37.5
1997–98	482.068	186.488	38.6

Source: Hamani (2000, 132).

Table 3. Female access to secondary/high school education in 1982–92 and 1996–97

Years	Boys	Girls	% Girls
1982–83	27.829	10.310	27.03
1983–84	29.103	10.897	27.24
1984–85	30.081	11.407	27.49
1985–86	29.106	11.286	27.44
1986–87	29.084	11.488	28.83
1987–88	32.191	13.175	29.90
1988–89	35.365	14.930	29.68
1989–90	35.692	15.437	30.19
1991–92	44.822	21.503	32.40
1996–97	48.156	26.199	35.23
1997–98	50.248	27.661	35.50

Source: Hamani (2000, 132).

graduate from that university (Hamani 2000, 137). Furthermore, the higher percentages of women in the faculty of education and in the faculty of health and social welfare (table 4) seems to reflect a pattern of women being channeled into those sciences related to "traditional" roles of socialization and reproduction.

Finally, according to UNESCO figures of 1995, the illiteracy rate in Niger stands at 86.6 percent of the overall population, of which women constitute about 93.4 percent. There is also evidence that even though the national literacy rate is increasing, the gender literacy gap is widening (Hamani, 2000 137–38).

Table 4. Percentage of female students by faculty at Abdou Moumouni University from 1985 to 1991

Year	FS	FE	FA	FHS	FEL	FLSH
1985–86	4	16	2	17	8	12
1986–87	8	20	17	19	7	17
1987–88	4	13	11	16	4	9
1989–90	8	24	11	15	7	9
1990–91	8	24	6	18	8	11

Source: Hamani (2000, 136).

Notes: (FS) faculty of sciences, (FE) faculty of education, (FA) faculty of agronomy, (FHS) faculty of health and social sciences, (FEL) faculty of economics and law, (FLSH) faculty of letters and human sciences.

Table 5. Percentage of class repeat and dropouts at primary school level in 1984

	1Gr	2Gr	3Gr	4Gr	5Gr	6Gr
Pass	95.34	85.37	82.52	84.11	79.52	25.52
Repeat	3.33	11.80	13.02	11.16	14.36	42.25
Fail/dropout	1.33	2.95	4.46	4.73	6.12	22.23

Source: Marcel Inné, L'éducation au Niger, 37, cited in Hamani (2000, 140).

Constraints on Women's Education in Postcolonial Niger

According to Abdou Hamani (2000, 140), in a cycle of six years of primary school, the dropout rate of students from the mainstream educational system dangerously amounts to 51.82 percent. Table 5, based on 1984 figures, demonstrates this trend. This syndrome becomes worse in the progression to the secondary and high school levels, especially with regard to female students. For example, a study by Koukou Adamou (1992; table 6) shows the following picture related to the progress of a group of students enrolled in the first grade in 1978 and those of that group who remain in the school system by 1991: Both male and female students have a remarkably high dropout rate. But there are factors that are specific to female dropouts arising from the patriarchal nature of the society.

In most Nigerien cultures, females are under pressure to identify with a normative social construction of womanhood—the preservation of virginity as the family code of honor, and early marriage (wifehood), childbearing, and childrearing (motherhood). Because the majority of educators of all streams have internalized this patriarchal ideology that equates womanhood to wifehood and motherhood, female students experience the least mentoring in their education and are not encouraged to be competitive with their male counterparts. In fact, in this regard, the profiles of the minority

Table 6. Student enrollment retention from 1978 (primary school) to 1991 (end of high school)

1978		1991	
Male	Female	Male	Female
22,600	13,800	542 (2.4%)	207 (1.5%)

Source: Koukou Adamou (1992), cited in Hamani (2000, 141).

of women who attended schools reveal that most of them ended up in the "traditional" professions of teaching and nursing, formally extending their expected roles as caregivers (wives or mothers) and agents of children's socialization.

Poverty is another factor that triggers girls to drop out of school. Under the circumstances, parents as well as the state prefer to invest more in the education of male rather than female children when confronted with economic hardships. This situation is compounded by the IMF's recommendations to privatize public education, a move that has shifted the burden of educational costs from the state to the parents.

The uneven distribution of upper-level schools in the country, which forces the state to assign students to advanced levels of training in regions other than their home areas, represents another major problem for the majority of Nigerien parents who oppose the idea of sending their female children away from home. Their opposition is tied to the strong determination to control female sexuality, to groom female children for early marriage, and to prevent childbearing out of wedlock. Consequently, parental objection to long-distance commuting for education also leads to early female dropout. Furthermore, there is a state law that denies unmarried, underage pregnant students any state sponsorship in education. While the law does not at all affect male students who impregnate underage girls, it severely punishes unmarried underage pregnant students.

Recurrent droughts and famines, in addition to the decline in the uranium economy, have led to rural-urban exodus, another destabilizing factor that has prompted early female dropout from schools. With men seeking greener pastures in foreign countries, abandoned wives become heads of families without the economic means to sustain themselves and their children. Some of these migrate to the city with their children, resorting to a struggle for survival through begging, manual jobs in households, and prostitution. Schooling becomes the lowest priority in this context regardless of the gender of the child.

Niger's experience with the civil war—the so-called Tuareg Rebellion (chapter 6)—from the mid 1980s to the late 1990s resulted in the displacement of families and the complete removal of female students from schools in the war prone regions. This national insecurity led to the disappearance, for example, of nomadic caravan schools that were designed specifically to accommodate nomadic populations. In short, then, specific cultural and economic factors combined to affect, in particular, school enrollment and dropout rates of female students.

It is noteworthy that Hamani's study did not incorporate Islamic education and its impact on gender. Perhaps this omission is tied to the discriminatory attitudes toward this particular track inherent in Niger's links with *francophonie,* which dismisses non-French education. Thus, female students of Islamic schools then face double jeopardy: first, vertical discrimination as a result of the dominance of the mainstream French system; and secondly, horizontal gender-based discrimination within their own Islamic educational system. This francophone discriminatory attitude persists even in the face of the failure of the national French inherited educational system. As Meunier observes:

> Qur'anic school is a mode of schooling and literacy in Arabic and *Ajami* which is not taken into consideration by education policy-makers, even in regions that are hostile to western modern schools. In this case it could have been an alternative substitute to the public school in highly Islamized regions given that there is no financial means, no human power to sustain formal education and mass literacy. (Meunier 2000, 14–15)

The French stranglehold, in the name of *francophonie,* perpetuated by the tiny francophile elite, has been so strong that the possibility of modernizing Qur'anic schools to serve the literacy needs of the nation has been constantly dismissed. After all, scientific studies such as those of Meunier (1997; 2000, 209–79), have provided insightful accounts of the diversified and differentiated pedagogies of these Qur'anic schools in Niger Republic as they reshape themselves in response to the developmental and religious realities of their changing environments.

From the colonial to the independence era, Islamic education in Niger has failed to enjoy the support of the state or of Western educational funding agencies, in spite of its cultural significance and resilience. The crisis of the mainstream French education, the World Bank's and IMF's urgent demands on Third World countries to privatize public services (which include education)[3] and the rise of political Islam since the early 1990s, however, have prompted a reconsideration of the place of Islamic education and literacy in Niger Republic. It is now a possible alternative solution and has been the point of ongoing negotiations between diverse interested constituencies with often divergent, if not oppositional, objectives and aims (Meunier 2000). As John Hunwick rightly observes, the current spread of Islamic schools in West Africa is "[a] response to a more general demand of education which national governments cannot satisfy" (Hunwick 1997, 51).

Women in Islamic Schools

Gender disparities in student enrolments are by no means limited to the secular streams of education. They also exist in (religious) Islamic schools. These are of various kinds and levels.

First there is the Qur'anic school commonly referred to as *makarantar allo* (wooden slate school) in Hausa, and *makaranta duDudal* in Fulfulde and Zarma-speaking regions of southwestern Niger. This is the first type of formal educational structure involving literacy that emerged in the country from the arrival of Islam, probably much earlier than the tenth century (Hamani 1989; Hunwick and O'Fahey 1995). It developed rapidly throughout the country and more especially in the mideastern regions (Meunier 1997; Gregoire 1991 and 1993). According to the 2001 Ministry of Education's report, there exist 51,168 Qur'anic schools in Niger with a total of about 562,148 students, of whom 35 percent are simultaneously attending the mainstream French-based school.

According to the same report, the census and pedagogic surveys of these schools were unduly delayed. The reasons were sociopolitical, having to do with the privileging of French-based school. This is in spite of the fact that these Qur'anic schools enjoy much community support by parents who believe that they strengthen their children's Islamic identity without alienating them from their social milieu, as is the case with the mainstream French school.

The *makaranta* schools welcome both sexes and all ages. Initially women's and girls' attendance suffered the same constraints as those experienced by female students in the mainstream formal French school system. However, beginning with the democratization process of the 1990s, Niger Republic began to experience the proliferation of mosque-associated schools, especially *female makaranta* and other modern schools *(madarasa* or *medersa)* in the urban landscapes. This development is discussed in greater detail in the next section.

In this type of school, learning mainly involves reading of the Qur'an and memorization of the entire text. The pupil is commonly referred to as *almajiri* (masculine) or *almajira* (feminine) in the Hausa language, or *talibi* in the Zarma and Fulfulde languages. Graduation involves the demonstration that one has fully memorized the entire *Qur'an* in various recitation styles, similar to the Qur'anic memorization training in Morocco described by Eickelman (1985, 57–71) and to the Qur'anic exegesis in Manding (Mali) discussed by Tamari (1996: 43–79). This final stage is commonly known as *saukar Qur'ani,* or *sauka* for short. In Zarma, the same process is referred to as *Kuraana Zumandiyan*. This event often involves a public performance at the neighborhood mosque where the parents and the community come to celebrate the success of the students and express their gratitude to the teacher, *Malam* (male) or *Malama* (female) in Hausa and *Alfaa* in Zarma.

While it is true that memorization of the Qur'an constitutes one of the main aims of this early stage of learning, which spans between the ages of four to eight, learners who do or do not succeed in memorizing the entire

Qur'an have also already been initiated into the Arabic alphabet and the reading of classical Qur'anic texts in the Arabic script even though they might not acquire the Arabic language itself. The meaning of Qur'anic texts is mediated through translation and interpretation in the local languages. Very advanced Qur'anic teachers may seek recourse to interpretative religious texts written in *Ajami* in Fulfulde, Hausa, Zarma-Songhay, Kanuri, or other local languages, depending on the native language of the teacher and the place of learning.

The second type of Islamic schools in Niger is the *madarasa (makarantar Ilimi)*, taught in Arabic and involving study of (1) the Qur'an; (2) the *hadith* (the sayings of the Prophet Muhammed); (3) *fiqh* (Islamic Law); (4) *sunnah* (the tradition of the Prophet as recorded by his companions); and (5) the classical Arabic language.

The third type consists of the modern bilingual schools in Arabic and French commonly referred to in Niger Republic as *medersa Franco-Arab.*[4] Its curriculum combines part of the national Ministry of Education's curriculum with Islamic education in philosophy and Arabic language. By incorporating the official language, French, the teachers and students are able to adapt their curriculum to the mainstream content-subjects as required by the Ministry of Education. As a result, its students are subject to the same national standards of evaluation as their contemporaries attending the mainstream French public or private schools.

From the 2002 enrollment figures provided by the Ministry of Education in table 7, we see once again that the gender gap is narrower in the lower levels and increases gradually at the higher levels of the school system.

Many graduates of the Franco-Arab schools opt to pursue further studies at the Islamic University of Say, established in Niger in the late 1980s. Before 2002, admission was restricted to male students. As a result, most of the female graduates from the Franco-Arab educational system terminated their education after high school and only a tiny portion joined the mainstream Abdou Moumouni University. In the latter case, the forced switch to a new educational track has had its own complications for the female students who would have had to compete with colleagues on unequal linguistic terms. As indicated earlier, because these students have been trained in

Table 7. Medersa Franco-Arab enrollments

	Male	Female	% Female
Primary	28,335	22,315	44.04
Secondary/High	3,956	2,205	34.91

Source: Ministry of Education Report on Medersa in Niger (2002).

schools where Arabic is the main medium of instruction and French only a subject of study, they are at a linguistic disadvantage once at Abdou Moumouni University. There is also a disadvantage with regard to their preparedness for tertiary education. Even though the *medersa Franco-Arab* track is required to follow the same curricular content as the French-based school in nonreligious fields, the fact that so much time has to be spent in Arabic and Islamic studies means that the time allocated to the secular dimension is less than what pertains in French-based schools. It was not until 2002 that a serious effort was made to look into the possibility of accommodating female graduates from Franco-Arab schools by opening a branch of the Islamic University in Niamey to cater to women only.

Grassroots Women's Responses to the Educational Crisis

The process of democratization in the early 1990s put an end to military and one-party authoritarian political culture in Niger. This development triggered a new consciousness that permeated other social constituencies such as women's grassroots organizations, which had hitherto been marginalized in policy-making processes and denied access to essential public resources. Combined with the opening-up of the political space, this new consciousness now encouraged the marginalized groups to enter into the public arena as active voices in the national educational debate in Niger, and as designers, implementers, and leaders of alternative schools initiated from within.

Most striking in this momentum of sociopolitical change is the sudden and dramatic visibility of grassroots women openly involved in activist work. They began to mobilize to raise funds for the creation of alternative adult literacy schools, *madarasas,* providing learning in Qur'anic studies and, informally, vocational training to women. Through their sponsorship of these neighborhood alternative schools, the women managed to exercise control over them. Institutionally, these schools were located primarily in available spaces in government-run schools that were not functioning or were temporarily closed down due to strikes, but they were also located in centers run by Islamic women's associations or in private homes. These successes in grassroots Muslim women's educational formations have attracted attention and support. Sponsoring international Islamic organizations and banks have offered scholarships to women graduates of *medersa* Franco-Arab high schools for pursuing further studies in Islamic education as well as in professional fields in modern Islamic universities and polytechnic institutes abroad (such as Egypt, Libya, Sudan, and Malaysia).

New women's sponsored neighborhood *madarasa (medersa)* in Niamey.

Young pupils from the new private and formal Arabic-Islamic school sponsored by Islamist organizations at Quartier Wadata.

These schools were partly a response to the crisis of education resulting from the effects of *francophonie* and World Bank and IMF privatization programs (Federici et al. 2000). The new policies produced a growing marginal population of school dropouts whose reintegration into the society was proving to be a serious problem. Since parents could no longer afford to educate their children in formal Western schools, it became important for their children to have access to an alternative source of literacy skills: the alternative that was acquiring renewed legitimacy was the Islamic school. With this development, mothers themselves began to participate as learners alongside their children in many schools.

The grassroots women's choice of the alternative schools was also a response to the alienating effects of the secular French-based education. In much of francophone Africa, many Muslim parents believe that the systemic failures inherent in French-based formal education (even before its crisis) had produced conditions for the development of social problems—juvenile delinquency and prostitution—and new social orientations that created a rupture in the normative and value system of the wider society. Islamic literacy therefore provided a basis for resisting this alienation and also became the paradigm for combating the discrimination that prevented most (Muslim) women in rural areas from having access to formal secular education.

During my fieldwork in Niamey and Kollo as well as in Maradi and Dakoro, I observed and participated in numerous women's religious associative activities involving the use of literacy skills derived from their *Qur'anic* education. These included: (1) women's Qur'anic reading and interpretation, called *tamsiri* (translation), and *wa'azi* (counseling) sessions led by women for women in neighborhood community schools sponsored by women; (2) *tamsiri* and *wa'azi* sessions by women as a new trend during marriage festivities, displaying women's Islamic knowledge and prestige; (3) women's development of economic initiatives through mutual support, with accounting and bookkeeping activities involving Arabic numeric skills; and; and (4) reading of Islamic poetry produced by women.

In the urban areas, the middle and upper-class strategies for women activism did not succeed in bearing fruit at the national level on fundamental issues such as women's rights in the domestic space, women's reproductive rights, and the right of access to certain basic public resources. This failure led some urban women educated in the mainstream French educational system to consider invading the conservative and patriarchal religious space in order to subvert its effects on women's oppression. For some educated women, this activism was partly inspired by the realization of the importance of knowledge of Islamic doctrine in a secular state that operates with both Islamic authority and secular power to interpret civic and legal matters affecting the woman and the family. The involvement of these women with the mosque could be interpreted as acquiescing to "Islamic fundamentalism." On the other hand, their achievement in coalition with other francophile women intellectuals in publicly promoting articulate Islamic women scholars—such as religious commentator Malama Dr. Zeinab Sidi Baba Haidara, a graduate of the Islamic University of Kuwait (see her biography in appendix 2)—who could challenge on Islamic grounds laws that violate women's rights, demonstrates their acute political awareness of the dangers of fundamentalist patriarchal entrapment.

The alternative schools must be regarded as a space with a disguised self-empowering agenda, given (1) the inabilities of the modernization project undertaken by most African countries in the aftermath of independence to ensure universal literacy to the majority of Africans and (2) the failure of the World Bank and IMF's policies to revitalize the educational system in Africa and to ensure the empowerment of African women through increased access to both literacy and formal education. In fact, the economic stresses engendered by the implementation of the World Bank and IMF's Structural Adjustment Programs contributed to the increasing denial of the right to education and literacy to women in countries such as Niger, where patriarchal prerogatives privilege men over women, especially in the context of scarce resources. Therefore, alternative *makaranta, madarasa,* and *medersa* are currently for most Muslim women and girls an affordable and safe space of learning and producing knowledge that responds to their needs.

To appreciate the relationship between resource allocation and the underprivileging of women, especially in education and literacy, one has only to look at the pattern of government expenditure. Mariama Bayard, the former president of Le Rassemblement Démocratique des Femmes du Niger (RDFN) and current president of an NGO called Femme et Famille (Woman and the Family) made the following poignant observation:

> In 1997, Niger's defence expenditure was 22 million U.S. dollars or 1.4 percent of the country's GDP, compared to 1.6 million of public expenditure on health. If defence money was directed toward education instead, the illiteracy rate among women in the West African country would not be as low as nine percent while that of men would be much higher than the current 19 percent. (Bayard 1999)

Given this apparent marginalization of women's education by both the government and international funding agencies, the women in Niger were forced to develop their own initiatives to promote their own and their children's educational interests. These initiatives are rooted in local knowledge systems and conceived within the limits of the material resources of the communities themselves.

For women in Niger Republic, not only are these local literacies affordable, but they also provide room and space for a curriculum beyond the religious, such as dressmaking, hairdressing in private homes or in salons, and other activities (incense making, cooking, and restaurants) that are income generating (UNICEF-Niger 1994, 62). Inspired by the experience of how women in northern Nigeria use local literacies in local languages, women in Niger have begun to experiment with the use of local literacies in the production of works in areas such as poetry and women-centered religious TV programs.

Given Niger's strong culture of patriarchal Islam and its military culture of government, a legitimate concern is to what extent a sociopolitical movement founded on religion and involving women's empowerment through education and literacy is capable of escaping from the very structures—patriarchal Islam and the system of governance—it seeks to subvert. In other words, has this newly evolved grassroots women's movement reached a level of consciousness that could resist the control of the powerful male-dominated Islamic associations that often regulate (by using religious and state authority) against women's right to formal education and literacy?[5]

The relevance of such a question must be evaluated in the context of what women in Niger Republic have successfully achieved in these few years since the country has opened itself to the test of a democratic culture. What is more crucial is to pay attention to the areas such as religion that women in Niger Republic (and in most countries of the world with autocratic regimes of governance, for that matter) seek first to transform without external intervention and, secondly, to use the space brought about by that transformation to act on other areas of primary concern to women, such as education, literacy, and health. As stated earlier, Niger is a secular state that functions within a patriarchal interpretation of Islam. As a result, any struggle for women's rights and gender equality within such a nation-state that underestimates the place of religion is doomed to failure, as most of the urban elite women strategies on women's rights agenda have shown. The use of Islamic-based literacies by grassroots Muslim women's movements is in part the women's attempt to create a framework for autonomy through the very heritage that was used against them, and at the same time a quest to go beyond it to interrogate the patriarchal nation-state in its manipulation of Islam. Furthermore, the interactions between women trained in *makaranta* and/or *madarasa* with Muslim women with university training in Arabic/Islamic learning will eventually transform old gender ideologies, roles, and expectations in multiple directions within the Islamic framework itself; certainly a dialogue with their francophile secularist sisters could lead to a Nigerien women's coalition that will pose a serious challenge to fundamentalist secularist and Islamist patriarchies.

Through the openings created by the country's move to democracy, the grassroots women find ways to speak for themselves. They present a challenge to both the developmentalist ideologies of the elite women and their sponsoring international agencies that impose alternative models of development without assessing the preexisting models or without engaging the people whose lives are affected by the imposed projects. Consequently, through the alternative schools, the grassroots women are calling for the reexamination of the resources available in the culture. This revisiting of the cultural heritage triggered by the failure of the French-only educational system in Niger Republic is gradually leading to the demystification of the hierarchy imposed by both patriarchy and (neo)colonialism on the literacies coexisting within the culture. For example, traditional literacy—*Ajami* in local languages—derived from Islamic education resurfaces as another important educational resource that can be used for secular purposes of development (as used in public health and agriculture, for example, in the German-funded rural development literacy projects in Tahoua in eastern Niger).

Today, literacy in French is accessible only to a few who can afford it, whereas the popular *madarasa* schools are the alternative structures affordable for the majority of Nigerien children and adults, especially women. Women who are literate in both Islamic doctrines and *Ajami* and who in the past decades had been silent or spoken for, are now speaking out on women's knowledge about Islamic jurisprudence in their roles as religious teachers and TV and radio commentators.

The ascension of "Islamicist" women in the public arena, exposing their astute knowledge and the multiplicity of literacies operating within the culture at large and in women's culture in particular forced Nigerien women political activists to rethink the question of women vis-à-vis education, literacies, and leadership. This led to the formation of new types of coalitions between secularist francophile Muslim women's organizations and Islamicist Arabic educated women organizations. This represents a step that both the Islamicist women scholars and their francophile educated counterparts are using for making connections and breaking the old barriers that used to set them in oppositional relations of power. Their coalition in the arena of the inherited literacies seems to echo Michael Oakeshott's interpretation of political education:

> Political education is not merely a matter of coming to understand a tradition, it is learning how to participate in a conversation: it is at once an initiation into an inheritance in which we have a life interest, and the exploration of its limitations. (quoted in Rinehart 1994, 42)

Nigerien women across class boundaries engage one another dialogically by using religious identity and literacies (Arab, Islamic-based and French, secularist-based) as interactional sites of mutual discovery and as important spaces for initiating a gradual inscription of a women-centered understanding of religion and construction of meanings. In this way, the women hope to develop new strategies for raising the national consciousness on gender equality within the framework of a predominantly patriarchal Islamic nation-state.

Part II

Women, Folklore, and Performative Identities

Chapter 3

Politics, Popular Culture, and Women Performing Artists

A Biographical Inquiry in a Francophone-Islamic Context

Introduction

My aim in this chapter is to continue exploring the reality of Nigerien women's identities by focusing on the biography of one of the most popular female artists in Niger, Habsu Garba. Through an examination of the interplay between cultural locations (ethnicity, culture, language, profession, and class) and the working of agency, I hope to demonstrate that Nigerien women like Habsu Garba not only "take on the gender" assigned to them by their cultures, but also can use their agency to "decide to participate" in the reproduction of the assigned gender ideology or can "choose" to stray outside the expected gendered boundaries of their cultures (Butler 1987, 132). Thus, through a (con)textual examination of the symbolic meanings of the series of transgressive acts in which Habsu Garba has been implicated, from childhood to adulthood, I will show how she has been contributing to challenging the workings of dominant discursive practices against herself as a woman visible in public space(s) as well as against marginal groups (such as people illiterate in the French language, high caste female dancers, and homosexual male dancers). In the process, she has been engaged in renewing Nigerien's cultural history of gender, class, and caste ideologies.

I argue, however, that the possibilities of acting to challenge the status quo or complying with the established authority are tied to how women understand their place in the culture and how they want to use that understanding. In this regard, I find Linda Alcoff's theoretical formulation of the interplay between women's identity, positionality, and the agency triggered by this positionality useful for analyzing the complex shift of identities that Habsu's life implies: "The concept of woman is a relational term identifiable only within a (constantly moving) context; but, second, that the position that women find themselves in can be actively utilized (rather than transcended) as a location for the construction of meaning, a place from where meaning is constructed, rather than simply the place from where meaning can be *discovered*. . . . The concept of woman as positionality shows how women use their positional perspective as a place from which values are interpreted and constructed rather than as a locus of an already determined set of values" (Alcoff 1988, 283–86). Taking into account temporal as well as cultural locations, is therefore crucial for understanding both Habsu Garba's actions as a historicized subject in a predominantly Muslim and francophone postcolonial space and the multiple identity shifts that her life journey displays. In the final analysis, then, I hope to offer a more holistic scope of this Nigerien woman's identities by applying positional and contextual analysis of the biographic narratives, songs, and dances drawn from recorded material during my fieldwork researching Habsu Garba's life—observing, participating, and filming her rehearsal performances.

Habsu Garba and Hybridity: A Critical Discourse Analysis

Habsu's introductory remarks at the beginning of our first interview offer a vignette for beginning the deconstruction of the subtexts underlying her cultural location. She begins by drawing my attention to the fact that the language of our dialogue should not be taken for granted, and how crucial it is for the two of us to agree, from the very beginning, on *our language* or *languages* of discussion. This clearly signifies the critical place and role languages play in defining how meaning is negotiated and processed in field research by both the researcher and the subject of research. That is why the following opening of our interview acquires great importance:

HABSU GARBA: Let me begin with my birthday [pauses] by the way, you know our *French* is not that strong [laughs] so can we do it in *Hausa* or *Zarma* because I express myself better in those [laughs].

OUSSEINA ALIDOU: Of course, we can use any of the languages that come naturally to us during the interview [laughs]. We always do this going back and forth with languages here [laughs]. It is the natural thing here. This is natural and it is fine for the interview. Please use whatever comes naturally to you and I will do the same as we are doing now, my dear.

On the surface of her statement, Habsu Garba is making a linguistic choice based on a self-perceived limitation in her French language proficiency. Above and beyond this dimension of linguistic competence, there are several layers of interconnected implications. First, the negotiation on the language of interview between Habsu, the subject of my research, and myself, the researcher who is also a woman from Niger, challenges up front the notion of "native essentialism" that too readily assumes our "commonality," including linguistic location in the "common" cultural space. For Habsu, the act of linguistic negotiation here regarding the choice of language(s) for our interactions highlights the relevance of her subjectivity in the construction of meaning about her life history.

Although educated in the French language, the official language of the country, Habsu Garba elected not to use it as the medium for discussing her life history. Given her knowledge of my educational and linguistic background as someone who grew up in the same cities as she did, Habsu sought to preempt the possible French linguistic hegemony that I might inadvertently impose on the process. Instead, she proposed Hausa and Zarma, the two mother tongues we had in common, which also happen to be the two dominant national lingua francas in Niamey.

Methodologically, therefore, the issue has arisen of the power of the research subject to determine not only her own location in the interview process, but also the linguistic location of the researcher. Habsu Garba clearly signifies that meaning about her life will be framed not only outside monolinguism in French or in one local language, but rather through polyglossia (fluency in multiple languages), in this case, in the Hausa and Zarma languages. I use "polyglossia" rather than "bilingualism" because even though Habsu specified Hausa and Zarma only, French did come up here and there in some passages in the course of our numerous interviews. We were thus forced to occupy a negotiated and negotiating space between three languages.

At the heart of the matter, then, Habsu Garba's attempt to shift the linguistic terrain of conversation illustrates an aspect of how the dynamic of power relations between the researcher and the researched is mediated sensitively in order to create adequate conditions for the voice of the "subaltern" to be expressed more freely (Foucault 1980; Spivak 1995). Methodological questions posed by the issue of languages (especially if polyglossia is involved) used by research subject(s) include the following: (1) What are the limits of mediating subjects' articulation of their subjectivities through translation, especially when this involves translators/interpreters who alter meaning, sometimes inadvertently, and other times consciously, for whatever reasons, especially when the topic of the research is considered sensitive, like the "woman question" in non-Western societies? (2) Are the meanings emerging out of polyglossia (multiple languages or multiple voices) sufficiently synthesized in the final text of the research?

Equally significant is the role of language in the (re)production, exercise, and maintenance of power across and within gender. Following Michel Foucault (1980), Kress (1997), and James Gee (1996), I would argue that underlying Habsu Garba's concern about our choice of language of interview is the subjectivity of women about the discursive social meanings associated with language policies and practices in Niger Republic. That interplay between power and the discursive social practices in language is the focus of Gee's notion of "Discourse" with capital "D." Discourse, in Gee's formulation, relates to patterns of using (and choosing) language(s) in social interactions and in contexts of power to (re)construct, recognize, negotiate, and contest meaning. While language practices conveyed in local national languages, such as Hausa and Zarma, carry less power in an interview situation, these practices reflect high, if not the highest value when conveyed in French, the official language of the country. This is a discourse that Habsu Garba inadvertently interrogates.

Moreover, Habsu's linguistic choice problematizes the issue of French-language policy in education in the so-called francophone African countries in general, and in relation to women in the dialectics of power and education more particularly. First, *our* in Habsu's phrase "our French" carries with it a paradoxical collective relational intimacy with the French language (and perhaps to the French culture and people) by virtue of the francophone identity label as applied to Nigeriens in general. In spite of this presumed *Frenchness* of the nation, Habsu regards herself as ill-prepared to function adequately in the society with that language. Here lie important questions about the entire French-language edifice in the educational system of the country.

Volumes of scholarship in psycholinguistics have been produced on the problematics of the teaching of French in francophone Africa. The work of Sido Issa provides a critical appraisal of the didactic weaknesses of the French curriculum in Niger. *Problématique de l'enseignement du français en Afrique* (Problematics of the teaching of French in Africa) (Issa 1982) is a required text that still resonates in my memory of my years as a student of linguistics at the University of Niamey. This course still remains a prerequisite offered in the Department of Modern Letters for both students enrolled in that department as well as those, like myself, studying to become linguists. The rationale for this general requirement is to produce a team of linguists trained to develop national language pedagogical materials that would serve as a bridge to the learning of the French language in the curriculum and to produce future teachers of French as a foreign language rather than as a mother-tongue as it was taught in the past.

Habsu's usage of the possessive adjective *our* in the phrase "our French" also raises the issue of a shared collective consciousness that vertically defines the educated elite in "francophone" Africa. Thus, the ambiguous semantics of "our French" could be at the base of the class ideology (Djité 1990; Weinstein 1976; Fairclough 1989) that sets a hierarchical divide between the small category of Nigeriens who had access to formal modern school inherited from the French colonial legacy and the largest group of Nigeriens who have benefited neither from the formal education nor from literacy in the French language (Moumouni 1964; Hamani 2000).

Furthermore, there is also the problem of distance between the majority of those educated (men and women) who are defined by early dropout from the formal educational track (the group to which Habsu Garba belongs) and the tiny minority of those who have managed to make it beyond the usual "expected" dropout point, especially women. As indicated in the last chapter, in a cycle of six years of primary school, the dropout rate of students from the mainstream educational system is 51.82 percent (Hamani 2000, 140). Among dropouts at all levels, there exists another internal split between an extremely tiny ratio of privileged French-educated Nigerien women and an overwhelming category of primary (and secondary) school female dropouts. This latter group of women is often referred to as *panthères blessées* (wounded panthers or wildcats) by chauvinist males.

The sarcastic tone of Habsu Garba's phrase "our French" is a bitter reminder of how the French language is still a *foreign language* that was used during the colonial time to divide and conquer various indigenous groups. The French language in francophone Africa, in general and in Niger in particular, represents the traces of that spirit of divisiveness installed by the former colonial master. As a language used for exclusion and division, the French language *could not be*, for many colonized subjects who have not developed a complex of their mother tongue(s), the language shaping intimate exploration of questions linked to one's identity.

I read Habsu Garba's request as, first, a reminder of the complicity of French colonial patriarchs as well as the local patriarchs in denying Nigerien women access to both the French language and formal education as well as the extension and reproduction of the same colonial policies in the postcolonial dispensation. Secondly, it expressed a need for both of us to achieve a resisting linguistic solidarity as women emerging from that common legacy. From the way my first interview with Habsu Garba began, I was quite pleasantly faced with the situation of exploring the potential of the research subject's subjectivity to influence the entire "gaze of the fieldwork"—to see whether the researcher is sufficiently disposed to observe and take into account this dialectic. Habsu Garba's act set the tone, emphasizing that she too must find the space in this process of engagement to add a dimension to the exploration of life histories of Nigerien women, perhaps to give the researcher a taste of her "own medicine," so to speak, while reminding me that I too am Nigerien: What about my own life trajectory in postcolonial Niger and now in the master empire, the United States?

I realize that like other ex-colonial languages, the French language can also be appropriated and used for counterhegemonic purposes. After all, as Ashcroft, Griffith, and Tiffin argue, "The belief that the English [or French] text is unable to communicate a non-English [non-French] cultural meaning is based on a misconception of the way language means" (Ashcroft et al. 1995, 284). An excellent study of the transformation of French for revolutionary purposes is of course the one provided by Frantz Fanon. In his study of the discourse of the "Voice of Fighting Algeria"—the radio broadcasting service of the Algerian resistance movement against French colonialism—Fanon shows how, in the hands of militant Algerian combatants, the French language gradually lost its "accursed" character as the language of imperialism to become a potent tool of anticolonial struggle:

> Still on the level of communication, attention must be called to the acquisition of new values by the French language. The French language, language of occupation, a vehicle of the oppressing power, seemed doomed for eternity to judge the Algerian in a pejorative way. Every French expression referring to the Algerian had a humiliating content. Every French speech heard was an order or a threat, or an insult. The contact between the Algerian and the European is defined by these three spheres. The broadcasting in French of the programs of *fighting Algeria* was to liberate the enemy language from its historic meanings. The same message transmitted in three different languages unified the experience and gave it a universal dimension. The French language lost its accursed character, revealing itself to be capable also of transmitting, for the benefit of the nation, the messages of truth that the latter awaited. Paradoxical as it may appear, it is the Algerian Revolution, it is the struggle of the Algerian people, that is facilitating the spread of the French language in the nation. (Fanon 1967, 80–90)

In the aftermath of French colonialism and into the postcolonial period, Algerian nationalists once again began to interrogate the place of the French language in an effort to construct an "authentically" Algerian nationhood. An Arabization project was rapidly put into place at the expense of the French language and, of course, of non-Arab minority languages like Berber. This nationalist project, however, has been regarded by some Algerian women with great ambivalence. While they do indeed appreciate the need to disengage the culturally hegemonic weight of the French language in the space of the Algerian nation, they see within this language avenues and spaces of women's empowerment that do not exist in the chosen language of Algerian nationhood, Arabic. This sentiment is clearly expressed by one of the leading Algerian feminist writers, Assia Djebbar (see Lionnet 1996, 331–32).

Yet it is true that the situation in Niger is characterized by a certain social enclosure of the elite due in part to the French language. The French language itself and the discourses associated with it are yet to be sufficiently democratized. As a result, those not equipped with this linguistic tool cannot participate and cannot be *in total* alliance with their sisters at the higher ranks of society through the mediation of the *French* language. A dialogue between them that admits equal partnership in the struggle can only be done in the local regional *lingua francas.*

Beyond the realms of political struggles, Habsu Garba's opening remarks about French also raise the question of language in the construction of knowledge in the process of studying "African realities." The produced knowledge about/on Africa is often a product of a mediated translation in the official metropolitan languages—English for "Anglophone" Africa, French for "francophone" Africa, Portuguese for "Lusophone" Africa—a path that Habsu Garba tried to avoid during my fieldwork. As Ngugi Wa Thiong'o observed during a lecture at Cambridge University: "Take the status of scholarship on Africa. Quite frankly there is nothing so contradictory in African scholarship today in Africa and in the wider world than the position of experts on African realities who do not have to demonstrate even the slightest acquaintance with an African language. Have you heard, for instance, of a Professor of French at a French university or any other place who did not know a word of French?" (Ngugi 1998, 93).

More recently, Achille Mbembe has made a similar observation about Africanist social scientists who focus on issues of social engineering but fail to master the African languages required for substantive fieldwork, research, and producing knowledge on Africa. "It should be noted, as far as fieldwork is concerned, that there is less and less. Knowledge of local [African] languages, vital to any theoretical and philosophical understanding, is deemed unnecessary. To judge from recent academic output, sub-Saharan Africa, wrapped in a cloak of impenetrability, has become the black hole of reason, the pit where its powerlessness rests unveiled" (Mbembe 2001, 7–9). Both Ngugi and Mbembe affirm the centrality of language in ways of seeing and (re)presenting the experience that is being studied.

My life as a Nigerien woman researcher working as an immigrant scholar in the United States is to a great extent determined by my "making it" through the French (francophone) educational system and my current negotiation of my way as a "Muslim francophone" within an Anglophone U.S. academy. Between Habsu Garba and me, there is a gap that is illustrative of the various levels of *unequal* commonalities among women in Niger. This divide, precipitated partly by the inadequacy of the adopted French educational system, certainly necessitates a mediation/negotiation of power relations between Habsu Garba, the subject of my research whose subjectivity I am exploring and me in my capacity as a researcher who is a "native-other" or an "insider-outsider." My experiences at "home," therefore, present some of the complexities tied to the interplay between identity (privileged native-other), fieldwork, and feminist theorizing and praxis that Jayati Lal (1999) incisively discussed in an article entitled "Situating Locations: The Politics of Self, Identity and "Other" in *Living and Writing the Texts*. Reading Lal's article before, during, and now in the process of writing this book has been an especially helpful "reality check" in challenging some of my assumptions about "insideness" while simultaneously resisting the potential inclination of excessive use of "otherness."

To sum up, then, the many implications that arise from Habsu Garba's phrase "our French" suggest a set of class power relations among Nigeriens, in general, and more sharply among women, in particular. It is, perhaps, this dialectics of power relations between two women sharing a common citizenship, but socially situated in different locations in the same national map which Habsu Garba was so conscious of and quick to address up front. Habsu Garba's intervention in this terrain of often unspoken class power relations entailed in the selection of language of interaction and my understanding and accommodation of her request created, perhaps, some space for both of us to negotiate the terms of transcending, at least for a short while, our point of difference in order to enter into a dialogue, rather than a one-way inquiry, into the "subaltern" life journey (Spivak 1995; Mohanty 1991; and Smith 1997).

Habsu Garba and Educational *Brassage*

Even today the French language is still acquired primarily through the school system throughout francophone Africa. The higher the level of education, the greater one's proficiency in the language is likely to be. Habsu

Garba's declared discomfort with the language, therefore, naturally led me to inquire about her educational background:

OA: Did you attend school at all?
HG: Yes, I did attend *école* [that is, the mainstream school run in French] up to CM1 [fifth grade]. . . .
OA: What type of school did you attend?
HG: From CI to CM1 [first grade to fifth grade], I attended the regular *école*. After that I attended the *Arabic* school for three years. After the three years, my parents wanted to *force me to get married*. I refused and I told them that I would rather return to a private school run in French, École L'Air. I was enrolled there for the CM2 [sixth grade]. After the CM2, I passed the typing examination at École Mission Catholique. I attended that school for two years and obtained my typing certificate.

What emerges from this account is a taxonomy of the various educational tracks that exist in urban landscapes in Niger Republic, as discussed in chapter 2. There is her experience in (a) the *école*, the French-inherited school system; (b) the *madarasa*, a product of Arab-Islamic influence in Niger; and finally (c) vocational training for women—offering secretarial skills—introduced by the French Catholic missionaries. This overlapping of educational systems reflects, once more, the concept of *brassage* (blending) in the realm of education, combining the secular and the religious. Within the religious, furthermore, we see the workings of a syncretism at the cultural level, if not at the confessional level. In other words, the interaction between Islamic and French-Christian values shapes the cultural identity of Nigeriens through the multivariate structures of the country's educational system. And mediating between these new religious and secular forces is the continuing influence of indigenous traditions born of processes of socialization outside the formal structures of the classrooms.

Here again, Habsu Garba's ties to Franco-Arab *madarasa* exposes a dimension of her life that brings back the question of language vis-à-vis education in Niger. For the very notion of *madarasa* in Niger entails the centering of the Arabic language, rather than French, as medium of instruction. In this system, the French language is taught more as a subject, although by the fourth grade it begins to acquire an equal status with Arabic in some schools. Yet because of the strong "francophilia," the French complex, the Arabic language continues to be regarded as inferior in educational status as compared to French; Nigeriens trained in the bilingual modern Arabic-French track have remained relatively disadvantaged with regard to employment and advanced educational opportunities. Before the new wave of Islamic revivalism known as *Izala* (see chapter 5), which revalorizes Nigerien Islamic identity partly through the pursuit of knowledge of Arabic language and the Qur'an (Grégoire 1992; Brenner 1993; Meunier 1997; and Masquelier 2001), many Nigeriens used to shy away from admitting that they had attended Arabic or Arabic-French *madarasa* for fear of being reduced to *marabouts* (mystic teachers) by fellow Nigeriens educated solely in the French mainstream.

Habsu Garba: Between Modern Education and Indigenous Traditions

Regardless of the diglossia between the Arabic and the French language—that is, the functional distribution between the two languages in which, one is regarded as having a higher status than the other—what is important for our understanding of Habsu Garba's life history is that the *madarasa* was the school she ran to as a child trying to escape the elitist French mainstream school that was not meeting her aspirations to sing. As she put it:

HG: The mainstream school in French was boring to me and I was very interested in singing. Singing as I used to hear it when passing by the *madarasa* on my way to or back from *école* was more attractive to me. So, I convinced myself to switch to *madarasa* without telling my parents. I went where pupils sing! That to me must be my kind of school. So, I dropped out of *école* at CM1 [fifth grade] and joined *madarasa* for three years.

When my parents realized what I did, they decided to marry me off. I protested and let them know that I would prefer to return to *école*. That is when my father decided to send me to the private school I mentioned earlier. I kept begging my father until he agreed to send me back to school. At that time the school fees were 1500CFA [about three U.S. dollars] per month. I was not successful the first year I took the primary school certificate exam in 1977. Thus, the same year, I took the typing examination at the Catholic mission school and passed.

OA: . . . Earlier you mentioned that you spent three years in Arabic school. Was it the Qur'anic school or the bilingual French-Arabic *madarasa*?

HG: It was the bilingual Islamic school, French-Arabic school, where the students learn Arabic. Of course, I realized it was not about learning how to sing once I enrolled [laughs]. I did not learn how to sing there as I thought I would [laughs]. But I stayed hooked to singing and there was some singing that was the recitation of the Qur'an. I used to listen to that a lot and it made me run away from the mainstream school. The French-Arabic school used to run until 1 p.m., so I stayed behind to listen to their singing while my young friends joined their parents [laughs]. That was childhood. I told my friend I could not stay in a school (the mainstream school run in French only) where I receive corporal punishment every day. I am switching to a more exciting school! So I dropped out without my parents' knowledge and joined the bilingual Islamic French-Arabic

> *madarasa*. My parents found out much later, almost toward the end of the year. They went to look for my report card because I was not bringing any from my school and they found out that I had opted for a different educational track on my own. I told them I wasn't going to be married off to a wealthy trader.

Habsu Garba's unilateral decision to enroll in *madarasa* as a child without provoking the concern of her *école's* teacher or her parents' awareness reflects the symptomatic disconnectedness between *école* and the lives of most Nigeriens, including the teachers of that system. In 1968, four years after Niger Republic became independent and around the time of Habsu Garba's struggles in primary school, Abdou Moumouni diagnosed the inherent structural problems of "francophone" education as follows:

> [E]veryone agrees sincerely or hypocritically in recognizing that rapid training of cadres on all levels and in every specialty, accelerated extension of schooling for children and literacy campaigns among the adult population, are all vital imperatives inseparable from any real progress in our countries. The inadequacy of the educational system inherited from the colonial era, in its conception, orientation, structure and content is at times vaguely realized, at times explicitly recognized and expressed. (Moumouni 1964, 12)

École might be, from the point of view of Habsu's parents, a temporary engagement while awaiting the "right" husband for their daughter. After all, it is very common that traditional patriarchal parents construct a view of womanhood for their daughters, whose identities are framed through the everlasting state of minorhood, wifehood, and mothering. While it is true that many women in Niger appear to live in conformity with patriarchal rules of behavior and sex roles defined by their cultures, there are some, like Habsu Garba, Malama A'ishatu (chapter 2), Azara (chapter 7), and many others, whose life histories clearly suggest heterogeneity of responses to the status quo—resisting, living through ambiguity and outright contestations or split affinities.

From the passage quoted above, we see that Habsu resisted being one of those women who drop out of formal school as a result of early marriage, a phenomenon discussed in many studies focusing on women's education in Niger. Indeed, Habsu had bargained her way out of being prematurely married to a wealthy man. Such a marriage was her parents' way of ensuring for her a life of security as a female who voluntarily dropped out of the new security path arising from the colonial and postcolonial "limited" formal education in the French language that did not meet her artistic aspirations. In short, Habsu Garba's remarks quoted above demonstrate her rejection of the ascribed patriarchal, colonial framing of her womanhood.

Perhaps, because they were born in the wake of Niger's independence from French colonization, the seeds of freedom and the desire to craft a "new" notion of independence even at the individual level permeated children's lives. Habsu showed a determination to have an active role in shaping the course of her life and acted accordingly, contrary to cultural expectations. These significant characteristics of a Muslim female child are often overlooked in many academic writings framed in Western epistemology about women in Muslim societies. Instead, many of these studies have sought to confirm their theories of the homogeneity of "submissiveness" of (African) Muslim women and their presumed surrender to (local and international) patriarchal order. Consequently, the eyes of the scholars have tended to see mainly those cases that confirm their a priori assumptions (Lazreg 2001, 321–44)

Brassage and the Urban Landscape

Let us now return to the conversation with Habsu Garba beginning with her birth.

> HG: Let me begin with my birthday. I was born December 25, 1958. I am Nigérienne by citizenship. Moreover, my mother is *Hausa* and my father is *Zarma*. Thus, *I am both of the two together* [laugh]. I reside in Niamey *in Quartier Médina Trois.*

This statement reveals how Habsu Garba culturally locates the complexity of her identity, at the intersection of religion, ethnicity, gender, and nationhood, within the boundaries of the Muslim francophone space of Niger Republic. For a person born in 1958, two years before Niger officially gained its independence, she has foregrounded her Nigerienhood around her *dual ethnicity,* of a Hausa mother from Maradi and a Zarma father from Dosso. Habsu is a person of plural ethnicities, a reality commonly and positively identified in Niger and in many other countries of the Sahel as *brassage sahélien* (blending of people from various ethnic and cultural backgrounds). Habsu's pleasant laughter after revealing that she is "both of the two together" is a pattern that is repeated throughout my interaction in the field with other women, from Malama A'ishatu to Azara. This phenomenon of mixed and plural ethnicity is particularly characteristic of urban and semi-urban spaces. Unfortunately, *brassage* is often overlooked, if not dismissed altogether, by social scientists of "African ethnicity." Many scholars persist on seeing and writing only *homogeneity* (ethnic or racial "purity"), ethnic clashes arising from intergroup animosities (thus suggesting an impossibility of interethnic peaceful coexistence), and binarism, none of which reveal the complex order of human experience(s) (Mbembe 2001, 8).

As for her residential biography, that is, the place where she shelters herself in the urban landscape of the capital city of Niger, Niamey, Habsu

Garba names the neighborhood of *Quartier Médina* (in French) or *Kàrcé Màdíinàa* (with *kàrcé* being the localized rendering of the French *quartier*). *Quartier Médina/kàrcé Màdíinàa* is a new reminder of how Islam has shaped the cultural and historical identities of Nigeriens who are predominantly Muslims. For *Màdíinàa* is the name assigned to her neighborhood in identification with a place of historical relevance in the collective imagination of Muslims throughout the world. *Màdíinàa* was the place of the big *Hijra* (migration) during the early stages of the consolidation of Islam as a new monotheistic religion to emerge in the Saudi Arabian peninsula in 622 AD. The word *quartier* and its domestication as *kàrcé* again reflect a linguistic *brassage* between the French language and local languages. Thus, *Quartier Médina* or *kàrcé Màdíinàa* are phrases that creatively reflect how urban Nigeriens assume the syncretism between local, Islamic, and French cultures in the naming of their landscape.

In Search of Professional Fulfillment

Habsu Garba's life developed into adulthood in her eleven years spent as a typist at a local bank. Here again she was confronted in the 1980s with the question of educational training as a condition for maintaining the job she held at one of the main banks, BIAO.

HG: After my graduation from the typist training in École Mission Catholique, I got the job at the bank BIAO where I served for eleven years. When BIAO and another bank called BICI wanted to merge, some of the workers had to be laid off. After awhile, they wanted to make some deals with us, such as proposing a voluntary early retirement for those who wanted or a resumption of work. I decided the former since I was already on the first black list—the list of people to be laid off. I said *wallahi* [in Allah's name], I won't stay even when they promised to offer us more formal training. I said, no. I requested that my legal benefits be given to me. I used that money to purchase a plot in Dosso [Southwest Niger, Zarmaland], my father's homeland, and built a house.

After this I began to do some trading and traveling back and forth between Cotonou (Benin), Lomé (Togo) and Niger to buy and sell goods. Before I was officially released from the bank job, I was given a job offer by the city hall as a cultural mobilizer *(animatrice)*, thus as a state civil servant. This is a position I still hold at the city hall.

Besides my job at the city hall, I founded my own private entertainment group called *Groupe Annashuwa*. In addition, I run sensitization programs for a private radio called *Radio Sarauniya*.

This period of job uncertainty for Habsu Garba requires cultural and historical contextualization. That was an era when major employers, including banks and corporations, had to undergo internal restructuring as demanded by international financial institutions such as the World Bank and IMF. This structural readjustment of employment agencies to better accommodate global networks of capital accumulation set new demands for computerized literacy, more business administration, and managerial skills and, quite often, the knowledge of the English language in francophone Africa. This was the period commonly referred to by the low-middle and middle-class Nigeriens as a *période de compression de travail,* that is, a period of labor reduction. Nigerien women, who for the most part filled the traditional clerical jobs (secretarial work, telephone tellers) in public or private administration sectors, were the hardest hit by Structural Adjustment Programs and the IMF's programs of liberalization. As a consequence, rather than reduce the gender gap in which by all liberal Western economic indicators women were located at the bottom, the restructuring pushed the majority of Nigerien women from the public formal sectors into the private world of domesticity. Forced domesticity of formally waged Nigerien women evokes Maria-Rosa Dalla Costa's (1974) concept of "housewifization" as the economic gender ideology of the IMF and the World Bank in their attempt to reconstitute women into the informal "free" labor for the benefit of local as well as international capital. Maria Mies (1989), the German environmental and economic feminist, incisively described the underlying goals of the IMF and the World Bank's promotion of housewifization as a model for the "integration of women into economic development" as follows: "The characteristic of this strategy [of housewifization through labor compression] is that it defines Third World women not as workers, but as house-wives. What they do is not defined as work, but as an 'activity.' By universalizing the housewife ideology and the model of the nuclear family as a sign of progress, it is also possible to define all the work women do—whether in the formal or informal sectors—as supplementary work, her income as supplementary income to that of the so-called main 'breadwinner,' the husband" (quoted by Sinith Sittirak 1998, 66).

But contrary to the World Bank, the IMF, and the state's design to reduce women to free labor in domesticity, Habsu Garba refused with dignity to be bound by this design and to be defined only by housewifization. She crafted her way beyond this imposed limitation by resorting to a trading occupation in major cosmopolitan African cities like Lomé, Cotonou, and Niamey, while also exploring her talents as a dancer and singer. She finally turned to a public life of professional performing arts. Habsu was thus able to draw from the various spheres of experience and talent in a transgressively creative manner, to forge a "hybrid" professional life. Gradually she moved into fields that are not stereotypically associated with women in Nigerien culture, especially those without higher educational background. These include (a) her involvement in international cosmopolitan trade (while waiting for a final termination of service from her former employer); (b) a settled career in the performing arts (crossing a caste boundary since the profession was traditionally restricted to people of *griot* lineage, and crossing a gender boundary by including gay members in her performing team); and (c) her hosting of a private radio talk show, subverting the gendered divide between the public and the private through radio waves.

The Becoming of a Performing Artist and Its Cultural Problematics

The emergence of Habsu Garba as a famous public performing artist in Niger was of such political significance that she quickly earned a state appointment as a waged civil worker at the city hall. This is a great achievement for a woman in Niger, given the autocratic and conservative political nature of the successive military governments from 1974 to 1991. This artistic-cum-political rise of Habsu Garba could be traced back to the era of General Seyni Kountché, the first military president who, in an attempt to forge a new national culture, stimulated the formation, in 1974, of neighborhood youth cultural and political groups that organized community projects known as *Samariya* (Dan Inna 1979; Beik 1987).

Kountché's regime imposed censorship on artistic expression, especially in the public performing arts. There was a ban on artist singers who praised individuals and this ban affected even the traditional *griots* whose very identity as (court) bards was tied to the patronage of the traditional rulers,

Habsu Garba *(center)* in performance at a political rally in Niamey.

Habsu Garba and her troupe, Shock, posing in Tuareg attire before a performance on national reconciliation in Niger following the so-called Tuareg Rebellion.

high-caste people, or wealthy people for whom they sang. This prohibition extended to Nigeriens who could produce oppositional discourses against the regime's political agenda. Only artists who produced "apolitical" art or the kinds of art that promote the government's political agenda were authorized to hold public performances in government theatres or other public places. In a sense, General Kountché's policy on arts was the Nigerien reenactment of the Policy of Censorship and Control Entertainments Act as implemented in Malawi by its former autocratic president Dr. Hastings Kamuzu Banda (Mphande 1996, 81). Performance licenses were authorized only after scrutiny by the bureau of arts located in the local city hall where Habsu Garba works. Habsu Garba was (and continues to be) a song composer and editor, a leading dance choreographer, and an active performer in her local *Samariya* cultural group she named Group Shock. She was famous during the Kountché regime as well as during that of his successor, General Ali Saibou, for her airport dance and song performances intended to welcome foreign dignitaries. Her role as an artist in Niger resembled that of the Malawian women praise singers and dancers discussed by Lisa Gilman (2001, 42–64) and the Zambian airport singers and dancers who promoted state ideology in compensation for its patronage under Kenneth Kaunda's regime (Crehan 2001, 253–72). Habsu described her involvement in the airport dance and singing group as follows:

HG: I am the one who welcomes any president of a foreign country who visits Niger. I am the entertainer or let's say the presidential cultural entertainer since the regime of the deceased General Seyni Kountché and that of Ali Saibou. . . . I am a crowd galvanizer and my performing group is called "Group Shock" [laughs].

OA: What type of entertainment is it?

HG: During the military regimes we had more than 1000 young men and women who entertained by singing and dancing at the airport before the visiting president and his guests landed and disembarked from their plane.

Habsu's appointment at the city hall came at a time when her job as a bank typist had been terminated. She negotiated a secure job at the city hall with the military regime, which was eager to reward her for exploiting her artistic talents to promote its political "developmental" agenda to the people, especially in local languages. But what was more significant with Habsu's appointment as a public civil servant was the security of tenure and retirement package that the job guaranteed. This development is unique in the life of a young woman artist in Niger where an older generation of women artists who had become national icons, like the ones she mentioned in the course of our interviews and some of those discussed by Aissata Sidikou (2001), are now forgotten and living a miserable life of poverty. With regard to the plight of such senior female icons in the nation, Habsu presented the following reflections:

OA: Do you know Hawa Bozo?

HG: She is alive!

OA: She is my grandmothers' friend. She used to visit them at home when I was young. My grandmother told me that she too did not inherit the art of singing. She began to sing in cultural functions in the military camp where she was married and her women friends enjoyed her voice. Thus, she became the principal entertainer at naming ceremonies, marriages, and other functions. This was how it seemed her career began, unless my memory of this account fails me. . . . Now she is one of the oldest female popular singers who, in my view, is a landmark in Niger's history of performing arts, especially singing.

HG: You are right, *wallahi*! She is alive and lives in *Quartier Aviation*. Our own challenge is that people like Hawa Bozo, even if they no longer sing, we must remember them in a special way given their contributions to the nation and how, through their work, Niger became known to the outside world. She must be remembered and respected, for up to this day people and the nation are continuing to use her art. But she does not benefit a penny from it. Thus, when we see what is happening to our senior colleagues like her who gave the best and are now neglected, we discourage our children from following our footsteps, especially singing or the performing arts.

So given what we see from the experiences of these senior artists, we the young ones are doing the best to save something for our children and ourselves for a time when we can no longer be active. Since Allah has blessed us now, and has opened the doors for us, we too must open the doors for our children in order to prevent them from living off people's mercy one day in the future. If we sit and wait for government's assistance, we will be in deep trouble. For once you stop performing, you become forgotten.

Clearly then, in spite of the fact that singing and performance were Habsu Garba's only personal choices about which she was very passionate, she was very wary of their limitations in providing her a secure future, given the prevailing attitude in the society at large. Neither the local communities nor the government are willing to provide the kind of material support necessary to insure a decent life of retirement for those who served the nation through the performing arts. Indeed, as indicated in the continuation of the dialogue below, even powerful women's associations have failed to come to the aid of their sister-artists:

OA: What support do women's associations like Association des Femmes du Niger and Rassemblement Democratique des Femmes du Niger offer you?

HG: They don't provide us any support. Except when they need us to sing and perform for them. Then they call us.

OA: Is this how the senior women artists are treated as well?

HG: Nothing is given even to the senior ones. They are not even made honorary invitees at events. This is a terrible shame. Senior female singers, like Hawa Bozo or Bouli Kakasi who are still alive, when you see them today, they live a miserable life, all forgotten. . . . This is why people stay away from this type of activity.

I believe in this world you receive what is planned for you. But there is a lot of rivalry. If you receive an international invitation or even a local invitation, colleagues working at the Ministry of Culture hide the letter sent to you or they eliminate you altogether by sending another person.

Thus, Habsu Garba's success in acquiring a job that guaranteed her a retirement package as insurance for an age when she can no longer make a living as a performer marks a departure from the life of the other female senior artists who were satisfied with instantaneous rewards of envelopes of money, a trip to Mecca to perform the *Hajj* (pilgrimage), or print textiles bearing propaganda slogans with distinct patriarchal messages.

Habsu Garba's achievements in this regard are quite remarkable for a woman with no formal training in the school of culture and arts known in Niger as Institut de la Jeunesse et Sport (INJS) (Institute of Youth and Sports) from which the majority of her colleagues working in the city hall arts bureau graduated:

OA: How did you begin to entertain? What drew you to the performing arts, especially to singing and dancing? And when did you begin to take it seriously as your career? How did you decide that this will be what you will embrace?

HG: Entertainment. . . . I grew up with entertainment. Since childhood, I was attracted to it. I did not attend any formal performing arts school like INJS as did most educated people involved in popular performing arts. My training came just as a gift from Allah. It is a gift!

Griotte(s) of Tradition and Modernity: The Struggle for Space

It was not only her colleagues at the city hall who revealed their jealousy. There was a similar reaction from traditional griots (griottes) who saw her as a noble usurping their culturally inherited roles:

OA: Is there a sort of rivalry between traditional griots/griottes and modern popular artists like yourself?

HG: For me, we are all equal. You see I have inherited this talent neither from my mother nor from my father's side. I am doing it simply because of my youthful attraction to *annashuwa* (entertainment). Some people inherited it [as a profession]. Some are annoyed when we meet. I never envy people in this world because I know one day I will leave this job as did others before us. This could be as a result of death or just by letting it go. But it is a very fulfilling and meaningful contribution from me as I see it.

This message offers a particular perspective on Habsu's bold subversion of caste ideology and the way this transgression is often condemned by both traditional griots and "nobles." The question of the origin of artistic talent and the problematics of crossing identity boundaries are what Habsu Garba seeks to highlight. As she acknowledges, her talent is neither a product of heredity as culturally inscribed for a singer (male or female), nor a product of training at INJS, the educational structure inherited from the Western colonial legacy in Niger. It is true that for most ethnic groups, including the Zarma-Songhay and the Hausa, singing is associated with the low-caste *griots* who are the inheritors of verbal praise artistry and performance, for praise itself is linked to the patronage of someone of royal or nobility background. Thus, although Habsu sees herself as a modern performer who is on par with the *griot*, the rigidity of the inherited professional caste boundaries set her against both the nobility and the *griots*. While for the noble, Habsu's rank in terms of a more traditional classification, she is violating the norms of their high status in the social hierarchy, for the low-caste *griots*, she is encroaching on a territory that by tradition is their exclusive preserve—a territory not only of their caste status, but of their economic survival.

It is interesting to see how Habsu Garba, a daughter of nobility, rationalizes her involvement in the performing arts in response to the hostility of both the nobility and the low caste of *griots*. By claiming that her artistic talent to sing and perform is a *gift from Allah*, Habsu Garba is inscribing a religious requirement in her life to put "the gift" to use for both personal fulfillment and collective good. This approach is in accordance with the Islamic tenet that Muslims must put to good use "the favor" bestowed on them by Allah: "Not equal are those believers who sit (at home) and receive no hurt, and those who strive and fight in the cause of God with their goods and their persons. God hath granted a grade higher to those who strive and fight with their goods and persons than those who sit (at home). Unto all (in faith) hath God promised good; But those who strive and fight hard (Allah distinguished above those who sit (at home) by a special reward" (*The Glorious Koran*, chapter 4, verse 95). If her art is her calling from Allah, then, Habsu regards it as necessary to galvanize it for the public good. That is why her art is used, in part, to promote developmental causes (including public health like her songs on HIV-AIDS, agriculture, and political welfare).

It is also significant that Habsu Garba eventually changed the name of her troupe from *Group Shock* to *Group Annashuwa* (Entertainment Group) instead of *Group Roko* (Praising or Begging Group, a name that would normally be associated with the *griot* caste). By deliberately avoiding an invocation of the *griot's* names and symbols on the one hand, and appealing to Allah's intervention for her talent on the other, Habsu was seeking to legitimize her place in the performing art space without offending the sensibility of either the nobility or the *griots*.

Functional Art: Between Orality and Literacy

Habsu informed me that she normally combines her oral verbal artistry with her literacy skills in the production of new songs and dance production. This ability to mix orality and literacy sets Habsu Garba's approach apart from those of the traditional senior female *griottes* who, in general, did not have access to formal education or adult literacy.

OA: How do you create your songs?

HG: I create my songs myself and craft them according to given themes. I am my own author, composer, and editor before I release them to my young colleagues who are in my group. Sometimes, if I am too busy at home, I create my song and the melody during rehearsal. I compose spontaneously, teach them the lyrics, and write the song as we are learning and composing it until the whole process of composing and performing is over.

With the appointment of her favorite candidate, the current president of Niger Republic, President Mamadou Tanja, Habsu Garba offers a rich and multivariate thematic repertoire of songs. While most of her songs are crafted around the political ideology of either the military regime or the Mouvement National de Société de Développement (MNSD), the political party in power to which she belongs, some of her songs are social commentaries on themes such as HIV-AIDS and family planning. For example, she composed the following song in Hausa, entitled *Sai Mu Taru Mu Zaɓi Tanja* (Let us gather to vote for Tanja), which she sang during the 1996 presidential elections.

'yen uwa	Brothers and sisters
'yen ƙasanmu Niger	The children of our country Niger
Sai mu taru mu zaɓi Tanja	We must gather to vote for Tanja
'yen uwa	Brothers and sisters
'yen ƙasanmu Niger	The children of our country Niger
Mai son rayuwar ƙasar ga	Whoever is committed to the welfare of this country
Mai son ya walwala da rainai	Whoever wishes to feel free with oneself
Ranar zaɓe mu zaɓi Tanja	We must vote for Tanja on election day
'yen Niger	Children of Niger
Kowa ya lura	Everybody must be aware
Jaggorar ƙasanmu Niger	—of our country Niger
In dai adali na gaske	If we are seeking for a true patriotism
Wanda ya ṣan ƙasanmu sosai	One who knows well our country
Mai hankali wanda ke da lura	One who is smart and observant
'yen uwa	Brothers and sisters
'yen ƙasanmu Niger	Children of our country Niger
Mai son walwala da rainai	Whoever wishes to feel free with oneself
Ranar zaɓe mu zaɓi Tanja	We must vote for Tanja on election day
Tanja	Tanja
Adali na gaske	True patriot
Tanja mai gaskiya da lura	Tanja the truthful and wise
Yay aiki ƙwarai ƙasag ga	He worked hard in this country
Har abada ba a mance Tanja	Tanja can never be forgotten
Tawa	Tahoua
Ba a mance Tanja	Tanja was not forgotten

Shi ya yi hanyal haɗin zumunta	He was the one who built the national unity road
Puroje Keita ma yana nan	He was also there for the Keita project
Maraɗi ba a mance Tanja	Even in Marad'i is Tanja not forgotten
Duk Niger ba a mance Tanja	Nowhere in Niger is Tanja forgotten
Yay aiki yabo ƙasag ga	He did a praiseworthy job in this country
'yen uwa	Brothers and sisters
'yen ƙasanmu Niger	Children of our country Niger
Mai son walwala da rainai	Whoever wishes to feel free with oneself
Ranar zaɓe mu zaɓi Tanja	We must vote for Tanja on election day
Kun ga halin ƙasanmu yanzu	You see in our country today
Mulkin danniya ake yi	They ran oppressive leadership
Komi ya taɓarɓare ƙasag ga	Everything is in a mess
Kaman wasan kara ake yi	Like a game of a puppet doll
'yen uwa	Brothers and sisters
'yen ƙasanmu Niger	Children of our country Niger
Mai son walwala da rainai	Whoever wishes to feel free with oneself
Ranar zaɓe mu zaɓi Tanja	We must vote for Tanja on election day
'yen ƙasam mu ne ga zaɓe	It is our people who are voting
Kar mu zaɓi mai gazawa	Let us not vote for an inept person
Mu zaɓi Tanja mai iyawa	Let us vote for Tanja the knowlegeable
Tanja gwani Tanja dodò	Tanja the maestro, the mystic
Zai maido arziki ƙasag ga	He will restore wealth to this country
'yen uwa	Brothers and sisters
'yen ƙasanmu Niger	Children of our country Niger
Mai son walwala da rainai	Whoever wishes to feel free with oneself
Ranar zaɓe mu zaɓi Tanja	We must vote for Tanja on election day
Tanja ya san ƙasanmu sosai	Tanja knows our country very well
Kauyukka zuwa burane	From cities to villages
Manoma ku zaɓi Tanja	Farmers vote for Tanja
Makiyaya ku zaɓi Tanja	Herders vote for Tanja
Ma'aikata ku zaɓi Tanja	Laborers vote for Tanja
ɗalubbai ku zaɓi Tanja	Students vote for Tanja
In dai Tanja munka zaɓa	If you vote for Tanja
In sha Allahu bai gazawa	Allah willing, he will not fail
Kowa harakasshi za ta yi kyau	Everybody's problem will be solved

'yen uwa	Brothers and sisters
'yen ƙasanmu Niger	Children of our country Niger
Mai son walwala da rainai	Whoever wishes to feel free with oneself
Ranar zaɓe mu zaɓi Tanja	We must vote for Tanja on election day
Ku zo ku zo mutane	Come on, come on, people
Ranar zaɓe mu zaɓi Tanja	Let us vote for Tanja on election day
In dai rayuwa muke so	If we are seeking for (our) well being

As a polyglot, Habsu also composes and sings in Hausa, Zarma, and French. In fact, the use of code switching in her songs, whereby the lyrics of a song are in Hausa and Zarma (and French), is one of Habsu's trademark. She attempts to build transethnic bridges by resorting to her polyglossia and by coming to terms with French as a lingua franca of the transethnic national francophile elite. Habsu Garba uses polyglossia to reach different national constituencies. An example of this code-switching phenomenon is evident in the following song, "Ranar Hwarin ciki Ranar Zaɓe" (Rejoice on election day):

(in Hausa language)	
'yen Niger	People of Niger
Ranar hwarin ciki ce yau	Today is a day of rejoicing
Sai murna	We feel joy
Za mu zaɓe yau	We will be voting
Na shugaba	For the president
(switching to Zarma language)	
Niger labiizay	People of Niger
Kuluuja nda farha hana ne ka	The day of happiness and rejoicing is here
Labiizay ir ma koy saafe	Citizens let us go and vote for
Ir gin bora	our leader
(switching back to Hausa language)	
'yen ƙasar Niger	People of Niger Republic
Sahiyar ga za ta yin kyawo	This morning will be a pretty one
Da maraice	In the afternoon
A ke ganin niyya	We will see what is commitment
Mun tabbata ƙasar Niger	We are certain in Niger Republic
Wadata za ta sabkowa	(that) it will be filled with bounty
Ni'ima ta lulluɓe Niger	Bounty will cover Niger
Mu ci gaba	So that we move ahead (we progress)

(switching to Zarma language)

Zaari hannaawo	This pretty day
Za day ciini gaa n go	It is up to the night
Niijeero sikka kullu si no	There is no doubt Niger
Suugin nda gwamni na zuure	(is) visited by goodness and plenty
kal zaadaya	What remains is moving ahead

(switching back to Hausa language)

'yen ƙasar Niger	Citizens of Niger
MNSD sabuwar Nassara	MNSD, the new power (leadership),
Ta yi kira	she is calling
Mu ba ta yarda mu da ko'ina	(so) that we give her our trust from everywhere
'yen ƙasar Niger	People of Niger
Bakin tahiya	The end of a journey [walk]
Ka zo cikin ɗaki	Is for you to get to the place [room]
Shirin namu	Our design (planning)
Ga shi ya zamna	has indeed materialized
Doki ne ram da kayanshi	It is a ready horse with its ornaments
Wane ne za a ba ragama	Whom should we give the lead
Ya tai da shi	for him to compete against

(switching to Zarma language)

Niger labiizay	Citizens of Niger
Ir soola karŋa kul si no	There is nothing left out in our preparation
A hima nda hu kan i soola	It is important for a house to be prepared
May no ga algano	Who will take care of it
di ir se kala	to hold it for us
ir ma koy	So that we move ahead

(switching back to Hausa language)

'yen ƙasar Niger	Citizens of Niger
MNSD sabuwar Nassara	MNSD, the new power (leadership),
Ta yi kira mu ba ta yardarmu	she is calling for us to grant her our trust
Mu ba ta yarda mu da ko'ina	(so) that we give her our trust from everywhere
'yen ƙasar Niger	Citizens of Niger
Sai zarumi cikakkenai	Only a strong courageous leader

Mai halin ƙwarai da adalci	Full of understanding and trustworthiness
'yen ƙasar Niger	Citizens of Niger
MNSD sabuwar Nassara	MNSD the new power (leadership)
Ta yi kira mu ba ta yardarmu	she is calling for us to grant her our trust
Mu ba ta yarda mu da ko'ina	(so) that we lend her our trust from everywhere
'yen ƙasar Niger	Citizens of Niger
Sai zarumi cikakkenai	Only a strong brave one
Mai halin ƙwarai da adalci	Who has great understanding and trust
Mai jinƙai	One who has compassion
Mai ganin tausai	Who has empathy
Mai son rayuwa da al'umma	Who wishes the well-being of the people
Mai son gaskiya da lissahi	Who likes the truth and understanding
Shi ne za mu ba ragama	He will be the one who will be enthroned
Ya tai da shi	For him to lead
(switching to Zarma language)	
Niger labiizay	Citizens of Niger
Gina ganjiya ga ba suuru	The spirits before us need appeasing
Kala kala cimi nda laasaabu	Only truth and understanding
Kala bor kan ga canse labo se	Only one who is proud of his country
No ir ga baa	Is the one we want
(switching back to Hausa language)	
'yen ƙasar Niger	Citizens of Niger
MNSD sabuwar Nassara	MNSD, the new power (leadership),
Ta yi kira mu ba ta yardarmu	she is calling for us to grant her our trust
Mu ba ta yarda mu da ko'ina	(so) that we give her our trust from everywhere
'yen ƙasar Niger	Citizens of Niger
Halay'aŋ ga kun ga	We saw those dealings
Mun gan shi	We saw it
Lalle mai wurin ga	Truly, the owner of this place (seat)
Mun sanshi	We know him
Mamadu Tanja	Mamadu Tanja
Ya kamance mu	He deserves us
Shi ne za mu zaɓanshi	He is the one we will elect as
Gaban ƙasa	Head of State

(switching to Zarma language)	
Niger labiizay	Citizens of Niger
Bora kulu	All the People
Ma koy ga foofo	Go greet
Mamadu Tanja no	It is Mamadu Tanja
Ga tir baako	Who loves us
Ma di algano	Hold the lead
Mamadu Tanja mir candi kala ir ma koy	Mamadu Tanja pull us till we reach
(switching back to Hausa language)	
'yen ƙasar Niger	Citizens of Niger
MNSD sabuwar Nassara	MNSD, the new power (leadership),
Ta yi kira mu ba ta yardarmu	she is calling for us to grant her our trust
Mu ba ta yarda mu da ko'ina	(so) that we lend her our trust from everywhere
Muna kirar kowa	We are calling on everybody
Ya amince	He is the right choice
Ya ba da yardarshi	He has given his trust
Kyawon ɗa	The beauty of a son (of the land)
Ya so masoyinshi	Is for him to love those who love him
Sannan hankalinshi	That is when his mind
Zai kwanta cikin ƙasa	will settle in the country
'yen ƙasar Niger	Citizens of Niger
MNSD sabuwar Nassara	MNSD, the new power (leadership),
Ta yi kira mu ba ta yardarmu	she is calling for us to grant her our trust
Mu ba ta yarda mu da ko'ina	(so) that we lend her our trust from everywhere
'yen ƙasar Niger	Citizens of Niger
Mamadu Tanja ne	It is Mamadu Tanja
Masoyinmu	The one who loves us
Ku zo	Come on
'yen ƙasar Niger	Citizens of Niger
Ku zo	Come on
Mu ɗau masoyinmu	To pick the one who loves us
Allah ya sa kun ji wanga kira	Allah (God) has made it that you have heard this call
Da munka yi	That we have made

(switching to Zarma language)	
Niger labiizay	Citizens of Niger
Mamadu Tanja no ga ba Niger	It is Mamadu Tanja who loves Niger
Nda yarda nda goy da imani	With trust, work, and humanism
Wa ka Niger labiizay	Let us gather people of Niger
Wa ka ir ma koy saafe	Let us go vote
Ir Koy Taalaa ma faaba dan ir se	May God bless
Jama ma to	May people Fill (the place)

In sociolinguistic theory, code-switching between two or more varieties of language is sometimes interpreted as a linguistic strategy for exclusion or inclusion. But Habsu's resort to code-switching is clearly intended for purposes of inclusion as well as a tool for celebrating her own *brassage* as well as the national *brassage*. This ability to move from one language to another, without violating the linguistic, cultural, and aesthetic rules and nuances of either language is demonstrative of Habsu Garba's strong multicultural grounding in the languages of her linguistic repertoire. Her openness to call upon either her nephew or her husband to assist her with the translation of her lyrics into French demonstrates her desire to make her art open and inclusive of others, to reach all sections of the population, including the predominantly male francophile elite. The phenomenon of code-swtiching is evident again in a videotaped song in which Habsu Garba uses Hausa, Songhay, and French in a performance at the Palais de Congrès in Niamey during HIV-AIDS awareness day. The song is entitled "Waƙar SIDA" (The song of AIDS).

Habsu's consciousness of building bridges across the national ethnic groups is also reflected in the dance choreographies she creates to accompany her songs, which I had the opportunity to videotape during her group rehearsal sessions that I attended during my fieldwork. The composition of her entertainment group Groupe Annashuwa is uniquely a *brassage* given its multiethnic and multigendered membership. It is composed of men and women artists as well as openly homosexual male artists, all from different ethnic groups. Though the musicians are all males from diverse ethnic backgrounds, each member plays an instrument typical of his ethnic cultural heritage. Habsu is the lead singer and dance choreographer. This profile of Groupe Annashuwa definitely embodies Habsu's engagement in praxis with *brassage* as a transformative concept of engagement with other fellow Nigeriens. *Brassage* for her goes beyond the usual rhetoric of *brassage sahélien* of "national unity" very commonly heard in political speeches by people in power who try to win over popular cross-ethnic national support in their campaigns.

The Tension between Performance and Politics

Habsu Garba's affiliation with the old military regimes and now with the MNSD—a political party that many Nigeriens consider reminiscent of the old military regime reenacted as the right-wing in the current multiparty dispensation—has drawn criticism from many opposition supporters. The latter perceive Habsu's "blind" allegiance to the regime in power that continues to control the political life of Niger Republic as the embodiment of a modern *griotage,* that is, a person who performs just for material gain.

I, however, find this negative assessment of Habsu's political consciousness as a woman who battled throughout her life from childhood to adulthood against patriarchal familial, educational, professional, and state assumptions regarding a female's place and life aspirations rather simplistic and one-dimensional. B. Roland Inden's critical perspective on how the subject's positionality in any given culture and/or situation determines how they choose to deploy and act upon their subjectivities is important to our understanding of what roles Habsu chooses to play and how she chooses to use her talents in the national political arena: "People do not act only as agents. They also have the capacity to act as "instruments" of other agents, and to be "patients," to be the recipients of the acts of others. . . . Yet we should not think of persons, or institutions, when they act as instruments or patients as mere adjuncts or even chattels of some superior owner. A person or institution, acting as an instrument or patient may be, from his, her, or its points of view, a more or less willing one. Indeed the idea that instruments and patients are both complicit and resistant is implied in the notion of hegemony" (Inden 1993, 23). Hence, Habsu is a complex modern Muslim woman whose identity reveals ambiguity in the arena of power, but at the same time reflects a woman quite *engaged* with her own subjectivity and the ways she uses it. She has placed herself in the space of power and exploits that space of power in order to interrogate power. So, yes, although in this context Habsu Garba might appear to have been an "instrument" of military regimes in Niger—to live as what Inden called a "patient or an instrument" of other agents (here the military regimes)—we see also that she has positioned herself in such a way as to reverse this role by acquiring, through her location in the circle of power, an agenthood that allows her to recenter the issue of women's rights in the national agenda, moving from the position of a "patient" to one of an "agent."

Habsu's life achievements in challenging patriarchal values by living as a successful female public performer, fulfilling her long held aspiration, stands, in my view, as a great success story of a Muslim woman. Her life history must also be read as a very powerful female political confrontation of both national and international male patriarchs of (right or left) political and religious persuasion, as well as of local and international female patriarchs. Habsu Garba's political consciousness takes form in her ability to creatively subvert oppressive traditional values that hurt both men and women. These include patriarchy, the boundaries that set apart nobles and caste members in a hierarchical manner (thereby hindering individuals, by virtue of their accidental birth in a given social order), and those boundaries that marginalize individuals such as homosexuals. Throughout her life, Habsu Garba has lived a series of subversive acts in order to transform the social order, not only for herself but for others as well, without forgetting to secure a material base for herself and her group members with whom she shares the financial gains of their performances.

Between Political Patronage and Political Representation

The democratization momentum of the early 1990s was also seized by Nigeriens interested in the development of private radio and television stations that could provide an alternative media culture. Habsu Garba became one of the first women who creatively curved for themselves roles of sociopolitical activism through their work as sociocultural and political commentators on radio talk shows. The new radio programs were commonly known as *faji karai* or *filin hira,* both meaning entertaining conversation in the Zarma and Hausa languages, respectively. In this way, Habsu Garba was thus able to bring her political consciousness to a wider public in her role as a popular radio talk show host.

The subversive efficacy of Habsu Garba's radio talk show is demonstrated by the large proportion of phone callers from her audience, especially women from the middle class who live in official or nonofficial *kulle* (seclusion in conjugal households). They call and make their views known on whatever topic is being debated and they intervene in the Hausa, Zarma, and/or French languages. Thus, the radio talk show programs give women an opportunity to inscribe their voices on national public airwaves and beyond. The domestic phones and public phones (at what are called *télécentre* booths, a relatively new phenomenon in Niger) have thus become the new vehicles for women's entry into traditionally nonfemale spaces in their attempt to engage the patriarchal listeners of the nation. This is how Habsu Garba speaks of her radio talk show that she cohosts with a male colleague who also participated in one of the interviews upon her own invitation:

OA: You are such a multitalented woman! What type of sensitization program is your radio program about? And since when did you start doing this?

HG *Radio Sarauniya* opened this December [2000]. This is less than a year ago. However, I was one of its pioneers. I was hired with John, who is here with us, to promote awareness, through social commentaries, on issues that negatively affect the life of the nation. These include youth issues, women's issues, as well as men's issues. I cover quite a wide range of topics.

The name of our radio program is *May ga no talo go?* (Who is responsible for this problem?) in the Zarma language, *À qui la faute?* (Whose fault is it?) in French, and *Riga ce ba wuya* (It is a shirt without a neck opening) in the Hausa language. The implication is that the social commentary can apply to anybody; it is not targeting any specific person. These commentaries can apply to me, you, or anybody, even though we do not mention names in order to avoid personal offense.

OA: Could you provide an example of a topic focusing on women you had on the program?

HG: For example, we had a session on the invisibility of women in executive positions in political parties and in the National Assembly. There are 53 percent women in Niger Republic and yet there is only one seat occupied by a woman in this government. So women are not given their *rights* in Niger. Look, for example, at the number of ministers. Some said that there are 23 ministers. If you go to investigate very closely twenty are all male and maybe two or three women. Check this out at the National Assembly. There is only one woman, Mme Ben Wahab sitting here with us, out of eighty-three national members of parliament. Thus, we did a program to focus on this problem in order to conscientize the women to tighten up their *zane* [clothing wraps or *pagnes*] and become very active in the political life of the country. They must stand up, play their cards well, and claim their rights by requesting to be heard. They must tighten up their *pagnes* and reclaim their right place. We are behind them. So we debated this on our radio program.

OA: Do you have an archive of your radio shows? Can one have access to them on tape if possible, with your permission?

HG: *Insha Allah* (Allah willing), I will bring you copies of what we did, especially on women, because I have up to three tapes produced on women's topics.

OA: How do other women respond to your radio program?

HG: You will hear us on the tapes. Women do encourage us a great deal. They call us by phone or write to tell us how pleased they are with our program. There are many radio stations with similar programs that receive bad ratings and at times even insults from listeners. We know this because the programs receive the phone calls live during the show. It is a direct interaction with the listeners by phone. However, this has not been our experience because our strategies of sensitization are different from others.

On my radio program, we introduce the topic and open the debate by freeing the lines to our listeners so that they can have their own input. We also read to the world the letters sent to us by our listeners. We allow listeners to take charge of the debate after we introduce the topic. We, that is, John and myself, consider ourselves as facilitators who galvanize the debate rather than control the waves. So the listeners prefer our program because of this democratic spirit of interaction.

> With debate or sensitization, one has to take into consideration that in this world there are plenty of bright people who need a space to speak up and who are worth listening to. Thus, a person with a radio program like ours must not monopolize the talking, thinking at the expense of the listeners, because we need to benefit from those intelligent minds as well.
>
> I ran the show with John as my radio cohost [John just walked in with Habsu's husband] John, I just mentioned your name. I was informing her about our radio program. She wanted to know how it started?. . . .
>
> JOHN: Radio Sarauniya started with us on December 12, 2000. Before that we were at another radio station and now we are at this one. We had to be very creative in order to attract a big audience given the number of radio (public and private) stations that preceded this one and which are still active. The competition requires more strategies. So we decided to be more aggressive by opening two lines. One line for the two of us and the other for us to talk to the audience so that we have spontaneous active participation from several directions. We have been very successful because of the large audience that is hooked to our program from 9:00 a.m. This is Habsu Garba's and my own innovation on radio shows.
>
> We focus on current issues without personal attacks. For example, one day we debated how people waste food in a country such as ours, which is always hit by famine, drought, and poverty.

Here Habsu Garba exposes the false promises of gender equity made by the multiparty order, the blatant exclusion of women in parliament. But her critique is not only focused on the patriarchal hegemonic nature of Nigerien multipartism; it also questions the basis of women's own lack of active public involvement in reclaiming their rights. Finally, Habsu Garba uses the platform afforded by the radio talk show to galvanize women toward greater political activism in the nation. Through her radio talk show, in other words, Habsu Garba is hoping to bring back to her sisters the spirit of solidarity that brought them to the streets in the capital city as well as in other parts of the country on the famous day of May 13, 1991, to protest the underrepresentation of women in the committee responsible for preparing the Sovereign National Conference (July–October 1991) that was supposed to set the foundation for a more just and democratic national political order. The disproportionate number of women in the executive and legislative bodies of the nation that Habsu Garba deplores can be seen in tables, 8 and 9 covering the period from 1997 to 1999.

By August 7, 2001, the date I had my last interview with Habsu Garba in Niamey, there was only one woman representative in parliament. It is precisely against the dangers of women's complacency and even complicity with the old patriarchal *ordre du jour* that one of Niger's most vocal feminist scholars and politicians, Aichatou Mindaoudou, the minister of foreign affairs in the current government, warned a few years earlier: "With regard to women, these silent actresses used as resonance chambers, we

Table 8. Political representation of Nigerien women in government from 1957–99

Political Regime	Number of government members	Number of women	Percentage of women
April 4, 1957–September 27, 1958, *Niger* as overseas territory	22	0	0.00
September 28, 1958–August 2, 1960, *Niger* as member of French Union	26	0	0.00
August 3, 1960–April 14, 1974, *Niger*'s 1st Republic	99	0	0.00
April 14, 1974–September 23, 1989, *Niger*'s *Régime d'exception*	377	1	0.20
September 24, 1989–July 28, 1991, *Niger*'s 2nd Republic	51	2	3.90
July 29, 1991–April 15, 1993, Democratic transition in *Niger*	63	2	3.17
April 16, 1993–February 20, 1995, *Niger*'s 3rd Republic	70	6	8.50
February 21, 1995–January 26, 1996, Cohabitation	16	2	12.50
January 27, 1996–August 7, 1996, *Niger* is Back to Military Régime—*Conseil du Salut National*	76	5	6.57
August 8, 1996–April 8, 1999, *Niger*'s 4th Republic	96	5	5.20
April 9–December 1999, *Niger* is Back to Military Régime—*Conseil du Salut National*	23	2	8.69
TOTAL	919	25	2.17

Source: Hamani (2000, 58).

often share responsibility for the precariousness of our status. We have often indulged in passive acceptance, capitulation, even when basic rights are held up to ridicule" (Mindaoudou 1995, 10).

The role that Habsu Garba plays as a social commentator on this radio program is to some degree an extension of her work with the theater group of women from various political parties. One of the most successful and provocative plays, entitled *Députè Balsa* (Corrupt deputy), produced by this women's group in 2000, is a political satire of a masculinist government, its abuse of state resources, and its total disregard of the women's agenda. The play not only exposes the shortcomings and the hypocrisy of the "new democracy," but it also serves as an additional platform for the struggle of Nigerien women to inscribe themselves afresh in the national

Table 9: Women's representation in parliament

National Parliament	Total of Number of Deputies	Number of Women	Percentage of Women
August 3, 1960–April 14, 1974,			
Niger's 1st Republic			
1st Parliament	60	0	0.0
2nd Parliament	49	0	0.0
3rd Parliament	49	0	0.0
Niger's 2nd Republic			
Parliament emerging from			
Dec. 10, 1989 elections	93	5	5.4
Niger's 3rd Republic			
1st Parliament	83	5	6.0
2nd Parliament	83	3	3.6
Niger's 4th Republic			
Parliament emerging from			
Nov. 23, 1996 elections	.83	1	1.2
Niger's 5th Republic	83	1	1.2
Parliament emerging from			
Nov, 24, 1999 elections	583	15	2.5

Source: Hamani (2000, 68).

space of politics of power. In essence, then, Habsu Garba is politically involved in struggles for women's advancement beyond the scope of her own political party, MNSD, as her participation in this women's coalition for political activism across party boundaries demonstrates.

When Fieldwork Connects the Present with the Past

Let me now return to a point I made much earlier in this chapter, relating to Habsu Garba's decision to "turn the gaze of the fieldwork" on the researcher, thus making me, the interviewer, the subject whose life is in focus. First, Habsu did not warn me that the interview would involve more than just the two of us. She wanted to give me a surprise after learning that her husband, Maiga, was an old friend of mine from adolescence. In fact, he, my twin sister, Hassana, and I used to belong to the same athletic team (from 1978 to 1980) that represented the Department of Niamey at the annual national cultural youth week competition commonly known as Championat National de la Jeunesse et Sport during the Seyni Kountché military regime. We were members of the same track team that brought pride to the region we represented. He competed in the 400 m and 800 m races and was part of the male relay team. I competed in the 400 m female team and was part of the 400 m female relay team, while my twin sister competed, just like Maiga, in the 400 m and 800 m track events. Hassana was also a member of the female relay team. Meeting Magia brought me back to the time when my twin sister and I first had to run from one family member to the other among the elders to inform them that we had been selected to represent the Department of Niamey and to ask for their approval, then to my adoptive parents, the Catholic nuns, who ran my school. For most of these guardians, the concerns were the same: "You will be sheltered in gender-segregated spaces? Just be careful, for some men will try to take advantage of your naivety. Don't shame us, please!" The thought that we too, the young women, might come back with "bright and shiny medals"—which we did win, by the way—just like our male counterparts, was of little relevance at that moment for our guardians. But my twin sister, the other young female athletes on our team, and I moved on in defiance of the patriarchal conservatism of our parents and school guardians to challenge the idea of seeing us only as sexual beings tied to their family honor. We were called all sorts of names—spoiled girls, prostitutes of the national stadium—by some chauvinist males as well as by some of our sisters whose minds were locked into patriarchal thinking or were just jealous for not being up to our daring decision. Yes, Habsu's "reversed mirror" was a chance to revisit my own struggle to inscribe myself within the system as "legitimate" in the national public arena of competitive athletics, side by side with other fellow Nigeriens who happened to be male.

Maiga, as far I can remember, was the most genuine male friend whom most of the women in the track team trusted and felt comfortable to hang out with. I still remember his humor as a way of helping the team relax before a race. As Habsu heard the sound of their car by our gate, she told my husband and my brother (who were around when we were conducting our interview), that she had a big surprise for me. Indeed, it was! Maiga and I had not seen each other since our last year in middle school in Marad'i in April 1979! This interview was conducted in Niamey on August 7, 2001: Over twenty years had gone by!

So here again Habsu Garba quite creatively subverted what I (the researcher) had initially set as the format for dialogue between the two of us by inviting both Maiga, her husband and my friend, and John, her radio talk show partner. Furthermore, her set-up to surprise me also became an arena for exploring my own life journey as a Nigerien woman among the ranks of female athletes who belonged to the early generations of national athletes, rewarded not with money, but with the honor of being on the sports field like our male contemporaries and of donning the official national sports attire. Habsu Garba thus crafted, in the context of this interview, a window into the "researcher's life," using what the African anthropologist Manthia

Habsu Garba posing with her husband and manager, Maiga, after her pilgrimage to Mecca.

Diawara called "reverse anthropology" when he set his camera on the life of the French Africanist anthropologist Jean Rouch (Diawara 1995). These glimpses into my own personal life outside of my identity as a researcher and that of her husband's younger years were revealed to Habsu and to my own husband from Kenya, through the following dialogue:

OA: Now allow me to ask some questions to our head of the household since he is supportive [teasing Maiga].

HG: OK! [big laugh]

OA [asked in Zarma]: Maiga, you and I and my twin sister practically grew up together as teenagers and worked hard to promote culture and sports in Niger. Now as adults, after so many years apart, our paths converge again, surprisingly on the terrain of performing arts and culture. I am just realizing that we have kept more or less that common old interest even though we are operating within different educational systems. I teach African languages, literatures, cultures and folklore in the Unites States now. Very often people read and write accounts of Niger as an extremely patriarchal culture where men control the lives of their womenfolk. In the West, I often enter into dialogue with my colleagues regarding the problem of excessive generalizations on patriarchal manifestation in Africa. Here at home, I find myself in dialogue (quite often a hurtful one) with our own conservative folks who see us women in sports and performing arts as deviants, prostitutes, etc. . . . What is your take on all this as a man given your close interaction with women on this cultural terrain from your teenage years to now?

MAIGA [answers in French]: Well, what you allow to affect you in life as an adult is often a product of your inner orientation. It is true that in Niger, culture has a gendered manifestation. However, women have a say with regard to the preservation and development of cultural patrimony more so than men. In the area of promoting cultural mores, traditions, women are not driven by money. In fact, they are much stronger nationalists. They have not commodified culture to the extent reached by men. Thus, through women, culture is promoted everywhere. In Niger, there are men promoting culture. However, the women outnumber them. The men are lettered; as a result, they study culture and even write theses on culture [that is, in contrast to practicing it].

Often here, people are conservative. So for them, unless you inherit this art of singing, they would make trouble for those artists like *us* who are in performing arts by attraction and gift. You hear all the gossip about it. Those who think this way then do not want to bear witness to the changing times and to the fact that modernity has taken its course, even on crucial areas of culture such as inherited traditions that include singing or performance. They believe that you, artists and singers [not by inheritance] are against tradition. Their analysis does not take into account evolution and the impact of modernity. We must do our best to safeguard our cultural patrimony, the tradition of the past, because this is what brings out and allows us to affirm our identity. A country or a nation affirms itself only through its culture. Through its culture, a people can identify where they come from. But culture also has it dynamism.

Negative understanding of our role in preserving our traditions and mores is what leads some individuals to misjudge the place of the modern popular artist in cultures such as ours. A committed artist, who uses the resources from our tradition, his or her motivation or goal is to preserve the past by bringing it to present memory through modern art. She or he can't be going against culture and tradition. The modern artist tries to promote her or his country's rich cultural heritage throughout the world.

The patriarchal men of our culture lead in making such negative portrayal within families. This negative portrayal of the modern artist, singer, performer, especially the female modern popular artist, totally disregards Allah's plan for the individual. That is, if your destiny is to become an artist, you will become an artist regardless of the traditional understanding of the art. As long as you are doing your art in a righteous way, there is no problem.

I myself was and have been since secondary school involved in culture, performing arts, and sports. When you find a male or female partner hooked to an activity or a career, you must not try to deny the person what they aspire to. As a man in a patriarchal society, you can take advantage of your culturally enjoyed privilege to exercise pressure on the woman to abandon her talent because she wants the marriage. However, the nation and its promotion must be prioritized before the individual. Therefore, if you love the woman you must encourage her to use her talent or her art by providing moral support in order for her to reach the goal she sets for herself.

OA: If all men think likewise, my friend, we would be saved! [laughs] I have more questions for you though. Now let me turn to the point of view of the husband, not all men. How did you meet? [laughs]

MAIGA: It is Allah's planning and circumstances. We met at the [political] party meetings.

OA: What is your political party affiliation?

MAIGA: Well, *Twin*, you have big questions! [laughs] MNSD-Nasara. It has been ten or eleven years that I have been a member of that party. That is how we met. Before party politics, we used to see each other from a distance in town. . . . [laughs]. . . But I don't know how it happened [laughs]. It is Allah's making.

From middle school on, I used to attend her rehearsal sessions with her group Shock because I love cultural activities. But we never spoke. I have been in performing arts circles with senior colleagues. I met so many people. I was always appointed as a coordinator and organizer of cultural events. And when party politics was instituted, Allah made this union possible as a way of strengthening my interest in culture.

Culture and the performing arts allow you to develop open-mindedness. It strengthens your intelligence and through it, when you go abroad, you grasp what is surrounding you as new. A person of culture survives wherever she or he goes. You cannot fail to be surrounded by old or new friends. You can get things that money would not provide. Culture and sport expand one's intellectual abilities and enhance adjustment with others. It is a channel for establishing ties with others.

OA: Do you have another profession?

MAIGA: That is correct! [in English] Isn't it what you say in English [laughs]. I used to travel a lot with national cultural performing groups. And that was very taxing for my pupils and myself as a teacher. Because of this, I searched for an alternative eleven years ago. I became the librarian of the school. So that this gives me time to travel for performance.

OA: There is another point that I think touches us women artists, more especially professional women in general . . . [interrupted]

MAIGA: [laughs] I know where you are going [laugh]. Do I act like *Sanussi Jacku* [an amusing political figure]? [laughs]

OA: [laughs]

MAIGA: No, I have no complex nor do I feel jealous. I am not jealous. Is it the question, Madam? [teasingly]

OA: [laughs] Not really, but you are quite close [laughs]. Yes, that is the question partly [laughs]. What type of pressure if any do you feel from inside or outside your communities? In communities, there are men who would complain that your wife travels a lot. . . . Like in my case as a scholar, I travel a lot and my husband, Alamin [who is sitting close to Maiga], commutes so that we can see one another because we work nine hours drive away from one another. If it were here, maybe this would not work because I feel there would be a lot of pressure reproaching our long-distance marriage life, especially because often, the expectation is for the woman to follow the husband and stay where he is. In our case, living in America, this marriage arrangement is not unusual even if it is not what we enjoy. We don't have a choice because both of us need to keep our careers while we are looking for other job openings that will bring us to the same place.

HG: Well, we travel together [laughs]. His feet, my feet [laughs]. I always take him with me wherever I go [laughs]. If you want to invite me, you must send two invitations [laughs].

MAIGA: So, she gave you a response [laughs].

ALL PRESENT: [Clapping and laughing . . .]

It is important to point out that while here and there Maiga used the Zarma language in his answers to my questions, French was the main language conveying his thoughts to me. Maiga himself saw no contradiction in talking about the importance of preserving indigenous cultures in a language that is still foreign. This is because the French language is by and large a male language resulting from men's disproportionate advantage in mainstream formal education in French. This, then, confirms how language is implicated in the gendered power ideology I discussed at the very beginning of this chapter and, in statistical detail, in chapter 2.

Moreover, Maiga's opening comments regarding the relationship between gender and cultural production in Niger are very insightful. He denounces the way advanced literacy skills have contributed to male appropriation of cultural production, the national "patrimony," for commercial ends, thus participating in the commodification of national cultural heritage. However, he contends that women, in spite of their limited literacy (or is it because of it?), endeavor toward genuine preservation and transformation of the cultural heritage for national popular uses and functions.

What is also revealed in the above dialogue with Maiga is an articulation of an unusual male voice from a man born into a patriarchal society with all the privileges it guarantees him, but who appears willing to give it up for the construction of a new social order. In Maiga's view, the new social order, although rooted in tradition, must take into consideration the changes and possibilities offered by modernity for both men and women.

Maiga's discussion of modernity in Niger through gender equity reminds us of Manthia Diawara's take on Mande modernity through his assessment of the contributions made by Salif Keita to build Mande's modern music. Diawara begins by appraising Salif Keita's heroism for being the architect of Mande's musical modernity, which he achieved through a series of cultural transgressive acts. As a son of the great Keita noble, Salif defies some dictates of the traditional Mande's social stratification into clan and caste that restricts singing only to the low caste of the *griot*. Then, through the use of his high-pitched voice as a male vocalist, Salif Keita transgressed into the gendered territory of female *griot (griotte)*. But more significantly, through the international recognition and the respect he earned as a great artist, Salif Keita succeeded in recentering himself, moving out of the marginalized cultural space assigned to albino people like himself in Mande society.

Diawara, however, contends that the disappointing aspect of Salif Keita's modern heroism resides in his problematic artistic rethematization of oppressive patriarchal values, frozen in the hegemonic masculinity of his thirteenth-century Mande imperial ancestor Sundiata Keita, for contemporary modern collective identity. In Diawara's view, the challenge to the construction of a new African modernity lies in hegemonic masculinist Mande ethos enshrined in the Sundiata image: "[T]he real challenge posed by Sundiata, . . . not only [to] Salif Keita but to all of us [Mande, African] who hail from the region [which includes part of Niger], is to avoid the griot's snare in our attempt to build *our* modernity on the ruins of the Mande Empire. [Sundiata] built institutions which were based on the autonomy of clans, the undivided authority of the king, and the superiority of men over women. These institutions far from collapsing under the influence of several centuries of Islam, colonization by Western powers, and recent trends towards globalization have in some areas been strengthened by them" (Manthia Diawara 1998, 98). For Diawara, then, "[t]he salvation of Africa lies in modernization, the creation of a secular public sphere, and the freedom of individuals [especially women]" (Diawara 1998, 55).

It seems that Maiga's vision of "African modernity" in both his theoretical formulation and his personal praxis demonstrates that what Diawara poses as a challenge to Africa is indeed attainable by Africans who opt from their "inner orientation" for modernity. Maiga's view of modernity itself is rooted in a spiritual design for the society as well as for the individual. This is what explains his meeting with his wife and the common interest they share in the performing arts. Thus, in his view, it would be un-Islamic to go against divinely inspired designs for the woman (or the man), to try to be other than what Allah has destined for individuals irrespective of their location in ethnicity, culture, clan, caste, socioeconomic strata, or educational background.

The use of religion by both Habsu Garba and her husband also has a subversive dimension. By resorting to religion, Islam, as a justification for their presumed multiple transgressions of cultural boundaries to inscribe themselves as modern performing artists and cultural critics of changing traditions, they are, in effect, challenging their detractors from the ranks of nobility and traditional caste of *griots*. At the same time, they are protecting themselves from charges of "immorality" from religious and secular sectors.

Perhaps Habsu's appreciation of the uniqueness of her husband's voice is the reason she wanted this part of her private life to be revealed, hoping that it would serve as a model for the positive transformation of society. Perhaps this collective interview she orchestrated was Habsu's way to record the life of men—such as Maiga, her husband, and John, her partner at work, my own husband (born on the coastal Swahililand of East Africa and on his first sojourn in Niger), and my brother (who was busy translating into English for his brother-in-law who spoke neither the local languages nor French)—who are linked to women who challenge cultural oppression and who are under the pressure of tradition for failing to conform to hegemonic norms. Thus, Habsu openly offers another dimension of herself as a married female artist whose husband is very much a partner in her artistic journey and with whom she continues the struggle to subvert cultural conservativism and traditions that entrap both men and women. Perhaps what the multidimensionality of Habsu Garba's life journey offers us is a new framework for looking at Nigerien Muslim women's identities beyond monolithic articulations.

Maiga is also unusual in his choice to work hand in hand with his wife in an area that often casts the woman performer in a negative light, regarding her as sexually loose or even a prostitute. In exploring the private lives of women singers and actresses in Zimbabwe, Liz Gunner and others present the following sad remarks regarding the tension between performance space (public) and domestic space (patriarchal private) from one of their interviewees: "If you are a woman, once you decide to become a musician, never, never get married. If you want to sing solo, he'll say "no." People will offer you places to perform and he will refuse. You will find all your time has been wasted. Your dreams have not come true" (Gunner, et al, 2001, 111).

This negative social stereotyping of female artists as "loose women" or "prostitutes" that affects female artists in Zimbabwe, leading to their marginalization and a life of loneliness in their older years, is a phenomenon that also hinders women from joining the performing arts in Niger Republic (Beik 1987, 60–62). In this regard, Habsu's private life and her husband's participation in it offer a refreshing departure from the plight of many other female artists in Africa in general and in Niger in particular.

Conclusion

In conclusion, I hope that by applying positional as well as (con)textual analysis to the ethnographic biographical narratives of Habsu Garba, I have demonstrated how her agency as a historicized female subject has been a determinant of the various identities she has taken and continues to take in the postcolonial national arena. Habsu has not only remained the woman as imagined by (pre)colonial and postcolonial traditions, but she has also moved (and continues to move) through her transgressive acts to comply, when useful, with her "old traditions," and/or to transform them when necessary. Additionally, there are instances in Habsu Garba's biographical narrative that clearly show how she has developed an understanding of dominant cultural ideologies. That knowledge, in turn, has assisted her in anticipating a strategy of counteracting the consequences of straying outside the normative tradition. This is well demonstrated when she invokes the power of religion, here Islam, to justify her crossing of caste boundaries by choosing to be a singer and a performer in spite of her "noble" background, to wade off multiple attacks from *griots*, the nobility, and religious groups.

The anguish of dislocation from one's gender assigned by prevailing and hegemonic social ideologies is captured by Judith Butler: "If human existence is always gendered existence, then to stray outside of established gender is in some sense to put one's very existence into question. In this moment of gender dislocation in which we realize that it is hardly necessary that we be the genders we have become, we confront the burden of choice intrinsic to living as a man or a woman or some other gender identity, a freedom made burdensome through social constraint. . . . The anguish and terror of leaving a prescribed gender or of trespassing upon another gender territory testifies to the social constraints upon gender interpretation as well as to the necessity that *there be* an interpretation, i.e., to the essential freedom at the origin of gender" (Butler 1987, 132). Our exploration of the complexities of Habsu Garba's life demonstrates that the concept of "gendered existence" as articulated by Butler can be used to interrogate the discursive representation of women in all spheres of society.

Habsu Garba demonstrates a consciousness of her subjectivity in crafting new identities and roles for herself as a woman from both the margins and the centers in Nigerien society. But more important with respect to Habsu Garba's life journey is her consistent struggle to inscribe herself in the national arena by giving equal weight to affirming her agency through artistic production, while not neglecting to secure a material base for her life, taking lessons from the misfortunes of the forgotten older generations of female national artistic icons who can now barely make a living economically.

Finally, focusing on one more situation of a woman's life in Niger, in this case a performing artist, I hope this chapter has achieved its objective of bringing to the center the marginalized knowledge produced by Muslim women who are dialogically participating, in their own ways, in the struggle to redefine the interplay between power, identity politics, and gender relations in the nation. This struggle for redefinition is explored further in the next chapter in the variant of the folktale of the wicked stepmother that Habsu Garba selected for narration on national radio. The unfolding of the analysis of that story will reveal further the workings of Habsu Garba's political consciousness as she continues to explore new avenues for the inscription of Muslim women in public space.

Chapter 4

Cinderella Goes to the Sahel

Introduction

In this chapter, I provide a discourse analysis of a variant of a popular folktale most commonly known as *Marainiya* (the orphan girl), which illustrates another area of Habsu Garba's contribution as a storyteller in radio broadcasting. The story is, in fact, a particular version of the *Marainiya* subgenre that Habsu selected for narration on the national radio. It is a choice she made precisely because of its counterdiscourse message on women's agency and acumen; furthermore, it reveals Habsu's creative appropriation of patriarchal symbols in order to subvert the hegemonic ideology of the time.

An important attribute of Hausa oral literature, as of Afro-Islamic and other African oral literatures in general, is improvisation. The tale exists only when it is narrated/performed, and with virtually every new narration it assumes a new life in response to the artist's interpretation of the new reality. A story changes depending on the time, location, setting, mood, and material conditions within which it is contextualized. I examine first the impact of Islam on a recent narration of "The Story of the Orphan Who Marries the Prince of Masar"—a tale of the "wicked stepmother" popularly known as "Cinderella" in the West. This takes place at a time of increasing Islamic resurgence and of growing participation by women in redefining Islam in Hausa culture of West Africa. Secondly, I show how Islam also has been affected and reconfigured in contact with indigenous African cultural practices and spiritual beliefs, especially as it has been appropriated by women.

Elsewhere I have argued that, in general, Hausa women's voices were marginalized in the precolonial as well as the colonial and postcolonial eras as a result of both local culture and colonial patriarchy. There was, of course, a tiny minority of women of upper- and middle-class households that did manage to make a contribution in public life, especially in the field of Islamic knowledge and literary production (Alidou 2004; Mack 2004). The cultural and political activism and literary works of the daughters of Sheikh Usman Dan Fodiyo, the Islamic founder and leader of Sokoto Caliphate, for example, of which Nana Asma'u's legacy remains one of the most remarkable, are already well documented (Boyd 1989; Boyd and Mack 1997; Mack and Boyd 2000). In general, however, women were heavily marginalized in formal education and administration, leading to men's control of economic, cultural, and political power, further exacerbating the exclusion of women in public spheres.

In the final analysis, then, traditional (Islamic) colonial and postcolonial educational structures combined to further disempower or marginalize women. In this process, Islamic knowledge—still primarily under the control of men—was continuously deployed to construct an ideology that justified the silencing of women, especially in the public sphere.

However, the wind of democratization that swept over the continent in the 1990s calling for pluralistic rights of social constituents in Niger Republic—for example, Christians and ethnic minorities—created room for women to seek Islamic knowledge on their own terms, even if still within patriarchal space, as a means of reaching a new understanding of women's rights within Islam and Islamic societies. Ever since, women have seized the political space of liberalization to expose their own knowledge of Islam, make their contribution to the sociocultural and political reshaping of the nation and to engage in the discourse of defining a "Nigerien" Muslim identity by providing a woman's perspective (Alidou 1999). This development has become particularly noticeable in the public sphere of both the print and electronic media.

Nigerien women's persistence to inscribe their voices in the public space, as the analysis of the radio storytelling of this version of "The Wicked Stepmother" will show, is a significant indication of their resistance against decades of marginalization by patriarchal forces in the nation that controlled the power of symbolic meaning—whether of a religious, cultural, or political nature—in the nation. Thus, Nigerien women's revisioning of this ancient tale, with a cross-cultural thematic resonance, demonstrates their willingness to use their knowledge of religion and agency to subvert the oppressive patriarchal elements that silence them in the nation. Furthermore, through their presence in the media and their appropriation of cultural fields of meanings such as religion and folklore, Nigerien women are creatively participating in the construction of a more gendered, balanced democratic order. This process of women striving to recenter their voices in the public sphere—religion, performing arts, and politics—of the construction of meaning (including self-definition) is a trend that is sweeping across many cultures of the world, especially the Muslim world. And the process itself has been engendered in part by forces of globalization, especially in its technological dimension. Thus, radio, for example, becomes both a tool and a site for women to engage their societies and the world that listens to their narratives.

The tale of the Wicked Stepmother is one that appears in different versions throughout the world. Its universality bears both multicultural and intercultural traits. The multicultural property is revealed in its thematic universality as it assumes culture-specific moralist accounts of how injustice, evil doing, and abuse of power are punished and how the weak triumph in the midst of numerous trials and tribulations. In spite of these variations of the tale, both from within a culture and across cultures of the world, there are still elements of commonality in the narrative, especially the psychological representation of the wicked character and the mechanism of her failure, and certain symbolic attributes that allow a cross-cultural recognition of the tale as that of the Wicked Stepmother or Cinderella (Manh Kah 1979; Climo 1989; Cox 1967; Dundes 1982; Gough 1990; Onyefulu 1994; Haviland 1966; Rustin 1994).

The intercultural characteristics of this universal fairy tale are manifested in the motifs of the narrative that reflect a confluence of cultures, indigenous and foreign, in the society within which the tale is narrated. It is on this aspect of cultural convergence that this chapter focuses by analyzing the impact of Islam on the crafting of this version of the story of the Wicked Stepmother. Consonant with a modern, woman-centered reinterpretation of Islamic culture, the analysis of the tale reveals how an abused female character uses her intellectual prowess to subversively attain her freedom from her oppressor as well as to skillfully manipulate the structure of patriarchal hierarchies to rise up the socioeconomic ladder.

Islam, Folklore, Gender, and Modernity

The Hausa people represent one of the largest ethnolinguistic groups in sub-Saharan Africa; this group converted to Islam probably much earlier than the Middle Ages. Moreover, as much as Islam is part of Hausa religious identity, it is equally an important marker of their cultural identity. Even the tiny minority of the Hausa subgroups who are still animist or Christian tend to be Islamic in cultural practice and they have been assimilated to the majority Hausa Muslim community in their mores and values, to the point of being mistaken for Muslims. The Islam practiced by the Hausa, however, reflects a syncretism between Islamic spirituality and pre-Islamic Hausa cosmogony that continues to prevail especially in *Bori* (spirit possession). This synthesis of spiritual worldviews is not unique to Hausa Islam, but is found in most other Afro-Islamic communities, such as those of the Somali, the Swahili, and the Bambara.

The impact of Islam on oral literary production in Hausa culture is multifold. First, the inception of Islam in Hausa culture affected its oral literature by infusing its themes, style, and language with an Islamic substance. Its mode of characterization also took a turn toward a more Islamic conception of personal conduct that defines a person as "good" or "evil." Furthermore, many modern Hausa epics and folktales contain metaphorical allusions to spaces relevant to Islamic history and experiences (Skinner 1980; Starratt 1993 and 1996). In the above-cited studies, both Neil Skinner and Priscilla Starratt provide detailed descriptions of the influences of Islam on Hausa oral literature, in general, and on the Hausa epic, more specifically.

Secondly, Islam brought literacy into Hausa culture (which had no writing tradition) in both Arabic and *Ajami*, the latter being a modified version of the Arabic script used in writing the Hausa language. This development had certain implications for Hausa oral literature. Hitherto, male storytelling took place in the public space and was associated with the narration of epics or factual events, current or past. This domain of "male stories" is known as *labarai*. Women's stories, known as *tatsuniyoyi*, on the other hand, were more akin to the fairy tale and were exclusively based on fiction and the creative imagination and performed in the confinement of domestic space. Traditionally, the custodians of this female folk genre were elderly women in the community who, through this cultural medium, both entertained and instructed the young. But because Islamic literacy was primarily the domain of men, the twentieth-century transcription of Hausa folktales was undertaken mostly by male scholars. This trend marked the beginning of male invasion of a female narrative space, in the process infusing it with a male voice and subverting some of its oral features (Alidou 2000; Starratt 1996). In addition, this male invasion of the female folkloric domain transformed both the language and style of the original tales by inscribing them within an Islamic Hausa linguistic and symbolic space. Islamic literacy thus came to mark the beginning of the seeming "degendering" of Hausa folktale production and narration in modern times.

The interplay between Islamic literacy, folktale, and gender was crucial to European cultural anthropologists who were interested in collecting oral folk narratives in Hausa culture during the colonial era. These scholars relied on the contribution of Hausa male literati who served as collectors, transcribers, and interpreters of the folktales (Schön 1886; Skinner 1968, 1969, 1977). But European colonization also had a modernizing impact on Hausa culture through the introduction of infrastructures and technology, such as the printing press, the radio and more recently the television. These modern means completely transformed the conception, transmission, reception, and interpretation of folktales in Hausa society.

This technological process also accounts for both the professionalization of folktale storytelling and the new trend of "regendering" the traditionally female narrative genre. The "regendering" results from the hiring of both male and female radio and TV storytellers, which offers opportunities for a gendered crafting and narrating of folktales and other types of folk stories. It is within this professional sphere of storytelling through Radio Amfani that this version of the story of the "Wicked Stepmother" was recorded. The narrator in this case was a young female radio storyteller working for one of the private radio stations in Niamey during the summer of 1997.

The Story of the Orphan Girl Who Married the Prince of Masar

What follows is my English translation of the tale from Hausa language:

"Here it goes, here it comes to you" (A formulaic opening in Hausa *tatsuniya*). Once upon a time, in a far away land, there was a trader with his two wives. One wife was called Delu and she had four children who were all girls. The name of the second wife was Rakiya. And Rakiya had only one female child, whose name was Facima. In this polygamous living arrangement, Rakiya was more favored than Delu by their husband. And this was the origin of the rivalry that defined their daily, shared living.

It is within these conditions that, one day, Rakiya fell sick and died.

However, before she passed away, she called her co-wife, Delu, and asked her if she could promise her to take good care of her daughter, Facima. A few days after her mother's death, Facima began to experience terrible hardship, for all the chores of the household became her sole responsibility. This terrible situation reached such an extent that she was not allowed to eat the food she had cooked. She was only permitted to eat the burnt parts or leftovers. And even when she pounded millet for porridge and made the beverage, she was not allowed to have a sip of it. She could only drink the soaked husk. On the other hand, Delu and her children took delight in living off Facima's labor and their father had no ear for anyone besides Delu and her children. Thus, during that time Facima's survival became awfully unbearable.

However, one day their father was preparing to travel to a land called Masar (Egypt) and as he was ready to take off, Delu's daughters rushed to him and the first one said: "Father, when you arrive in Masar, buy me a wrapper"; the second one said: "dress"; the third one said: "Father, buy me shoes"; and the fourth one said: "Father, I request you to buy me a headscarf." When the father was done with Delu's children, Facima approached him. She had a *dala* [a penny] in her hand. She said: "Father, here is my *dala*. When you arrive in Masar, buy me the Prince of Masar with my *dala*."

When the father arrived in Masar, he got busy first with his trading business. After days and days, when he was done with his trading priorities, he remembered his children's gift requests and he spontaneously fulfilled each of Delu's daughter's wish. And when it was Facima's turn, he went to search for where the Prince of Masar was on sale. When people realized that what he was looking for was not to be found in the market, they told him to go to the king of Masar's palace. Maybe that would be the most appropriate place for him to get what he was looking for.

He rushed to the king's palace and announced himself and asked to speak to the Prince of Masar. And the guards indeed took him before the Prince of Masar. Then he transmitted his daughter Facima's request. When the Prince of Masar heard that, he asked Facima's father to return home and tell his daughter that "He himself, the Prince of Masar, will be coming to visit that same night; therefore, she must look for a place to hide herself for he is visiting that night."

When he reached home and rested a bit, Facima's father gave every daughter what she requested. And when it was Facima's turn, he told her in detail what he discussed with the Prince of Masar. When Facima's rival sisters heard this, they said: "Serves you right! May they come to kill you." Facima, then, entered her room and started to cry and kept saying that she called this upon herself. She kept thinking that if she had known, she wouldn't have made such a request, to have the Prince of Masar.

When night came, the Prince of Masar showed up at Facima's as he promised. Even though Facima's room was closed, that did not prevent the Prince from entering it. Moreover, as he was so determined, he entered the room through its roof. As soon as he entered the room, Facima entered into a trance and began to cry and shake her body. When the Prince saw this, he asked her to stop crying because he wanted her to know that he understood her intention. When Facima calmed down, they began to talk, she and the Prince of Masar. When the conversation became sweet (interesting), Facima began to notice that every time the Prince of Masar spat, a piece of gold dropped from his mouth. So every day, after their night meeting and courting, Facima collected the drops of gold pieces that came out of the Prince of Masar's mouth and hid them in a closed jar.

They had been meeting for six months and things were as they were, when one day, one of Delu's daughters who was very naughty, entered Facima's room and out of her nosiness found a piece of gold. She couldn't wait and as soon as she got out, she rushed to show it to her mother, Delu. And when Delu asked her daughter where she found the piece of gold, the daughter replied, "In Facima's room." When Delu heard this, she asked, "Who would give gold to Facima? Or has she begun stealing?" When the father came Delu informed him by saying, "Now, Facima steals. Nowadays, only a thief can get gold." At this point they rushed into Facima's room and searched her entire belongings and collected all the gold that Facima had amassed. But this was not satisfying to Delu who wanted to see the person who brought this gold to Facima. She mounted surveillance until she understood the way by which the Prince of Masar got into Facima's room. With this knowledge, Delu looked for needles and threads that she planted on the route followed by the Prince of Masar.

That same day, the Prince of Masar came to visit Facima as usual. He was not aware of the mischief planned by Facima's stepmother, Delu. Then, kwaram [boom!] he fell down on those needles she set to destroy him. These needles penetrated deeply into the Prince's body to the extent of causing him to vomit blood. When Facima saw this, her heart was shattered because the Prince, her lover, was on the brink of dying. On that day their nightly meeting was cut short and the Prince of Masar, feeling very sick, returned home quickly. Once he arrived home, the Prince of Masar fell extremely ill.

When the king of Masar saw that his son was sick, he became very preoccupied and sought for help to heal his son. This led him to gather all the *Malams* [learned Muslim teachers] and all *Bokas* [the traditional healers], who possessed the secret of healing. However, all the people gathered failed to cure the Prince of Masar. This increased the king's worries. When the king realized this failure, he called upon experts beyond national boundaries for a cure. The king also promised to reward the successful healer with a great deal of wealth.

Facima became very concerned, for the Prince of Masar had not visited her for several months. She began to think that probably the disease was sucking her lover's strength. She then said, "There was no rest for me." She decided first to shave her hair to complete baldness. Then, she looked for traditional Muslim male attire, a pair of white pants, a white *jallabiya,* and a white turban. She put on the clothes and wrapped the turban. Then, Facima looked for a small Islamic slate, a gourd of water and disguised herself as an *Almajiri* [a young male Muslim student wondering to proclaim devotion to Allah while living on *sadaka* (charity)]. She was all in white. She went into exile from her land and headed for Masar without notifying her family or any other person.

She walked for a long, long time across forest and bush areas. When she became totally exhausted, she sat under a tree that offered great shade in order to rest. While resting she overheard some birds chattering up in the branches of the tree above her. They were telling one another in song: "May a holy person pass by and collect our excrement spread here on the ground below this tree, mix it, and give it to the Prince of Masar. Once he drinks the potion, he will be cured." The birds kept repeating the song and Facima made certain to catch its details. Once the birds finished their conversation and flew away, Facima got up and collected their excrement. She filled up her gourd and resumed her voyage to Masar.

As soon as she arrived in Masar, she headed for the king's palace. She announced herself. As she introduced herself to the guards of the palace who mistook her for an *Almajiri,* they asked her what brought her to the palace. And *Almajiri* replied, "I came to heal the Prince." When the chief guard heard this, he said, "Please, *Almajiri,* turn back if you want to keep yourself alive and in peace. How can you, a mere *Almajiri,* succeed where famous *Malams* and *Bokas* failed?!" But the young *Almajari* insisted that he must be introduced to the king. Once the guard saw how determined *Almajiri* was, he took his hand and led him to the king.

The guard informed the king of the child's intent. After the king listened to *Almajiri's* story, he told him "All right, boy! I heard you and I agree. However, if you don't succeed in healing my son, I will kill you. And if you succeed in healing him, you can request anything you would like, even if that means granting you my throne." At this point, *Almajiri* asked to be led to the Prince of Masar.

When *Almajiri* arrived at the Prince's place, he saw his lover, meaning "she" saw "her" lover in great pain, completely worn out, and, worst, he was close to dying. He then asked for water. After the water was brought to him, *Almajiri* asked the crowd to leave him alone with the Prince of Masar. Facima did not reveal herself to her lover. Once in privacy with the Prince, *Almajiri* opened his gourd and poured the bird excrement in a vessel and mixed it up for him to drink. As soon as he drank the concoction, the Prince vomited until all the needles in his body came out. And he was instantly cured!

Once the king saw his son cured, he asked *Almajiri* what reward he would prefer. Right there, *Almajiri* replied, "Nothing extraordinary," but he listed three simple items. First, he wanted the Prince's finger ring; second, he wanted the Prince's turban; and third, he wanted the Prince to promise him to punish whoever afflicts him anytime, except *Almajiri* in case he wronged the Prince. Right there, *Almajiri* was granted all his requests: the turban, the Prince of Masar's ring, and the Prince's oath to keep his promise. After this event Facima, disguised as *Almajiri,* returned to her homeland where she resumed her old life of hardship in the hands of Delu, the cruel stepmother.

However, Facima's rival half-sisters were not happy with her return. In fact, both her stepmother and her half-sisters wished she had died. They would have felt relieved of her presence in the family household. A few days after her return home, the Prince of Masar decided to visit Facima's homeland in order to kill her. For he believed she was the cause of his sickness. Upon arrival at her house, he took out his sword and was ready to cut off her head. When Facima realized that he was determined, she rushed to say to him: "Forgive *Almajiri* in the name of the promise you made to him. Please, for Allah's sake, forgive *Almajiri.* Prince of Masar, spare me, *Almajiri,* who cured you!" When the Prince of Masar heard this, he was deeply surprised and dropped his sword. Then he wanted to know who informed Facima of *Almajiri's* story. Right there, Facima began to tell her story to her lover of her life with a cruel stepmother to her entry into his father's palace to save him from the wicked doing of her stepmother.

After she finished narrating her stories, the Prince of Masar, not quite convinced, told her, "If you are telling me the truth, you must show me a proof of that!" Facima then quickly fetched his finger ring and his turban and showed them to him. Even with this proof, the Prince was not convinced. So, he told her, "But *Almajiri* was a boy!" Facima then took off her headscarf and showed him how she had shaved her hair to baldness. When the Prince of Masar saw that, he was so touched by Facima's truth and commitment to their love that the blood running in his body cooled down. He believed Facima. The Prince told her: "I must return home to talk to my people. They must come to ask for your hand. We must get married."

As soon as he reached home, as he promised, the Prince of Masar sent his people to Facima's parents. When they arrived, they introduced themselves and informed Facima's parents of the purpose of their mission. As the stepmother heard them, she jumped and warned them to go away, for they misunderstood whose hand they were to ask for, not Facima's. She told them, "You must have been sent to ask for one of my daughters' hand. Go back to the Prince and ask for more clarification!" And the go-between said, "No, the Prince was clear and we clearly heard him. He asked for Facima's hand." The stepmother, Delu, sent them off and Facima's father did not intervene one way or the other.

After he heard his representatives' account, the Prince of Masar decided to go himself to ask for Facima's hands in marriage from her parents. He made it clear to Delu that he was not there for any of her daughters. The marriage was celebrated before the evil eyes of Delu and her jealous daughters. The Prince of Masar took Facima to his father's palace in Masar and they are still living there to this day enjoying life! In fact, they gave birth to five children. "Well, well! Tale return on the head of Hyena." (A formulaic ending of Hausa folktale).

Analysis of the Tale

In this section, I turn to an analysis of the symbolic meaning of motifs within this fairy folktale that reflect the syncretism between Islam and African spirituality and the ways it also inspired the narrator who developed this version of the story. The folktale begins with an introduction of the main characters and provides the names of the major players of the story, such as the cruel stepmother, Delu, her co-wife Rakiya, and her stepdaughter, Facima. These three names are important for understanding the Hausa naming system. While Delu is a name of non-Islamic origin given to a child born shortly after the death of her father, the names Rakiya and Facima are clearly of Islamic derivation. Here then we witness a dual heritage of naming, part Islamic and part indigenous. But the name Delu also symbolically opens up to the possibility of "non-Islamic" conduct on the part of the stepmother.

The husband is introduced simply by his occupation, trading, and we know that Delu has four daughters whose names are not revealed. The failure to name the husband foreshadows the decline in his authority and reduced function in the story. As for the four daughters, since their actions and attitudes toward Facima are dictated by their mother, Delu, their identification by name is less important than their actions.

However, the identification of the husband as a "trader" from a forest and bush land who goes to Masar for trading transactions has another significance in the story. One can argue that the narrator introduces the motif of trade in reference to the trans Saharan trade that linked the Sahelian population and the populations of North Africa, Middle East, and Europe, all of which exchanged goods during the Middle Ages. Moreover, as historians such as Ibn Battuta reported, trade is always associated with the inception of Islam in sub-Saharan Africa as well as in other parts of the world visited or conquered by Islamic people.

We also learn that the wickedness of the stepmother evolves as the result of an unfair treatment by their polygamous husband. Polygamy is a matrimonial practice that was prevalent among the Hausa before their Islamization and the practice continued after their conversion to Islam. The practice allows a man to marry up to four wives. However, Islam demands fair and equal treatment between the wives (Qur'an, Sura 4:3). By violating this tenet, by favoring Rakiya, that is, Facima's mother, the father set the stage for the animosity and cruelty that was to develop.

Rakiya's death creates favorable conditions for Delu to regain her husband's attention and avenge herself even against him. Delu's rivalry against her co-wife and bitterness against her unfair husband leads her to develop such venom against the innocent Facima, a living reminder of what she went through during their polygamous marital life. Expectedly, that venom led Delu to break the promise to Rakiya at her last hour to care for her daughter. In Hausa Islamic understanding, this represents the breaking of *amana (cin amana)*, that is, a violation of trust. This type of violation has a negative moral implication especially when it involves the violation of an orphan. After all, the Qur'an makes it clear that orphans are to be maintained with fairness and justice and spoken to with kindly speech (Sura 4:2–4).

It is ironic, however, that Facima's mother, who enjoyed preferential treatment over her co-wife, should have asked Delu to make and abide by the *amana* to take care of her orphan daughter upon her death. One would assume that given the rivalry and the jealousy endured by Delu, Facima's mother would not expect such a promise to be fulfilled. But the myth suggests Delu's acceptance of the *amana* to care for Facima. By failing to abide by that pledge, Delu was acting contrary to Hausa Islamic conception of *mutumniya mai kirki* (a kind woman) or *mutumniya wai zuciya d'aya* (a woman with one heart) meaning a "good" person endowed with *imani*—compassion.

In the aftermath of Rakiya's death, Delu's internalized bitterness begins to unfold, as does Facima's tragic fate in her hands from that point on. Moreover, Facima also experiences her father's distance, silence, and complacency in the cruelty of her stepmother and stepsisters. There is a *hadith,* a saying of the Prophet Muhammad, that when a Muslim sees a wrong being committed, one should stop it with his or her hands; if one cannot, then one should stop it with words; and if one cannot, then he or she should at least feel bad about the wrong being done. And that is the lowest level of faith in Islam. The narrator obviously put Facima's father outside the referential conduct of this *hadith.* The father is oblivious of Delu's wickedness and Facima's suffering in his household.

As already mentioned, the depiction of the father as a detached character is important for the unfolding of the tale. This depiction allows the stepmother's cruelty to evolve out of an unusually excessive desire to avenge herself and her daughters against her husband's past unfairness to her. Thus, while the death of his preferred wife pushes the husband to lean on Delu's affection and pledge to care for his orphan daughter, this new monogamous restructuring of the household and Delu's status as a surrogate mother to Facima provide her with the means to dominate everybody. Facima is thus left alone in her struggle.

Equally important in the Afro-Islamic construction of the story is the journey to Masar from the land of forest and bushes that corresponds to the Sahelian savannah where the Hausa live. The place Masar is an important Islamic motif that could be interpreted from several angles. First, Masar (Egypt) is the first Saharan region in Africa where Islam set foot. This resulted from its conquest by the forces of Umar, the second khalif of Islam, in the first half of the seventh century. Because of the cultural affinity between the Hausa people and the rest of the populations of the Saharan region, this historic beginning has special meaning in the religious imagination of the Hausa people.

Secondly, Masar was historically one of the resting sites in North Africa for sub-Saharan Muslims on their religious pilgrimage to Mecca, known as *Hajj,* in the early days of Islam before the development of modern transport system. In more modern times, Masar also became an important site of Islamic learning and cultural activities for Muslims throughout the world. It is the home of the leading and one of the oldest Islamic universities, Al-Azhar, and of some of the most influential Muslim thinkers in modern times. Thus, in Hausa culture, a journey to Masar is both an act of religious significance and a means to exhibit economic status, for Masar was also a major site of trade for merchants throughout the Muslim world. All in all, then, Masar represents a site of cultural convergence where Afro-Islamic populations interact with other African and non-African populations.

Thirdly, Masar has a Qur'anic reference that goes back to Egypt's era of pharaohs. This is when Moses told his followers: "Get ye down to Masar (Egypt)—for ye shall have what ye have asked" (Sura 2:58). This remark was, of course, made by way of rebuking the Jews who were complaining about their hardship in the desert in the course of their migration to Jerusalem. But it also alludes to Masar as a place where one can secure any form of material desire—the good, the bad, and the ugly. In the spirit of this verse, the daughters of Delu in this Hausa version of the story expect to receive the gifts they had requested their father to bring them from Masar. But more important, it is from Masar that Facima hopes to gain the freedom she was yearning for. Unlike her sisters whose choices are drawn by blatant materialism, Facima sees the material opportunities of Masar as a means to a higher ideal of freedom and as a possible site of transformation of power relations. Moses failed to humble the pharaoh. But in her assumed identity of a "mere" *Almajiri,* Facima succeeded in humbling royalty. In his desperation to find a cure for his son, the king of Masar was ready to give up his throne to *Almajiri,* while the Prince became eternally indebted to his lover from the ranks of the downtrodden. On the other hand, it is through Masar that Facima was able to emerge as the victor against her wicked stepmother, Delu.

Unlike her half-sisters, Facima offered her own money for the purchase of her gift from Masar. In this way the narrator signifies Facima's autonomy from her father and her lack of expectation of receiving free gifts from him. This contrasts with her other siblings who are close enough to the father to feel comfortable enough to request gifts without offering any money. As the storyteller puts it: When the father was done with Delu's children, Facima approached him. She had a *dala* in her hand. She said, "Father, here is my *dala.* When you arrive in Masar, buy me the Prince of Masar with my *dala.*"

Facima's autonomy is further illustrated by the type of item she ordered in the story. Although requested innocently, the item of her desire, that is, the Prince of Masar, symbolically epitomizes power whose acquisition, in Facima's psyche, might eventually lead to her liberation from the claws of her cruel stepmother. In most versions of the story told in Hausa culture, the mistreated stepdaughter is depicted as a weak, sorrowful, and unimaginative character waiting for the assistance of either the ghost of her deceased mother or a God-sent savior to liberate her. This modern version, however, offers through Facima's actions an alternative representation. Here we see a young woman creatively using her mind to create the conditions for her freedom from subjugation.

Facima's daring request for the Prince of Masar, her father's search for him, and the Prince's belligerence in meeting this audacious young woman from the forestland, his nightly secret visits to Facima, and his spitting of gold pieces are all elements that add more mythical meaning in the construction of the tale. Here again the spitting of gold could be interpreted as symbolic of the role that gold played in the trans-Saharan trade and exchanges between Muslim populations of the Sahel where the Hausa live and their partners from the North. In addition to reenacting the era of plenitude of gold in Afro-Islamic transaction, the incident also foregrounds the significance of gold as a gift of love from the man to the woman.

The gold that was spat from the mouth was also used as a pretext in the story for yet another exploration of Delu's wickedness. This new revelation in Facima's life leads Delu to plot to eliminate the Prince with poisoned needles planted on his route. The Prince becomes seriously ill after falling prey to Delu's machinations, compelling Facima to undertake a journey to Masar in search of a cure to heal her lover. An important Afro-Islamic element is again introduced at this point. In this attempt, Facima cross-dresses and shaves her head bald to pass as a male. In addition, she carries an Islamic slate and gourd, items that usually characterized itinerant *Malams,* religious Muslim priests. In the narrator's imagination this disguise was most likely inspired by the form of attire often worn in a quasi-Islamic parody called *Taushe.* This could involve comic disguise, female-male dressing, or male-female dressing and cross-gendering by young people during the month of Ramadan to entertain the fasting community. The parody is often a satire of the religious literati and a social commentary against wrongdoing in the community. To this extent Facima's disguise is also a symbolic message against the prevailing oppressive order in her life. The Islamic male disguise, then, allows Facima to escape from her hometown without the suspicion of her relatives and members of the community. It also assists her in fooling the guards, the king, and even her beloved Prince to gain access and administer the cure that eventually heals him.

The color of Facima's disguise attire, that is, white, may also have an Afro-Islamic symbolic meaning. In Hausa *Bori,* spirits that appear in white are identified as positive and benevolent. White, in Islamic culture, on the other hand, is also repeatedly invoked to represent purification of the soul, body, and action. Facima's choice of white clothing, then, is not only in conformity with a Hausa Islamic male dress code, but it is also a projection of the purity of her intentions and actions in relation to her planned trip to Masar to visit and cure her lover. Hers is a whiteness of declared innocence.

It is also important to look at how the narrative compresses time and space. The Prince of Masar pays a daily visit to Facima, who resides in a far away land; outside the mythical imagination, the trip might involve weeks and even months of travel on the back of a camel or a horse. This seemingly unreal characterization of space-time accords perfectly with the magical realism orientation of Hausa and other African oral literatures that in more recent times has also influenced some modern African imaginative writings.

But this shrinkage of time and space could also have been inspired by the Islamic tradition of *mi'raj*, of Prophet Muhammad's journey to the heavens and back. In one version of this account, the angel "Gabriel came to Muhammad at night, mounted him on a winged beast called *Buraq*, and took him to Jerusalem, where Muhammad led all the prophets [of the past] in prayer. Then Gabriel took Muhammad up through the seven heavens, introducing him to all the angels and the prophets [of old] residing in each of them and then to hell and paradise. Finally Muhammad went alone into the presence of God" (Chittick 1995, 117). By morning the prophet was back in Mecca. Within a single night, therefore, the prophet traversed the horizontal distance between Mecca and Jerusalem, and the vertical distance between the earth and heavens, all in the age of the camel. He further traveled centuries backward in time, all the way to the time of Adam. It is within this Islamic tradition of *mi'raj* and the indigenous tradition of magical realism, therefore, that the daily trips of the Prince of Masar seem to have been framed.

Another important Afro-Islamic convergence relates to Facima's ability to hear the language of the birds. This is partly derived from the African cosmological worldview that presumes a symbiotic relationship between the living and nonliving, and between humans and nonhumans in the universe. As Dorothy Blair puts it: "In the traditional animistic beliefs and mythology of Africa there is no dividing line between life and death, between animate and inanimate objects, between animals and humans. All these partake of the same essence and contribute to each other's total experience of existence. An animal, a child, or a wooden statuette can obtain the spirit of a dead ancestor" (quoted in Larson 1997, 27). Facima's experience with the birds, then, essentially reflects this African spiritual understanding of the world we share.

But the incident of Facima and the birds may also have an Islamic origin based on the Solomonic tradition. The Qur'an tells us that Allah granted Solomon the ability to hear birds and learn from their wisdom. As the scripture says, "And in knowledge Solomon was David's heir. And he said. 'O men, we have been taught the speech of birds, and we are endued with everything. This is indeed a clear doon from God.' And to Solomon were gathered his hosts of Djinn and men and birds, and they were marched on in bands" (Qur'an, Sura 27:16–17). Like Solomon, then, Facima is endowed with the ability to hear and understand "bird language."

Within the Islamic imagination, the bird also has some special significance. This myth goes back to the time of the Prophet Muhammad when he was fleeing from Mecca to Medina—the event that marks the beginning of the Muslim calendar. On the way, the prophet hid in the cave. When his pursuers from Mecca arrived at the site, they could not suspect that the prophet was hiding within partly because there was a bird, a dove, sitting on its eggs right at the entrance of the cave. Inspired by this tradition, then, the bird has come to represent in a number of Afro-Islamic narratives a kind of a "savior" of the oppressed.

Just as Facima understands the birds, the birds have some comprehension of the goings-on in the world of humans. They are fully aware that the Prince of Masar is critically ill and that only their excrement could cure him. Within some indigenous healing practices, it is not anathema to use excrement of animals for medicinal purpose. In Islam, excrement is *najs*—a religious impurity. But here too what is illegal becomes legal under critical conditions of life and death. Within this Afro-Islamic perspective, then, the use of *najs* to cure the Prince of Masar further underscores the extent of his seemingly incurable disease.

The narrator consistently continues to develop Facima as an intelligent character with tremendous foresight. Thus, she was able to anticipate that her own beloved Prince might not believe her story of innocence in his sickness or her disguise as a male during her successful quest for a cure to heal him. When the Prince eventually confronts her and demands that she prove her version of the story, Facima is able to present the three intimate items she requested from him, namely, his turban, his ring, and his promise not to harm *Almajiri*. This demonstration of innocence, intelligence, anticipation of problems, and design of solutions to handle them adequately is what earns Facima, the abused orphan, her freedom from the claws of the cruel stepmother and the complicity of a father who abandons her as well as her escape to the heights of Masar's hierarchical structure. Her crucial role as the successful healer who saves the life of the Prince of Masar situates her as the most powerful woman within the palace. And just as Sura 2:58 of the Qur'an commanded "Get ye down into Egypt (Masar),—ye shall have what ye ask for," Facima did go to Masar and through humbling the power structure, she acquired her freedom and lived happily ever after as the wife of the Prince of Masar.

Conclusion

In recapitulation, then, this is a version of the story of the Wicked Stepmother that demonstrates a cultural syncretism that heavily incorporates an Islamic dimension. For all practical purposes it is an Afro-Islamic narrative. Given the former predominance of the male in Hausa Islamic literacy, the initial "Islamization" of this and indeed many other Hausa folktales from the female domain of *tatsuniya* may have originated from male transcription of the tale. The narration of this particular version in the 1990s, however, also took place in the context of new attempts to reinscribe the Muslim woman as a significant player in Islamic discourse. Facima, the main character of this story, is perhaps ultimately a product of this reconfigured Afro-Islamic space in Hausaland, enhanced as it is by the new technologies of communication. What emerges in this Hausa version of Cinderella is a tale of liberation in which women's agency over their destiny and their triumph over oppression is evident.

Part III

Women and Overt Political Contestation

Chapter 5

Islamisms, the Media, and Women's Public Discursive Practices

A'isha reported that Saudah bint Zam'ah went out one night. 'Umar saw her and recognized her and said, "By God, O Saudah, why do you not hide yourself from us?" She went back to the Prophet (peace be upon him) and told him about it while he was having supper in her room, and he said, "It is permitted by Allah for you to go out for your needs." The predominant idea in the teachings of Islam with regard to men and women is that a husband and wife should be full-fledged partners in making their home a happy and prosperous place, that they should be loyal and faithful to one another, and genuinely interested in each other's welfare and the welfare of their children. A woman is expected to exercise a humanizing influence over her husband and to soften the sternness inherent in his nature.

Commentator of the *Hadith*, Abdur Rahman I. Doi,
Professor and Director, Center for Islamic Legal Studies,
Ahmadu Bello University, Zaria, Nigeria

Introduction

The dynamics and counterdynamics of the democratization momentum of the 1990s inspired the women of Niger to interrogate their historical location in this predominantly Muslim West African nation of about eleven million people.[1] This self-reflection eventually led to efforts by the women to organize themselves in new ways and, partly through the use of the electronic media, to situate themselves as agents in the Islamic discursive space. What has emerged in the process are not only new challenges to patriarchal authority and patriarchal readings of Islam, but also a reconceptualization of identities for women, men, and the nation at large. The experience of the Nigerien women examined here confirms what Dorothy Holland and her colleagues have suggested: "[P]ersons and, to a lesser extent, groups are caught in tensions between past histories that have settled in them and present discourses and images that attract them or somehow impinge upon them. In this continuous self-fashioning, identities are hard-won standpoints that however dependent upon social support and however vulnerable to change, make at least a modicum of self-direction possible. They are possibilities for mediating agency" (Holland et al. 1998, 4). In the wake of the new politics of organized Islam in the 1990s, then, and while continuing to play into "their domination by social relations of power," women in Niger—cognizant of the fact of their womanhood—also found new "possibilities for (partial) liberation from these forces" (Holland et al. 1998, 5).

Democratization and the Rise of Political Islam in Niger

What is at stake here is not religion (in this case Islam) *qua* religion, but how people take recourse in religion in an attempt to come to grips with the anxieties resulting from unsettling socioeconomic and political uncertainties and insecurities. After all, religion cannot be divorced from the historical, political, and material conditions that (re)produce it and within which it is situated. "[T]o understand the role of religion in women's lives, we must identify the conditions under which it emerges as a significant factor, as well as those that limit its scope. In addition, we must address the ways in which religious symbols are manipulated by both women and men in everyday life as well as in institutional settings" (Lazreg 2001, 333).

What will unfold in the remainder of this chapter is how different aspects of Islam in the urban landscape are appropriated and mobilized, especially by women, often with symbolic effects to address particular needs and concerns. The results of these religious appropriations and manipulations have been ambiguous and contradictory, seeming to reinforce (internal and external) patriarchal hegemonic dispensations, on the one hand, and to open up potentially emancipatory space, on the other hand.

Although the existence of religious leaders, *'ulema (Malammai),* was noticeable in Niger during the first Republic under the presidency of Hamani Diori (1960–74), the regime did not grant them authority to organize into associative organs with a power to influence political life in the country. This ran parallel to the banning of all organized forms of political opposition in the country. As Robert Glew rightly points out: "Law number 64-034 which was passed in November 5, 1964 required all [political and social] associations in Niger to receive approval from the government" (Glew 1996, 187). Under these circumstances, the authority of the religious *'ulemas* was felt more at the village level where they represented and continued to function as *Alkali (Qadhi),* or Islamic jurists who preside over family law issues or minor religious matters. They were prohibited from any political involvement in government affairs and were under the authority of the traditional chiefs who were themselves administrative auxiliaries of both the colonial regime and the postindependence government.

In 1974, the civilian regime of Diori was overthrown in a military coup that was led by Seyni Kountché. Recognizing the crucial place of Islam and the stronghold of the religious *'ulemas* in Nigerien social psychology, he opted to restructure the religious leaders into a single national association, Association Islamique du Niger (AIN). With a strong *Tijaniyya* hold,[2] the AIN has been presided over by Sheikh Omar Ismael since 1974 in spite of the recurring changes in governments and leadership of the country. Significantly, however, throughout the military presidency of Seyni Kountché and the successive military regime of Ali Saibou (1987-91), this national organization did not create any room for women's involvement and leadership representation, even of the very learned ones. Women were regarded as no more than recipients, consumers, and followers of decrees delivered from above by the male clergy.

This association increasingly became a de facto organ of the state, expected to foster links with Islamic donor states and to counteract internally the rising tide of "Islamic fundamentalism."[3] Precisely because of this dual role (part external and part internal), the AIN soon won a virtual monopoly over Islamic oriented newspapers, television, and radio programs of Niger's broadcasting stations. This national religious association became the regime's police for discrediting and censoring any oppositional religious attack against the government. For example, in 1975 it backed the military regime's decree on the house arrest and repatriation to their rural homes of *Malams* (teachers or healers) of mystic order and power, culturally known as *'Yen Cibbo,* as well as the banning of itinerant Qur'anic *Malams* (teachers) and their *almajirrai* (students).[4] Moreover, this censorship led to the establishment of a law by the Ministry of Interior that gave the AIN the sole authority to grant license to individuals intending to engage in certain Islamic activities (such as mystic healing and presiding over naming or marriage ceremonies) in urban areas. The holder of the license was under serious scrutiny of the Islamic association. The AIN thus became a political watchdog of the successive repressive military regimes.

The opening up of the political space in the 1990s, under local and international pressure for democratic pluralism, prompted the formation of several other Islamic associations, as duly licensed by the Ministry of Interior. Within this climate, Niger experienced the consolidation of a number of Islamic associations (Glew 1996, 187–204), among which was a new *militant* Islamic revivalist movement in the urban space under the name of *Izala* (Removal) or *Ahlal Sunna* (People of the *Sunnah*),[5] dedicated to the eradication of *bida* (innovations) in the Islamic body politic and to a return to the fundamentals of the religion (as seen, of course, through the eyes of its followers). An excellent and important contribution to our understanding of *Jama'at Izalat al-bida wa iqamat al-sunnah* (the Society for the Removal of Innovation and Reinstatement of Tradition), or *Yan Izala* movement for short, is the recent work of Ousmane Kane (2003). He draws a distinction between reformist and Islamist articulations of Islam in sub-Saharan Africa: "I call reform movements those Islamic movements that attempt to reform social and religious practices whereas those movements that attempt to capture political power and establish the rule of God, I call them Islamist movements. This is not to say that reform movements are not engaged in political struggle. Rather, the priority of reform movements is to reform social and religious practices, whereas Islamist movements believe that the rule of God must be established first, and then, the reform of religion and society will follow" (Kane 2003, 8). Within this paradigm, Kane clearly locates the *Yan Izala* of Nigeria, which is the main focus of his work under the reformist umbrella. Furthermore, *Yan Izala* is seen as a nationalist movement. It serves as a postcolonial response to what is perceived as Western hegemony (in both its global and local manifestations) and draws on modernist reading and praxis of Islam. Both these features of nationalism and modernism constitute the basis upon which the *Izala* distinguishes itself not only from the "orthodoxies" of the dominant *Tijaniyya* and *Qadiriyya* orders but also in its critique of the orders as essentially departures from the *Sunnah* or the "authentic" tradition of Islam as lived by the prophet Muhammad (Kane 2003, 104–48).

The *Yan Izala* movement in Niger shares many common features with the experiences of Nigeria as described by Kane. For example, the local intellectual foundations of the two variants of *Izala* are essentially the same, drawing primarily from the philosophical stimulus of Shaykh Ibrahim Gumi. In addition, there are crucial similarities between the two in their social base, recruitment patterns, and gender policies, as this chapter will demonstrate.

In fact, the *Izala* movement in Niger Republic both conforms to and participates in modernity through its innovations, contrary to its rhetoric about the return to "authentic" Islamic traditions. As Victoria Bernal concludes with regard to Islamic revivalism in a Sudanese village: "It is only when Islamic fundamentalism [i.e., revivalism] is recognized as a facet of modernity that we can understand, for instance, why its earliest and strongest proponents in many societies are urban and educated. Modernity, in the era of postmodernism, is itself, a contested ambiguity; here it refers to the process of incorporation into the nation-state and into the capitalist world economy. These processes are multifaceted, involving transformations, not only of societal institutions, but also of identities" (Bernal 1994, 38–39). Aihwa Ong (1990) makes similar observations with regard to the situation in Malaysia. This argument, as the rest of this chapter will show, is supported by a number of elements, among which are (1) *Izala* ties with cosmopolitan adherents of (low- and upper-) middle-class and upper-class backgrounds; (2) *Izala* introduction of imported *hijab,* an improvisation in the culture associated with women's modesty in the "modern" age; and (3) *Izala* transnational connections to other militant Islamic revivalist groups in Asia (Malaysia, Indonesia), the Middle East, and the Western world.

Niger's *Izala* experience, however, poses a challenge to the distinction drawn by Kane (2003) between reformism and Islamism. There is every indication that if the conditions are right the *Izala* leadership and constituency in Niger seeks to capture the state and impose laws based on the will of God (*Shari'a,* on the interpretation of Islam that would respond to their ideology). For example, during the National Conference of 1991, Izalaists and their sympathizers came out strongly to challenge the then prevailing separation of religion and state, advocating instead the institutionalization of an Islamic Republic partly on the ground that Niger is predominantly Muslim (more than 90 percent). Indeed, had it not been for the strong opposition to the call for the establishment of the Islamic state, the Izalaists might have ventured to seize state power.

In the final analysis, then, the distinction between reformist and Islamist attributes may depend less on the inherent nature of the movements themselves than on the realm of political possibilities within which the movements are operating. Some of the factors that interact and define the space of possibilities permitting a movement with a reformist agenda, such as *Izala,* to become politically Islamist include the demographic distribution of different religious constituencies within the nation-state, the ideological orientations of these constituencies, their historical relationships, and the colonial and postcolonial mediations.

The new revivalist *Izala* movement has a militant orientation and links to global Islamic trade networks that set it fundamentally apart from the earlier revivalist order known as the *Wahabiyya.* With this new revivalist movement began a new era for "political Islam" in Niger with new performative identities that threw away old cultural principles of peaceful interdenominational and interfaith cohabitation. Under mounting economic and political stresses, therefore, the democratization vision led to the diversification of organized Islam, in the process producing oppositional discourses and a social fragmentation of the Nigerien urban landscapes into secular Muslims, Islamicists *(Tijaniyya)*, Islamicist revivalists (early *Wahabiyya*), militant Islamicist revivalists *(Izala 'Ahalal Sunna)*, minority Christians (Catholics, Baptists, and other Protestants) and minority traditionalists *(Arna)*.

The main promoters of the *Izala 'Ahalal Sunna* movement in Niger are linked to the network of Nigerien traders who have business partners in northern Nigeria who in turn are part of a trade network with militant revivalist traders in places like Saudi Arabia, Iran, Pakistan, and Malaysia. These are the names of the countries that seem to appear repeatedly on brand tags of commodity items from abroad—clothes, Islamic literature, and so on. These foreign groups impose their brand of Islamic practice as a condition of business on their African partners and even offer a number of scholarships for students and academics who embrace the movement. In this context of vested interests, the African players eventually assume (or even appropriate) the more militant Islam in order to create economic, political, and educational advantages for themselves. In Niger, the town of Kollo, near the capital city Niamey, and Maradi, the commercial capital in Hausaland, are the main headquarters of operation of all the Nigerien traders across ethnic boundaries who are dealing with *Izala* of Northern Nigeria and other parts of the Muslim world. Each Nigerien trader becomes a member of a lobby that operates around a sponsored mosque and a trade monopoly of a commodity (grain, cloth, oil, construction material) manufactured or produced in promilitant revivalist countries such as Sudan, Iran, Pakistan, Malaysia, and other countries, including the United States, where the leaders of the networks operate. The network, both locally and internationally, is made hierarchical in such a manner that the traders with huge investments are surrounded by a group of traders of average means; and the latter have their own auxiliaries, most of whom are desperate unemployed urban young males in search of subsistence. The role of the youth within this militant Islamic movement in Niger is comparable to that played in places like Malaysia (Aihwa Ong 1990) or in the Sudan (Simone 1994).

The emergence and subsequent consolidation of *Izala* had obvious political implications. Clearly it had become a force to contend with, given both its stronger financial base and its local and international network. It had the power and resources to influence political directions and outcomes, sometimes in unsettling ways. As much as successive regimes continued to favor the politically "moderate" national Islamic association, they were also forced to seek the patronage of the revivalist *Izala*. This delicate balancing act of the state was achieved partly by confining Islamicist discourses to religious affairs. And because of the patriarchal foundations of all these organizations, as well as of the state itself, religious issues that often dominated electronic media were heavily inclined toward topics that affected women.

It is clear from the above description of *Izala* in Niger and certainly in Nigeria, given the analysis provided by Kane (2003, 140–43), its conception of modernity is essentially masculinist and patriarchal. Neither in its ideology nor in its *modus operandi* does it seek to create a gender equality based on its proclaimed mission of egalitarian inclusiveness of all the marginal ized groups in various societal institutions. It is this masculinist gender ideology of *Izala* that explains the sentiment of the main *Izala* ideologue, Alhaji Abubakar Gumi: "There are things that women should do. Things that are suitable to them like teaching children. They can be clerks or they can be in their own homes and those things that keep them isolated from men. They can be very useful but to make them mix with men like Europeans is not acceptable. . . . I don't hope to see a Nigerian woman leading me when I am alive" (quoted in Kane 2003, 142). In spite of its pretension to embrace the Islam of the *Sunna,* the *Izala* movement goes against the very history of that tradition, effacing the important leadership roles played by Muslim women, beginning with Khadija whose role in the very formation of Muhammad's prophethood was indeed critical. It is in this context that the work of Muslim scholars such as the legendary Nana Asma'u, Nawal El Saadawi, Ayesha Imam, Saba Mahmood, Margot Badran, Amina Wadud, Fatima Mernissi, and others becomes significant in Muslim women's struggle to reclaim their place in the history of Islam.

In their discourse on egalitarianism, the *Izala* betray great selectivity in its reading of Islamic doctrine, especially in matters of gender. For example, they ignore the Qur'anic verses that emphasize the equality of men and women in regard to their respective duties, rights, virtues, and merits, such as in the following: "Not equal are those believers who sit (at home) and receive no hurt, and those who strive and fight in the cause of God with their goods and their persons. God hath granted a grade higher to those who strive and fight with their goods and persons than those who sit (at home). Unto all (in faith) hath God promised good; but those who strive and fight hath He distinguished above those who sit (at home) by a special reward" (*The Holy Qur'an,* chapter 4, verse 95, translated by Abdallah Yusuf Ali). "Whoever works righteously, man or woman, we shall assuredly give him/her to live a goodly life." Yet, in spite of the fact that both verses are balanced in their gender consideration, Izalaists are blind to that fact and continue to advocate the seclusion of Muslim women under *hijab* in public or in *kulle,* secluded domesticity.

The masculinist and patriarchal nature of *Izala* and other Islamisms that have emerged in Niger are, of course, directly related to their nationalist thrust. Because it is so fundamentally defined in terms of a reaction to the hegemonic patriarchal Western "other," it refuses to interrogate hegemonic relations that are internal to itself. Indeed, any such introspection is quickly dismissed as part of the discourse of the "other," absolving itself of any responsibility to address fundamental issues of inequalities and disenfranchisement from within. The same pitfalls of a restricted nationalism account for why Muslim women (whether reformist or secularist) have not fared any better even within secularist masculinist orthodoxies.

But how do women within the *Izala* movement and its variants articulate their own realities and exercise their own agencies, if at all? Kane's (2003) study is fascinating and comprehensive, offering a detailed description of the broad features of *Izala* in Nigeria as a whole. Unfortunately, it sheds little light on women's voices within *Izala* movement. As suggested in the introduction of this book, women's experiences in (alternative) modernities are different from those of men. This observation holds true as much in the secular world as it does in the religious realm, including the world of *Izala* and beyond. It is this alternative voice of women that this study of Muslim women in Niger attempts to capture.

Democracy, Islam, the Media, and Women's Activism

The place of women and women's issues in the public media and discourse, however, must be understood against the background of the interplay between democratization, Islam as a social movement, and the media. The democratization process gave rise to the emergence of private TV and radio stations that are granted some space for airing private religious and secular programs. These new media stations provide an arena for political opposition and civic leaders to respond to the views or discourses aired on the national media that are for the most part controlled by the party in power. The AIN authorized by the government still continues to enjoy a monopoly of Islamic programs of the state broadcasting station, while the dissident *Izala* airs programs on private media stations or alternatively distributes its messages through cassettes sold in the markets and their mosques.

By the late 1980s, the state itself was severely weakened as a result of the conjuncture of a variety of developments. These include the fall of the uranium price in the world market, the backbone of Niger's economic well-being, France's economic disengagement from its former colonies caused by its incorporation into the European Economic Community system, the adverse effects of Structural Adjustment Programs (SAP) imposed by the

World Bank and the International Monetary Fund (IMF), and the devaluation of the local exchange currency (CFA). A crisis of legitimacy of the Nigerien state was indeed in the making.

Under these circumstances, the impoverished state began to exploit the confrontation between moderate Islamicist and the Izalaists to prevent any potential uprising by a discontented and economically deprived civil society and to divert the populace whose welfare it had failed to provide for. Increasingly, the people of Niger began to witness a shift in news coverage from explosive national issues, such as the prolonged delay in the payment of civil servants' salaries, students' stipends, and national strikes, to matters of religion and religious relationships both locally and internationally. However, because the government prohibits any political religious commentary that is critical of its authority or that calls for its overthrow, the religious confrontation in the media between the AIN and the *Izala* ended up focusing on issues affecting women and the Family Code (hitherto, popularly referred to by Nigerien men as the Women's Code). At times, these denominational confrontations directed at women assumed abusive proportions, especially those by the *Izala,* to which the state remains complicit and silent. But Nigerien women of all Islamic and other religious persuasions were not intimidated by such aggression. On July 17, 1992, more than two thousand Nigerien women throughout the country marched, demanding that the government take measures against the perpetrators of religious Islamist violence against schoolgirls wearing styles of clothes objectionable to the *Izala* (White-Kaba and Alidou 1994, 8). Early in 1994, the women of Maradi also protested against similar Islamist religious aggression seeking to impose a dress code on girls and women (Niger Ministry of Social Development, Population and the Promotion of Women 1994). Tension tied to the politicization of religion continued to manifest itself through the politics of fashion and the place of women within it, leading the government this time to react in a more vigorous manner. According to the *Europa World Year Book,* "Violent protests broke out in Niamey and spread to Maradi in mid-November 2000, following a demonstration by Islamist protesters in the capital and its attempted dispersal by the police. The demonstration had been organized in response to a fashion show [promoted by Alphadi], which Islamist leaders had condemned as an incitement to debauchery. Some 270 people, reportedly including prominent religious leaders, were arrested, although around 240 of the protesters were released promptly without charge. Islamist extremists were investigated in connection with the killing of a U.S. diplomat in Niger in December" (2002, 2:2981).

This patriarchal complicity during the democratization era inspired Nigerien women to fight for their rights of political association in political parties, religious organizations, and NGOs headed by women and operating with women-centered agendas. Nigerien women saw their demographic size (52 percent) and their economic contributions as workers and often as heads of the household as a compelling argument in their struggle for their rights to be part of the political debate over the democratic future of the nation, as well as the right to head political associations and national and international organizations. It is important, however, to emphasize that women's mobilization and political activism during the democratic transition involved mainly the urban sections where those educated in the mainstream French system visibly retain the leadership. The rural women, who represent more than 85 percent of the women's population and who are major contributors to the country's farming and herding sectors, were not active participants in this dimension of the political transformation of the nation.

As the urban women began to succeed in their struggle to gain access to powerful political leadership positions of the state, they continued to strengthen their mobilization structures and multiply their domains of political intervention. From the early 1990s to the present, Niger's urban women also saw the religious sphere as a crucial terrain of action. In spite of the hostility they faced from the patriarchal religious leaders of the old guard as well as from those of the *Izala,* women eventually succeeded in inscribing themselves in the public arena of religious discourse.

Women's more prominent participation in religious structures and discourses can, of course, be read as a resort to a conservative terrain under the control of men, implying that women are consenting to patriarchy. However, given the power of Islam in the national consciousness of the majority of Nigeriens, women's subjectivities in the religious terrain become a critical mode of quest for empowerment within the cultural frameworks that shape their identity. In fact, then, what may appear as consent may mask a range of possible consciousnesses and political activities, from active support to passive acceptance, in order to emerge as resistance. Consent emerges as a more complicated interaction than it first appears, highlighting the need to rethink the question of such ideological struggle in cases of gender inequality as well.[6]

As indicated earlier, this move by the women evolved from their understanding of the complicity between a patriarchal state and a patriarchal religion, both objectifying the subject woman in their attempt to outdo each other's authority in their quest to dominate life in the nation-state. Consequently, the urban women's movements were sandwiched between the patriarchal technocrats within the state's administrative structures, on the one hand, and the militant patriarchal Islamicist groups who use violent threats against them, on the other hand. This is clearly demonstrated in the following comments from one of the former woman ministers interviewed: "At the beginning of the democratic transition, a woman minister experienced the sabotage of her authority by male officers who had found it hard to execute orders given by a woman irrespective of the merit of her appointment. However, we women in administrative and legislative leadership positions felt that we had proven ourselves in competitive endeavors in the school system that these male colleagues attended and therefore the task is not ours to handle patriarchal egoistic feelings. On the other side, we consider the Izalaists complete schizophrenics whose desire resides in locking us in the back of their "shops/houses" and rendering us invisible and mute. We women consider that while there are no rational grounds for engaging with complete "schizophrenia," we could afford to continue the dialogue over power and national resources with the male secular officers whose problems lie not in the denial of women's right to work in the public sphere, but in her right to hold leadership positions in a non-sex-segregated workplace."[7] This is how the "women question" in urban areas in Niger began to assume a serious dimension at the religious, intellectual, and political levels. The rural women, however, continued to remain outside this gendered dispute over political power.

Plural Islamisms and the *Hijab* Discourse

Another factor that parallels the development of religious association is its continuing gendered politics and Niger's experience with what is popularly called the "*hijab* woman" or "no-*hijab* woman" phenomenon. Hitherto, the *hijab* had not been an issue in urban areas and to this day it continues to have little relevance in the rural areas. The "*hijab* woman" phenomenon is linked to urban politics in its ties with capitalist Islam and women's unconscious or conscious participation in its performative identification. More significant, however, have been the multilayered responses of the women themselves to the patriarchal *hijab* project.

The *hijab,* in the framework of political Islam in Niger, is different from the traditional Muslim women's attire of modesty that involves the *kallabi* or *adiko* (a headscarf), *mayafi* (a light wide scarf over the neck or on the top of the headscarf), and *zane* (long wrap or skirt stretching to the feet). The traditional *mayafi* is symbolically associated with married women. Unmarried women do not use *mayafi,* especially if they do not want to reduce their chances of finding potential mates. Thus, in the period before democratization and the consolidation of political Islam in the 1990s, wearing or not wearing *mayafi* represented a cultural symbol setting apart married women from unmarried ones, especially in the urban areas. Furthermore, the code of dress for both men and women in Niger Republic reflected heterogenous tastes, especially for the urban, secular youth, and no state or religious body censorship was imposed. The unmarried individual men or women chose

Malama Khadija providing Qur'anic literacy classes to a women's group at Quartier Wadata.

the quality of the traditional attire to fit their own tastes, values, and financial means. The new veil called *hijab* is the *caddor* imposed on the women following the dress code prescribed by Middle Eastern, Persian, or Asian militant revivalists who supply their African business counterparts with commodities for trade.

The *hijab* has both multiple and ambiguous meanings for women of secular as well as religious persuasions. Imposed on all women in Niger and symbolizing Islamic modesty and physical seclusion, the *hijab* came to blur the traditional cultural code of dress that distinguished unmarried from married women. For women in the urban areas it has acquired ambiguous connotations. While reinforcing the patriarchy's image of the woman, the *hijab* is also a subversive performative device against the exploitative patriarchal political and religious bodies of the nation that subjugate them. Similar phenomena were also observed and analyzed in other predominantly Islamic countries, such as Malaysia (Aihwa Ong 1990), Sudan (Victoria Bernal 1994), and Egypt (Lila Abu-Lughod 1998; Nawal El Saadawi 1997).

Early revivalist *Wahabiyya* women, on the other hand, see the *hijab* as a crucial element of their religiosity. In their case, the concept of *hijab* includes both its narrow association with the veil as a piece of fabric fashioned to carry a religious meaning, and *hijab-purda* (or *kulle* in Hausa) signifying a woman's vocal and physical seclusion to the gender-segregated matrimonial and family household.

All the women civil servants interested in Arabic and Qur'anic courses offered in mosques wear the *hijab* to attend lectures. As they step outside the lectures, they drop the *hijab* and return to either the traditional *mayafi* or whatever attire they have beneath the *hijab*. Some maintain it at the workplace as a tool against uncooperative, abusive male colleagues (Nawal El Saadawi 1997, 95–96). As female heads of institutions, and in the absence of any concrete government protective measures against assaults on women at the workplace, they use the *hijab* to legitimate their secular authority and spare themselves the unwarranted abuse from male colleagues. By seeming to submit to the patriarchal construction of the "ideal Muslim woman," therefore, these otherwise secular women in administrative authority achieve their goal of ensuring productive work behavior in the workplace partly by silencing and counteracting their male aggressors.

Women called *gabdi*—these are essentially "modern sophisticated prostitutes" who pass as "cultured" women of class—use the *hijab* as a symbol of their transformation from a supposed "outlaw" life to one of total submission to the new religious moral code of *Izala*. Through the new attire of the *hijab,* they thus manage to attract those *Izala* traders who sponsor violence against women who fail to conform. As one male interviewee put it: "These *Izala* traders fall in their own trap by marrying the *gabdi hijab* women they try to denude. Man desires the hidden and his curiosity increases as he tries to appropriate a mysterious being wrapped in the imported *hijab* he sells. Thus, both achieve their goals: the veiled *gabdi* excommunicated by society becomes reintegrated through marriage and the militant revivalist trader acquires access to the object of his desire."[8]

Finally, the *hijab* women in Niger include some Western-educated women who are tired of being victimized for their educational pursuits and academic achievements and who want to have "legitimate" children through marriage. These wear the *hijab* to attract their young contemporary males who are oriented toward the *Izala* movement.

What is striking once again is the absence of rural women in the new politics of the *hijab* identity and women's responses to it. The fact is that even political Islam of whatever order is aware of its irrelevance to rural women whose poverty and struggle for subsistence are unattractive for market-driven and profit-driven religious prescriptions. When asked about the new religious trend, a rural woman interviewee commented:

> I wake up by the first call of the rooster. We walk about seven to eight kilometers to work on the farm. Then we come back at night to pound millet and make the night meal and the *hura* (porridge for breakfast and lunch) on the farm tomorrow. By the time we finish all this labor I am dead asleep. It is the women who retire from farm work who attend Qur'anic learning with the young children left behind at the nearby *Malam*. As a female child reaches puberty, her Qur'anic learning is interrupted unless she is married

> to a *Malam* who teaches her and if her mind is up to it. Male children can continue learning because after the harvest season they can travel with their teachers. We women can't because we are married off and become bonded to farm labor and childbearing. . . . We pray, for some of us are Muslims and the Arna (traditionalists) continue their practice here.[9]

As for the clothes worn by their female relatives who visit from the city, she added: "They are pretty nice. If you bring them to us we will wear them during *Sallah* (Islamic celebrations, such as Eid). You know we wear our rugged clothes for our dusty work . . . [laughter]. But we do like nice things too if you bring us some . . . [laugh]. . . . May God provide for us all. . . . Some things happen only in the city. . . . May God help and bring peace." These spontaneous responses of Niger's Muslim women to the imposition of *hijab* in the culture clearly speak to what Holland and her colleagues refer to as individual "improvisation in heuristic development," which suggests that "one's history-in-person is the sediment from past experiences upon which one improvises, using the cultural resources available, in response to the subject positions afforded one in the present. The constraints are overpowering, yet not hermetically sealed. Improvisation can become the basis for a reformed subjectivity" (Holland 1998, 18). By both accepting the figured meaning of *hijab* as it is linked to women's modesty and seclusion and rejecting it through symbolic subversion, then, Niger's Muslim women are claiming agency by displaying malleable subjectivities (Holland 1998, 5).

Women's Islamic Literacy and the Public Display of Knowledge

Connected with the debate on *hijab,* of course, has been the patriarchal image of the woman as a "good" wife, mother, daughter, and sister. Accompanying these messages and images, therefore, was the call for the education of women to better enable them to play their religiously defined roles within patriarchal Islam. This call coincided with a trend in Niger's Islamic history that increasingly encouraged the study of Arabic as part and parcel of Islamic education. Women thus came to take up this educational call by pursuing the learning of Arabic and Islam for varied reasons that do not necessarily corroborate the original patriarchal vision.

The urban Islamist establishment continued to gain political legitimacy largely because Islam is such a crucial aspect of identity construction in Nigerien culture, even for the minority of the Nigerien *Arna,* traditionalists and Christians.[10] As the urban political landscape continued to exploit religion as a tool of patriarchy to push women back into the shadows and out of public visibility, new alliances between women themselves began to emerge. The urban French-educated women who in the past did not embrace some of the educated Islamicist women now saw them, in the wake of Islamicist revivalist aggression, as partners who could (1) dispel the patriarchal myth that only men can attain Islamic knowledge (2) articulate their own Islamic interpretation of society, and (3) influence the laws by enforcing the proper Muslim individual conduct. The new coalition of women elite from both sides of the educational divide encourages the Islamicist women intellectuals, especially those of the moderate *Tijaniyya* orders, to enter the stage of public intervention on religious matters.

This led to the emergence of religious TV and radio programs run by Nigerien women who had graduated from Islamic institutions of higher learning in North Africa (Egypt, Morocco, and Tunisia), Sudan, Saudi Arabia, and Malaysia. Some of these women who were inspired by Islamicist women activists in the countries of their training now quickly rose to national prominence and became influential commentators on Islamic matters on television and radio programs. Significantly, however, it is only women scholars associated with the *Tijaniyya* order who came to establish a visible presence in the electronic media. The Izalaists have been essentially opposed to such a public display of "their" women and to women's leadership in Islamic affairs. This Izalaist stand on women in public media was presumably welcomed by the state, which regarded it as an opportunity to divert people from rising up against its own failure to deliver basic public welfare to the nation.

The appearance on television and radio of such learned Muslim women commenting with unprecedented authority on a wide range of nonpolitical Islamic issues had a great inspirational effect upon other women throughout the broader society. Islamicist women began to organize themselves around important mosques in their communities to offer instruction to their sisters. A significant proportion of the student population in these new schools is comprised of women educated under the French system, especially married women who are civil servants. Other students have been single urban women of marriageable age. The number and variety of students in the mosque schools have been increased and compounded by the young women from the mainstream French schools which, since the 1980s, have been experiencing long and recurrent closures and have failed to meet the expectations of the population. And in response to the general trend in the country, these women-run mosque schools also made the learning of Arabic a virtual prerequisite to the acquisition of Islamic religious knowledge.

On the question of learning Arabic language and script for Islamic knowledge, however, a major ideological difference persists between Muslim men associated with the *Tijaniyya* order, the Izalaists and the elite women students of the alternative schools. The *Tijaniyya* male scholars continue to believe that Islamic learning for the laity need not involve rigorous study of

Arabic. Within this linguistic dispensation, then, women have simply been expected to accept the male interpretation of the scriptures and accede to the patriarchal interpretation of Islam. The Izalaists on the other hand, favored the acquisition of Arabic as part of the *Sunna* path toward Islam. But they also have another motive. By discouraging *Harda* (rote memorization of the Qur'an) and *Tamsir* or *Tafsir* (a mediation of Islam through local non-Arabic languages), and by insisting on the value of Arabic, the *Izala* men are seeking to legitimize their own authority in the eyes of their revivalist brethren in parts of Asia and the Middle East. To some of the women, however, the motive for learning Arabic is decidedly different. For in Arabic, some of them have discovered a tool for understanding Islam in its original. And by so doing, they hope to be better placed to challenge and combat some of the patriarchal interpretations of Islam.

For Nigeriens in general and women in particular to immerse themselves in the learning of Islam through its original language, therefore, suddenly had an unforeseen outcome. With their growing knowledge of Islamic scriptures in their original and the instrumentality of the modern electronic media, women involved in the new Islamic learning were indeed beginning to search for new readings that challenged the prevailing order and to advocate for the centering of the rights of women within local syncretic manifestations of Islamic religion and culture while at the same time being mindful of the rights and freedoms of other non-Muslim women in the nation.

Women, Islamisms, the Family Code, and the Media in Niger

Let us turn now to the interplay between Islam, women, the Family Code, and the media debate in Niger Republic. The United Nations' declaration of 1975 as the Year of the Woman had a major impact for women throughout the world and more especially in the Third World. Nigerien women's participation in the various international and national forums organized and sponsored by various internal and external sociopolitical bodies seeking to empower women created a terrain for the Association of Niger's Women (Association des Femmes du Niger—AFN)[11] to begin to act openly on issues pertaining to the violation of women's and children's rights in the nation. The military regime, under local and international pressure, allowed the AFN, the association of women jurists of Islamic law known as Association des Femmes Juristes du Niger (AFJN), and the religious leaders from AIN to form a committee to work on formulating a new Family Code (Villalon 1994; Reynolds 1997 and Dunbar 1991, 69–89). From 1975 to 1990, the work of this committee was never really taken seriously and the committee itself had not yet officially issued any finalized document. However, already by the mid-1980s the few debates on national TV and radio on the conception of this document and the implications of its outcome had begun to fuel tensions and oppositions by the majority of men of Niger who were not ready to give up the privileges ascribed to them by patriarchy.

Following Seyni Kountché's death in 1987, tremendous local pressure—from student and labor union protests against SAP—and international pressure were pitted against the military rule and called for democratization of government with a multiparty system. The unprecedented determination of the populations to break out from under the shackles of auto cratic (civilian or military) rule culminated in the National Conference in Niger from July 29 to November 3, 1991 (Malam Adji 1991; Robinson 1994; and Ibrahim and Niandou 1996). This opened the new doors for unraveling Niger's political future through increasing formation and participation of civil societies. However, the exclusion of women during the preparation for the conference triggered another unprecedented event in the country's political history. On this remarkable May 13, 1991, women protested against patriarchal democratization and rallied for multipartism. This patriarchal hold on politics during the national debate on the political future of the nation led women's organizations to mobilize and put pressure on the politicians to renew their focus on the issue of women and children's rights and the Family Code.

The Family Code document was eventually finalized and presented to the nation during the democratically elected regime of Mamane Ousmane in 1993. However, the question that arose at the time was how to push for its constitutional adoption given the rise of the militant *Izala 'Ahalal Sunna* movement in Niger. No consensus was reached between the parties—the women's associative bodies, the patriarchal secular men, the government, the moderate (male and female) *Tijaniyya* Islamicists, and the militant *Izala* groups. The groups had conflicting vested interests in its constitutional ratification or otherwise. These conflicts once again relegated the issue of the Family Code to the bottom of the national political agenda. Moreover, this international pressure must not be seen as one intended to empower women; rather it was a strategy for creating space to inscribe a specific agenda related to population control.[12]

In 1996, General Ibrahim Bare Mainassara led a coup against the democratically elected government of Mamane Ousmane that was trapped in a power struggle with the opposition that pushed the country into a climate of political, economical, and social inertia. General Bare Mainassara's regime, which was perceived both nationally and internationally as an insult to efforts to build a democratic culture of governance, sought to legitimize itself by calling for new elections that would reinstate his rule democratically.

Thus, in order to win the electoral support of the powerful pro-*Izala* traders, associations and the powerful national capital investors and sponsors of political activism, General Bare Mainassara saw himself unable to support the Family Code. As a result, the document remained dormant during his regime as well.

The *Izala* traders supply jobs to a growing body of desperate urban youth seeking employment. These traders who operate through the exploitation of political Islam are very well known in the country and their orders are executed by both the youth groups whose livelihood is at their mercy as well as by leaders of the nation whose power is tied to their support. Politicians from all parties, including General Bare's party, feared retribution from *Izala* partly because their parties are financially weak. Thus, in this climate of economic austerity and competition for political power, what is at stake is not religion as tied to religiosity, but vested economic and political interests that use *Islam* and women (and their agenda) as pawns in a national political game.

On April 12, 1999, as General Bare was struggling to hang on to power and the nation was calling for his impeachment for his excessively autocratic and ineffective governance, he was brutally murdered by his elite presidential guard. The commander of that unit, Daouda Mallam Wanke, became the leader of the all-military National Reconciliation Council to rule Niger. As a result of the *coup d'état,* the Wanke regime was immediately boycotted by the international community, and economic sanctions were imposed against him. All the international bodies (such as the United Nations Fund for Development, the World Bank, and the IMF) that sponsor (national) programs dealing with the promotion of women's empowerment and family planning formed a coalition to put pressure on this regime. In addition, they made the ratification and implementation of the Family Code and family planning programs a condition for granting further financial loans to the country. However, these international bodies were also cognizant of the force of the fundamentalist *Izala* opposing their demands. Consequently, they decided that since the new regime came to power through undemocratic means, the regime must devise a strategy to pacify the *Izala*.

Given this pressure from international funding agencies and the potential for civil unrest against his regime, President Wanke requested that all the religious bodies of the country take a look at the document and highlight the problematic parts that conflict with Islam and/or the *Sharia*. The "symbolic" meetings between the conceivers of the Family Code document, government representatives, and the religious bodies were publicly displayed on national TV and aired on national radio. This was Wanke's way of showing to the nation that a consensus was in the making, and soon, without any revisions, the Family Code was declared ratified. The signatures of all religious associations that appeared in the register of participants at the meetings (not in the document itself) were used by the government as evidence of their endorsement of the Family Code and family planning campaign projects.

In spite of what was clearly a stage-managed exercise, at the legal level, the official public announcement of the adoption of the Family Code and the family planning projects did not provoke any mobilization and mass action against it. While the official announcement of its ratification helped President Wanke's regime appease the bilateral donors in his quest for their support, his regime did not go further toward its implementation. And the current democratically elected regime of Mamadou Tanja (1999) has yet to demonstrate any intention of going beyond the present status quo. The failure of the Family Code after its ratification can be accounted for by the unwillingness of menfolk to give up patriarchal privileges and the patriarchal state's endorsement of their position. As one interviewee puts it:

> Women see their rights violated within the social practice of family life, especially with regard to the management of family resources in both monogamous and polygamous households. The polygamous men often abuse their right to polygamy at the expense of the women married to them. A man can divorce his wife after she has given him children and with no serious reason can ask her to leave because he wants to take another wife. If the woman refuses, she is simply repudiated and within the Niger legal system no witness or protest is manifested toward the man. Moreover, the provision of the Family Code that requires that the man who repudiates or divorces his wife on no reasonable ground must take care of the woman until she remarried is constantly ignored by Niger Muslim as well as non-Muslim men. For the Muslim men, they believe that their Islam requires them to take care of her only for three months of *Idda,* and not until she remarries.

Let us add, however, that even this Islamic provision that requires men to support the divorced women during the *Idda* period is generally never fulfilled.

Another aspect that many Niger men find problematic in the Family Code that makes its implementation culturally inconceivable relates to the issue of distributive justice over the apportioning of family resources/production in the event of divorce, especially in a polygamous context. The patriarchal men see the Family Code as promoting socialist values over Islamic values and over a traditionalist conception of partners' rights by promoting both equality and equity across gender and other members (including children) of the family over the sharing of resources acquired during matrimonial life.

The new Islamist women's dynamism (especially of the *Izala* movement in Niger) presents a challenge to the classicism characterizing secularist (privileged) Muslim women elites.[13] The point made here can well be supported by the wide range of Muslim women's responses to the heated national debate on the constitutional adoption of the Family Code (Reynolds 1997, 125–27; Dunbar 1991 and 2003, 24–27). As Roberta Dunbar points out:

> In 1992, six Muslim women's organizations publicly opposed the Family Code. The *Union des Femmes Musulmanes* demonstrated its willingness to ally with secular organizations and government's ministries to support the rights of women, although its leaders stopped short of advocating the Family Code. In July 1995, the Association of Muslim Women of Niger petitioned the government to begin teaching Islam in the public schools. . . . The organizers of the 1996 conference on women's rights and responsibilities in Islam demonstrated an interesting shift in strategy that perhaps anticipated future developments in language, discourse, and organizational styles. Speakers at the conference appeared in conservative Muslim dress and spoke in African languages about sensitive issues facing Muslim women. Both choice of dress and language defused the capacity of opponents to levy charges of Westernization against them, and open up debates on issues of family law within the context of Islam itself. In these debates some women emphasized that women have important rights under Muslim law (and therefore don't need a Family Code), but said that they are being denied them by current interpretations. Others argue that the reason the Family Code is needed is because of this denial. (Dunbar 2003, 26–27)

UN Family Planning Campaign and Muslim Women's Activism in the Media

The militant *Izala* rejects family planning on the ground that it is against Allah's order for a person to stop reproduction. Furthermore, some of them are in denial that HIV-AIDS exists, even though it is devastating a large proportion of rural-urban migrant laborers returning from neighboring countries such as Ivory Coast and Burkina Faso; others among them argue that it is a disease imported by the West (the white men) in order to prevent them from reproducing. As a result, the fundamentalist *Izala* campaigned against women's use of contraceptive pills and men's use of condoms, both of which are regarded as *haram* (forbidden) in their Islamic doctrinal interpretation.

In order to counteract the *Izala* protest, and aware of the importance of Islam in the country, the UN Family Planning agency recruited, by providing substantial stipends, a number of moderate *Tijaniyya* teachers, both male and female, such as El Haj Sani and Malama Zeinab Haidara,[14] to be their spokespeople on national TV and radio. They produced discourses stipulating that Allah requires one to seek medical care to prevent or cure sickness, especially that of an epidemic nature such as AIDS, and quoted relevant passages of *hadiths* that justify the spacing of birth. Thus, contrary to the claims of *Izala,* these commentators on the staff of the United Nations and other *Tijaniyya* Islamicist women's NGOs were able to establish that the campaign on family planning and HIV and AIDS prevention was in perfect conformity with Islam.

Through these religious programs women commentators also got the space to respond to questions from women viewers and listeners on a wide range of topics touching on the abuse and violation of women within the family and in the society at large. These question-and-answer sessions became particularly critical in creating new public opportunities for women's interrogation of patriarchal interpretations of Islam and for setting the stage for women's activism around their rights and freedoms in the culture.

While thematic programs dealing with more graphic discussions of sexuality, such as how condoms are used and where to acquire them for free, are presented on male-led programs, the women religious commentators handle the less explicitly sexual themes, such as the health impact of rural-urban migration of men on the family. For example, according to one interviewee, Malama Zeinab Haidara's program debated the case of men who are migrant laborers who return home sick because they have contracted the HIV virus. The programs, sponsored by the UN, were then followed by TV sketches dramatizing the plight of co-wives who are infected by their husband and the suffering that the entire family experiences as they begin to witness the death of the sick. Malama Zeinab Haidara was considered the most visible *Tijaniyya* Islamicist intellectual and public defender of women on issues related to HIV prevention and family planning in Niger.

These sensitization programs on prevention against HIV-AIDS and birth planning led to an uproar of *Izala* protest in Niamey one day when a UN-sponsored religious commentator displayed a condom on national TV and proceeded to demonstrate how to use it. The *Izala* struck back, equating the program with the appearance of Satan himself on national TV and his attempt to teach women prostitution by providing them with the tools to protect themselves in case of adultery. What followed was the launching, by the leaders of the *Izala* mosques, of anti-condom and antifamily planning programs on private radio and on audiocassettes sold in mosques and the main markets in urban areas.

The *Izala* also protested against the appearance of women on TV or the use of their voices on radio; in their views both women's images and voices on public display through the modern media violate the Islamic prohibition against reproduction of an image of animate beings and the requirement that women remain in the *hijab* even in the context of promoting religion.

It is important to mention that while the *Izala* and the *Tijaniyya* Islamicists are engaged in the production of oppositional discourses over what is allowed or forbidden in Islam, the focus of their contention is strictly social and is under government censorship against any political substance. For example, the *Tijaniyya* religious programs aired on national TV and radio cannot reply to the *Izala* questions over the interplay between Islam, the rise of prostitution in urban centers, and the campaign for giving the public access to free condoms in HIV-AIDS prevention centers in a predominantly Muslim country. Questions of this nature, often asked by the public sympathetic to the fundamentalist *Izala* concerns or with a different type of argument, usually of a secular nature, which nonetheless is opposed to the UN campaign for family planning in the country, remain unanswered by the moderate Islamicist commentators on national TV or radio. Part of the fear here is that such questions are inherent provocations of issues of a political nature.

The *Tijaniyya* Islamicist programs on national TV and radio give voice and space for women in Niger to interrogate the integrity of patriarchal Islamic praxis in the culture where men violate even the rights granted women and children. One interviewee provided the following question that an anonymous female interlocutor asked Malama Zeinab Haidara on national TV: "When my husband goes out after dinner, he returns at 4:00 a.m. Am I obliged to give myself to him?" Another question related to the issue of gambling. The father of a woman asked if it is right for his daughter to divorce her husband who is addicted to gambling. He has stopped performing his prayers after their marriage and has insisted that his wife behave as a good Muslim wife. Can he take his daughter away and help her perform the *Hajj* (pilgrimage to Mecca)? Both questions speak directly to the pervasive abuse women are subjected to in the "Muslim" culture and the double standards on what is deemed a good Islamic behavior for women in contrast to men.

Thus, the intervention of Islamicist women as authorities on Islamic knowledge on public media (TV and radio) has produced a new consciousness among Niger's urban women who now expose patriarchal Islamic abuses while also negotiating ways to "speak back" at their oppressive partners and intolerant male colleagues at the workplace. As authoritative public mediators, the Islamicist moderate women commentators extend their solidarity to the other women of the society by including a question-and-answer component in their programs and by supplying their TV and radio audience the exact passages within the Qur'an and *hadiths* that speak to Muslim women's right to a fulfilling life in the society as well as in marriage or at the workplace. This is clearly shown in the following question a woman asked in her attempt to question the integrity of her husband who is involved with a young *hijab* woman: "Is it Islamic to use the *hijab* in the daytime and drop it at night to go to a nightclub with a man even if he happens to be one's husband?" Of course, the Malama's response was "No. It seems that both the man (if he is the husband of the *hijab* woman) and the woman herself have given a new meaning to the *hijab*. I mean maybe she is not wearing it for religious purposes. But I cannot speak on her *anniyya* (intention). . . . But you cannot play with Allah . . . right. . . . Both of them if they have been raised in a Muslim family know the relationship between *hijab* 'modesty' and going to a nightclub in our culture. . . . You cannot hide anything from Allah. . . . Truly. . . . You need to tell this man to desire/love you as you are . . . for Allah's truth."

This dialectical as well as a dialogic cultural interaction between the public display of proficiency in Arabic, Islamic knowledge, and the advocacy of women's rights in Islam, especially as it relates to marriage, has naturally created new tensions between partners, with women developing a new consciousness of themselves and their rights and men developing an unwillingness to surrender privileges long guaranteed them by patriarchal Islam. Many men who once favored the presence of revivalist Islam in Niger are now retracting this view as the women move on to learn Arabic, master the Qur'an, and defend and reclaim their rights. This is not to suggest, of course, that the entire body of the women of Niger was suddenly absorbed by this new articulation of Islamic learning and activism. Certainly not. The face of the Muslim woman in Niger continues to be heterogeneous, manifesting different trajectories in the continuing tension between the "old" and the "new." At the same time, however, there is little doubt that the new momentum has become predominant and has captured the imagination of very many women. But how long will these doors of women's agency in Islamic *Ijtihad* remain open in Niger? Only time can tell, as the forces unleashed by the democratization momentum of the 1990s continue to unfold, sometimes in the most unsettling ways.

Chapter 6

Through the Eyes of Agaisha

Womanhood, Gender Politics, and the Tuareg Armed Rebellion

Historical Background

Between 1985 and 1990, the Tuareg—a nomadic pastoralist people inhabiting the Sahara—launched sporadic attacks from their military camps in Libya and Algeria with arms supplied by France, Germany, and other foreign countries.[1] These attacks provided grounds for the Nigerien government to implicate all Tuareg indiscriminately and to order the national armed forces to lead a merciless crackdown on Tuareg civilians. Both the Tuareg rebels and the national armed forces operating in the north of the country violated the human rights of innocent Tuareg and other ethnic groups. The appalling silence of the rest of the population aggravated their fate.

The Political Context of the Uprising

In this chapter I try to develop an understanding of the so-called Tuareg Rebellion in terms of the interplay between power, gender, class, identity politics, and the contest for the legitimization of the postcolonial nation-state. In addition to secondary sources, I make extensive use of excerpts from an interview I conducted in December 1998 with Agaisha, a Nigerien woman from the north of the country. Her journey is one of self-discovery, one of coming to understand women's social position and political possibilities. She also learned the effect of conflict on relationships among women citizens of the same country. Agaisha was born in the war region and experienced the conflict first hand. Also participating in the interview was Mme Aishatou Ben Wahab, known in Niger as the first woman ever to be designated to represent her party, UDPS AMANA, in the government; she held the post of minister of commerce and arts. *Agaisha* is a fictitious name used to protect the identity of our primary interviewee.

French colonization is widely perceived by some Tuareg to have been the initial cause of this conflict because it imposed mobility constraints within "fixed borders," a concept not compatible with Sahelian nomads' traditional way of life. In this regard, Agaisha—a leading female Tuareg activist (see introduction for full biography)—made the following observations when asked to provide her personal assessment of what seems to be the "Tuareg problem" in the Niger Republic:

> Well, the Tuareg problem is really a vast problem that does not evolve from the present. The Tuareg problem began with the colonizer. If there is someone who created the Tuareg problem, it is maybe the colonizer because the Tuaregs are herders who have always been mobile. They were nomads who do not know these problems of borders. A nomad can move from Niger to Mali. For him he is always at home. He can go from Mali to Algeria, this is still home for him. However, now with the problems of (national) borders, there is of course a limit: Tuaregs from Niger must remain in Niger. If you want to cross to Algeria, you must possess a national identity card, a concept they don't understand. They don't understand the concept of a national identification card, let alone that of a passport. Therefore, this is the problem. . . . It is an old one and I think the issue has been the focus of well-documented studies over the years.

Thus, the impact of European colonial balkanization of Africa, leading to the creation of the modern nation-states, is what, in Agaisha's assessment, accounts for the crisis confronting nomadic Tuareg populations in whichever postcolonial state they may be regarded as citizens, and more particularly in Niger Republic. The colonial border configuration stripped them of their cultural and survival rights of access to natural resources (water, herding sites, animals, etc.) and broke the cohesion of a unified ethnic group by scattering its members to several distinct "sovereign countries," thereby imposing new "national" identities on each disjointed unit of the old entity.

The quest for green herding areas often led to tensions with other native agricultural sedentary communities sharing and competing for the same natural resources. Numerous tragic conflicts were registered as the herds of pastoral groups invaded agricultural lands in response to severe long lasting periods of drought and the lack of natural resources for survival in the newly enclosed pastoral lands (Charlick 1991). At the transnational level, nation-state borders led not only to the political and cultural marginalization of nomadic Tuareg populations (and other nomadic groups including the Tubu), but also to their being perceived as "violators" of immigration regulations. Lack of adequate understanding of the laws due to the high rate of illiteracy from their resistance to assimilation into the new colonial and postcolonial social order made the Tuareg particularly vulnerable to criminal charges related to immigration.

After independence, most nation-states retained (and still do) the administrative apparatus installed by the colonial authority. Thus, very little has been done to establish some political, economic, and social parity between the various ethnic and social groups in the country in the management and utilization of national resources.

From 1960 to 1991, the political leaders of successive civilian and military regimes in Niger maintained their rule through an authoritarian and centralized system of government. The leaders maintained patron-client relations with organized social groups—such as the union of civil servants and student organizations—which had the potential to oppose state authority (Charlick 1991; Gervais 1997). Both regimes marginalized rural farmers and nomadic and/or non-nomadic pastoralists. The most alienated groups among those excluded from formal participation in the national decision-making process were the nomadic Tuareg, Tubu, Fulani, and Arabs, as well as almost all women.

Various regimes neglected the development of rural economies and, worse, misappropriated the international foreign aid allocated to Sahelian regions that were severely affected by prolonged drought and famine. Also, the revenues generated by uranium and coal mines benefited mainly the ruling political leaders who used them to maintain their power by satisfying the interests of the urban professional middle class and the students. Meanwhile, the regimes ignored the most basic needs of the people who produced the mineral wealth.

Moreover, the problem of integration of nomadic Tuareg into national citizenship in Niger Republic was aggravated by the rush to modernize through the use of financial revenues acquired from the exploitation of mineral resources in the Sahara and, in particular, in the areas inhabited by the Tuareg and other native ethnic groups living in the northern part of Niger. These populations were deeply affected by the privatization of their native lands to uranium and charcoal companies strongly dominated by European investors with controlling shares by the French.

In the meantime, technologically skilled or economically more powerful migrant groups from other parts of the country attracted by the opportunities offered by the industrial transformation of the Nigerien Sahara began to move in and settle as new residents. The industrial Nigerien Sahara landscape assumed a new face, becoming hierarchically occupied by Europeans and elite Nigeriens (from all ethnic backgrounds) in the most urbanized and modern housing areas, with the native residents being pushed into housing quarters with minimal infrastructural facilities (health centers, schools). These socioeconomic disparities in areas like Arlit and Anou Ararem were flagrant even in the late 1970s to mid-1980s when Niger Republic was faring well from uranium revenues from the Sahara region as the native populations (Tuareg and non-Tuareg, nomadic or sedentary) continued to be denied the benefits of the resources extracted from their native region.

Severe famine and lack of government assistance forced many nomadic populations to abandon their rural settlements and seek assistance elsewhere. The Tuareg were the most seriously affected, and 1984–85 saw the mass exodus of nomadic Tuareg and Fulani whose livestock had been decimated by the drought. They moved south toward the cities and north into the neighboring countries of Algeria and Libya. The failure of their own government to assist them in the prospect of a bleak future made thousands of frustrated Tuareg and Tubu vulnerable to Libya's Mu'amar Qaddafi's imperialistic designs couched in revolutionary rhetoric. They became easy prey to the Tuareg guerrilla force he had established and were at the service of his expansionist appetite in the region. Similarly, border disputes between Niger and Algeria led the Algerian government to organize a Tuareg insurgency against Niger (Charlick 1991, 141–42), while containing the Tuareg at the southern gate of Algeria itself. Tuareg refugees (men and women, militants or not) were constrained within enclosed areas at the Algerian border with Niger.

Libya and Algeria finally expelled Tuareg refugees from their territories and forced them to return to Niger. This expulsion came at a time of intense sociopolitical crisis and economic austerity resulting from the fall of uranium prices, France's disengagement from Niger, and the antisocial "economic recovery" measures imposed by international donors through structural adjustment policies. This crisis triggered a painful disillusion with the promises of an all-inclusive national integration made by President Ali Saibou in the late 1980s.

The Saibou regime became conscious of the fact that a significant number of returning Tuareg had received military training and was extremely suspicious of them. The regime's authority was already weakened by the opposition of the middle class and student organizations, which saw their interests compromised by the austerity measures imposed by the International Monetary Fund and the World Bank. Against this backdrop, Tuareg men and women became the target of harassment and repression and were subjected to mass political arrests and brutalization. Once more they were treated as outcasts in their own country. The resulting rebellion was the response of the marginalized to their plight in a situation in which no other solution seemed open to them.

In the meantime, the narrow ethnonationalism of the Tuareg elite made the Tuareg struggle vulnerable to ideological attacks from various fronts. First, the government successfully created a propaganda campaign to counter the rebels' request for the decentralization of power. The regime depicted the claim as an unpatriotic disengagement from the nation on the side of the Tuareg, bound to split the country along ethnoregional lines. This propaganda was particularly successful in light of the silence of the ruling political classes—the civil servants and the students—in the face of growing harassment, and their lack of compassion or solidarity with the victims of the armed conflict. Second, the leaders of the rebellion tactlessly embraced French and German racial accounts that portrayed the Tuareg as "white nobles" oppressed by their former "black slaves." This convenient myth spared France from facing its responsibility in shaping the colonial history of the country and in controlling its postcolonial destiny. Rebel advocacy of federalism on racial grounds failed to galvanize the support of Nigeriens, many of whom are a product of Sahelien ethnic blending. Finally, the majority of poor Nigeriens, who had been equally deprived of access to the privileges generated by the exploitation of natural resources, found it difficult to sympathize with rebels who explained their plight in terms of "racial" discrimination.

Brassage Sahélien: Women Dispel the Myth of Ethnic Purity

The Tuareg are a nomadic people and are believed to have originally descended from the Berber of North Africa. Now they can be found in Algeria, Burkina Faso, Libya, Mali, and Niger. Migrating with their tents from region to region in search of grazing pasture for their camels, goats, and sheep, most became Islamized. Eventually they expanded into regions bordering the Sahara Desert and assimilated into their society various sedentary farming and trading peoples. From their early formation as a community, therefore, the Tuareg showed signs of multicultural affinity, even though they continue to be mistakenly regarded—especially in the Nigerien context—as a homogeneous ethnic unit. The mistake is partly attributable to the internalization of the colonial and postcolonial paradigm of racial and ethnic purity.

Traditionally, the Tuareg family was matrilineal and monogamy was the most common marital practice. Although women did not work in the public sphere, they were the heads of household by virtue of the fact that they were very often the owners of the settlements, and very skilled in leather crafts and processing of dairy products that the men would take to the markets and other trading centers for sale. Unlike in other Nigerien cultures that are predominantly oral, in Tuareg culture literacy in *Tifinagh*—an indigenous alphabet with its own rules—was very prevalent among men as well as women, who creatively used it in producing rich Tamajaq poetry. Tuareg women play an important role in the maintenance, preservation, and transmission of traditional values as well as in managing the financial and herding assets of the family. Agaisha described the status of Tuareg women in the following terms:

> The status of the Tuareg woman before the conflict or even as far back as I can remember it has been that of the head of the household. When I say head of household it does not necessarily imply involved in domestic work, but I mean her husband cannot take any decision without her consent. She has always been associated with the decision-making process. The woman controls the family affairs and dictates what the man ought to do in the public sphere and bring into the household. She owns whatever is in the household, including the herds, which usually combine what she owns on her own and what the husband brought in during the marriage. When there is divorce everything remains with her and the man leaves her house empty-handed unless she offers him something. But now everything has changed. Things have changed for all Nigerien women, even the Tuareg women. The Tuareg women and the Nigerien women suffer because the men have abandoned them. Social and cultural norms have been changing to the detriment of women and children with the economic crisis and worsened by the armed conflict.

Rural-urban migration of families and coexistence in deprived urban quarters with other native ethnic groups led to the development of new cultural practices among the various groups as a result of interactions of the various cultures. Thus, while influencing their neighboring ethnic groups, the Tuareg also assimilated new cultural values from other ethnic groups. Polygamy, an attribute of patriarchal cultures, for example, began to infiltrate urban Tuareg family formations. Women whose herds were destroyed by famine or other factors were now forced to live as dependents of their husbands or to migrate to squatters' areas in cities where an overwhelming majority of them resorted to begging. In rural areas where Tuareg women still remain heads of household, multiple divorces have become common as new male-centered values began to clash with the monogamous ways.

One such encampment that accommodated huge populations of migrants from the rural areas was Tudu where Agaisha grew up and which she described as an urban neighborhood of the marginalized poor.

> Tudu is a very well-known section of Agadez. It is inhabited by many different people. There are some Hausa, but it is predominantly inhabited by the Tuareg who lost their cattle and moved here because they did not have enough resources to settle in town where they have to pay rent. The same explanation accounts for the Hausa who live here. Those who did not have money came here and pitched their tents next to the Tuareg and settled down. There are also Fulani, another pastoralist group. For many of the Tuareg, Arabs, and Fulani, it was not always poverty that made them settle in Tudu; it was habit and culture, because for them living in mud houses is like living in a prison. They prefer to live in tents. In Tudu, there are tents like in the countryside. The men go back and forth between Tudu and Agadez looking for money that will help them reconstitute their herds. They buy one or two goats here and there, sometimes three, and lead a country life in Tudu, which still has some pastoral resources. Many people who live in Tudu are nostalgic because they did not want to leave the rural homeland; they were forced out of it.

Tudu, which really means "the hill" in Hausa, is in fact located on a hill on the outskirts of Agadez City. It is a site that was strategically chosen by the disenfranchised almost as a declaration that they too can engage in symbolic surveillance from the "top" against a state that was forcing them into urban sedentary life. The state tried to put them in enclosures within the city to contain them. They can now use their new geographical location to "fortify" themselves against a hostile "enemy."

Agaisha's narrative about her childhood in Tudu is also significant: it informs us about the land dispossession suffered by the Tuareg and other groups of the Nigerien Sahara, and it provides some evidence for transethnic, peaceful cohabitation even in a time of crisis. This coexistence is striking, for it reflects a regional multiethnicity predating European colonial rule. It survived the postcolonial governments in the form of class solidarity among people who shared a common socioeconomic fate. It suggests that ethnicity is not likely to have been the root-cause of the crisis in Niger in the mid-1980s, as the Western media would have us believe. In fact, peaceful cohabitation and interethnic exchanges permeated the intermarriages that characterized the Sahelien identity. Agaisha herself is a living example of this complex Nigerien identity, which she believes is "l'avantage d'être Nigerien":

> I was born in 1960 in Tigida n Adagh in the county of Tchirozerine in Agadez Department. My mother is Targui (female Tuareg) and my father is Hausa-Ba'adare from Tahoua. My father told me that if I am asked about his ethnic background I should say he is a sedentary Tuareg because the Ba'adare are originally Tuareg who became Hausa through settlement and intermarriage. His mother is Targui from Talamses and his father is Ba'adare. My father was a forestry officer. He and my mother divorced and I stayed in the village with my maternal grandmother until I was seven, when I joined my mother who was living in Tudu after the divorce. I learnt Hausa there with the other children.

From the foregoing quote and reflecting on her first marriage, which took place in Tudu, Agaisha reveals more of her feelings about the meaning of Nigerien identity and the multidimensionality of Nigerien Tuaregness:

> My first husband was in the military. He is from Ader, a Ba'adare. . . . But he himself is quite a mixture [laugh]. . . . Well, his mother is Ba'adara, but his father is from Dancandu, so he is Zarma [laugh]. . . . His father is Zarma and his mother is from Tahoua, a Hausa-Ba'adara. And here we are—he married me, a Tuareg [laugh]. This is quite a distinctive characteristic of Niger [laugh]. . . . Here is this *brassage* (blending). . . . This is Niger. . . . The *brassage* is even the advantage of being Sahelien, that is Nigerien, because all people are interrelated and one feels at home wherever one is. There is no one ethnic group today that can claim it is only Hausa or Tuareg. . . . That is the fact . . . not being mixed does happen, but . . . that is how I describe the common *brassage*.

"Tuaregness" in the context of Niger, then, can be in the form of a *Targui,* that is, a Tuareg not assimilated to any other non-Tuareg ethnolinguistic groups, or it can mean Tuareg "mixed" with other Nigerien ethnic groups. If her mother could be said to be a Tuareg-Targui, Agaisha and her father belong to the other connotation of Tuaregness as *Ba'adare,* that is an ethnic blending of Tuareg-Targui and Hausa of Ader, a region that is next to Agadez in the southern fringes of the Sahara. Both Agaisha's and her mother's Tuaregness underwent reconfiguration through the institution of marriage to husbands who brought additional features to their identity, including a shift from rural life to urban life.

However, it is important to point out what Agaisha referred to as *brassage sahélien* is not simply a mixture, for mixture does not necessarily produce the kind of comfortable blending highlighted by Agaisha. *Brassage sahélien* is a positive blending of cultures and ethnicities, which leads to the invention of new identities. This is why Agaisha had to laugh as she deconstructed the reality of her own identification to Tuaregness. The question is what happened to "l'avantage d'être Nigerien"? Why didn't *brassage* help prevent armed conflict?

Tuareg Women Entrapped by Identity Ties

What emerged from my interviews with Agaisha and Mme Wahab is that warring parties use propaganda to manipulate the concept of collective identity and play it against women, giving them no space to make a choice during the war. Biological determinism, which depicts women as mothers, daughters, or wives, becomes the basis of a bondage that offers no real option for the majority of women who look Tuareg—those whose lighter complexion reveals their Berber ancestry. They have no opportunity to make an independent decision to side with one or none of the various parties in the civil war. Agaisha's response to the question of whether Tuareg women were consulted about, or alerted to, the possibility of armed uprising reveals this lack of choice:

> We women were not consulted about the impending uprising. We were taken by surprise when the attacks were launched and the national armed forces started to raid our homes. The women knew that Tuareg men had left during the harsh drought and famine for Libya, Algeria, or France to find work and provide for families left at home. Most of the men who went to Libya were recruited by the Libyan army. We knew that. They worked hard there, but then they were expelled. They returned home empty-handed and the majority of them were very bitter. Bitter because the Nigerien government promised to assist them on their return but failed to deliver. These men became the rebels. They did not consult us because they knew the women would protest against violence. So they decided not to alert us and as a result we were very shocked by what we had to face. But they are our men, fathers, husbands, and brothers, so I guess we have to understand them.

While it may indeed be true that women were not consulted in the decision to launch the rebellion, some of them became major actors in popularizing its causes. For example, a female Tuareg poet by the name of Lalla of Kidal, who was exiled in refugee camps in Algeria, creatively transformed the classical *tende*—a poetic genre sung across gender that was based on classical metaphorical composition. Lalla of Kidal created a more overt nonmetaphoric form in an attempt to convey more clearly the plight of the misunderstood young Tuareg males known as the *Ishumar* (derived from the French language "chomeur," meaning unemployed) from Niger and Mali. Later, this new poetic genre innovated by the young Tuareg woman would be appropriated by the male artists among the *Ishumar* natives of Niger and elsewhere beyond Niger Republic. From exile in Algeria, Libya, Europe, and the Arab world, the *Ishumar* announced through the reconfigured *tende* the impending armed rebellion to end their political and economic disenfranchisement in their country of origin.

In fact, for the majority of the civilian population and Tuareg women especially, the armed conflict became a reality only when the national armed forces and security agents began to raid their homes and viciously subject them to intimidation, arrest, and torture. This operation against women was undertaken in the hope of squeezing out confessions about their complicity in the rebellion or knowledge of key rebel agents and the source of their military support. Agaisha, for example, recounts her terrifying experience with the Nigerien gendarmerie in the late 1980s and early 1990s:

> Everybody was targeted, not only me. But, maybe because as a woman I couldn't just watch what was happening to innocent people, I made a point to denounce what was going on in Agadez whenever journalists from British Broadcasting Corporation (BBC) or French International Radio (RFI) inquired. It was risky for me because I had a secure job as a secretary at the municipal office and I could have been killed just like others. But my conscience did not allow me to just watch the violation of innocent people's human rights. I used to gather women together to ask them to break their silence. We need to do something. We must write letters to the préfet of Agadez, to inform the nation about what is going on. But because he feared being implicated as sympathizing with the Tuareg rebels, the préfet (who is himself a Tuareg) did not react. He advised me to be careful. From that moment on, I continued to be the target of arrests and interrogation by the national security services, until I escaped to Algeria.

In Agaisha's account this reprisal was particularly violent toward women. The women saw themselves being victimized by their menfolk who, without warning, abandoned them and left them with the responsibility to provide for the needs of the family. In these conditions Tuareg women were forced to sell their valuable belongings and use whatever money they got to help the family survive.

The rebellion resulted in the loss of thousands of lives, leaving behind widows with large families to support and orphans who lost entire families. It became yet another factor in the move to urban areas, forcing many dispossessed Tuareg women to migrate to the urban centers with their children and live as beggars, often at the mercy of the humiliating and unsympathetic urban population. The urban reception was hostile, as the residents were captives of government propaganda that portrayed Tuareg migrants as traitors and betrayers of national unity.

Other groups of women risked their lives to seek refuge in a more sympathetic neighboring country such as Algeria, where Tuareg with Algerian nationality shared their cultural affinities. Agaisha sadly recounts the conditions under which her friend Dijal and other relatives perished in the

Ténéré desert in their attempted escape to southern Algeria: "Dijal is a comrade who was committed to the Tuareg people wherever they are. I would say her struggle was for the future of all Nigerien women, not only Tuareg women. Her death in the Ténéré desert came as a result of the confrontation between the government armed forces and the rebels who forced her to leave her home in Agadez. She was forced out. Initially, she refused to go into exile. She believed in staying in Niger with the other women, children and the older people left behind; she preferred to die here. But as the killings and the government harassment intensified, I pushed her to leave for the refugee camps in Algeria. But she did not make it."

Women of other ethnic groups in the North were also greatly victimized during the rebellion. Some were abandoned by husbands who either joined the army or the rebellion or prolonged their seasonal labor migration in neighboring countries or in urban centers of Niger for fear of being ambushed in the conflict. Some women were dispossessed of their meager commercial goods at trading checkpoints by either government soldiers or combatants from the rebel camps. Yet others were fortunate and succeeded in making their way to refugee camps in Algeria.

Women also began to demonstrate that even victimization can be transformed once one is immersed in a war. Whether in reaction to their victimization by the government, or because of their affiliation with male kin in combat, or because they were rejected by many Nigeriens who accused them of complicity, some women embraced the Tuareg rebels by lending their services as spies. As Agaisha reveals, "despite the harassment, expulsion from their homes, humiliation, and torture, Tuareg women resisted. We were no longer afraid of being imprisoned or killed. To the contrary, we reinforced our contribution by spying for and coordinating the rebellion. Tuareg women endured a great deal and contributed fully, yes fully, by every means they could till the final victory."

Tuareg women in refugee camps in Algeria played active roles by nursing wounded combatants and by working at odd jobs to provide supplies necessary for the battle. Women's organizational abilities were not overlooked by the leader of the rebellion who solicited their contribution through Agaisha. Her activism led to her rise to leadership in the refugee camp in Algeria. In Agaisha's own words, "One day the leader of the rebellion approached me. He said, 'I have noticed that you women are very organized. Now, I think it would be better to assign well organized women in the refugee camps in Algeria to a well defined mission.' He told us that he wanted us to take care of the wounded combatants. Moreover, if at the military base they needed something, they would let us know. Till the end of the rebellion we cared for the combatants. We bought the supplies needed at the military base paying for them with money some of us brought from Niger or earned by working at odd jobs in Algeria."

The contribution of Tuareg women in the camps was carried out at high risk; they could have jeopardized the safe-haven granted to them by the Algerian authorities who opposed any form of political gathering. Though restricted, Tuareg women devised strategies to conceal their transactions with the rebels on foreign soil. Agaisha describes some of the ways she and other women avoided any suspicion of their active role in the conflict by the Algerian security service: "How did we acquire medical supplies (drugs and bandages) without arousing the suspicion of Algerian pharmacists? If they knew that we were assisting the combatants, they would inform their government. We devised a strategy. As soon as we received a list of the supplies needed, we assigned a woman's name to each product and the designated person was in charge of acquiring that item. In this way we collected the necessary supplies during the conflict."

Despite harsh conditions in the refugee camps and the extreme hostility expressed toward them in Niger, Tuareg women transformed themselves from victims into active players through their involvement in the armed conflict. Some women like Agaisha came to realize women's importance and their power through their contributions. This realization led them to craft a new identity and new roles to play in the national political arena. It is in this context of conflict that both Agaisha and Mme Wahab emerged as political figures. They contributed actively to the mediation of peace agreements between the rebels and the Nigerien government and were present at both local and international negotiations. Among the influential parties that were constituted during Niger's fragile transition to a multiparty system of government was the Union Démocratique pour le Progès Social (UDPS-AMANA), a predominantly Tuareg party or one supported by Northerners. The party nominated Mme Wahab to the post of Minister of Commerce and Arts in the democratically elected government of the Second Republic. In the opinion of Mme Wahab "it is because traditionally women were the heads of decision-making in Tuareg traditional culture that the members of my political party, whose constituency is heavily Tuareg, was very much at ease with nominating me, a woman, as their representative in the government" (interview with the author, January 9, 1999). But because so much had changed, even among the Tuareg themselves, Tuareg women who assumed a political role at the national level, as Agaisha points out in our interviews, were subjected to verbal abuse, disrespect by government and media, and continuous suspicion, intimidation, and harassment by government security agents.

Agaisha's conclusion on how war affects women is that women carry a heavy burden regardless of the roles they assume or the gains they achieve in society in the process. For a woman who lost her children, husband, and relatives, no material gains or new titles can heal the void created by the horrors of war. Thinking retrospectively about our dialogue on women's experiences during the polarized national crisis, Mme Wahab agreed with Agaisha: "Who is in pain? The one who dies? Or the ones who are left behind to mourn the loss of the loved ones? The memories of this nightmare are painful to go back to even though they are part of what we have become now as citizens, mothers, wives, daughter or friends of the belligerents. . . . War has no winners; we are all losers one way or the other."

Sisterhood during War

Patriarchy defines most Nigerien ethnic and cultural practices. The patriarchal interpretation of Islam, the centralization of political power in patriarchal hands, and allegiance to patriarchal ruling classes are some of the factors that have historically prevented Nigerien women from being actively involved in national politics. According to Agaisha, neither of Niger's most popular women's organizations—the Association des Femmes du Niger (AFN) founded in 1975 under the Kountché regime and the Rassemblement Démocratique des Femmes du Niger (RDFN), which was created in 1990—opposed the armed conflict or lent solidarity to women in the conflict zones. Although both associations make women's rights and empowerment a central part of their platforms, their silence betrayed their class-based gender politics.

Women's participation in Niger's political parties is determined by identity politics, which thrives on the manipulation of ethnic and class differences. Women leaders in the opposition alliance, many of whom were elite Tuareg or Northerners, did indeed express their sympathy with northern women's struggles. They publicly protested against the manner in which the government dealt with the rebellion. But Agaisha's interpretation is that they did so only to position themselves as leaders and mediators in the peace process, seeking to become powerbrokers in the shadow of male politicians. Agaisha commented that Tuareg women did not receive anything from either the AFN or the RDFN, but women in the AFC—a coalition of political parties—"lent their moral support to us since our party, UDPS-AMANA, was a member of the coalition." In effect, therefore, Tuareg women who were entrapped in the daily agonies of war became pawns, not only in men's game of power and control, but also in women's agenda. Women politicians and activists in civil society sought to gain privileges in the male dominated order—locally, regionally, and internationally.

Conclusion

An important misconception that this chapter sets out to dispel is the binary stereotype of the roles that men and women play during wartime—men as active agents and women as passive participants. The many experiences of Tuareg women during the so-called Tuareg rebellion are further evidence that the stereotype is inaccurate.

What we learned from Tuareg women's experiences during wartime, on the other hand, is that Nigerien women have not conquered the differences that divide them—ethnic identity, regional and political affiliation, and class allegiance. As a result, many Nigerien women did not respond to the horrors of war confronting Tuareg women and other women in regions affected by the conflict. Identity politics led Nigerien women to pay blind allegiance to one or another warring party. They responded to "imaginary" identities, forgetting the principles and experiences of *brassage sahélien* that truly defined them. They sacrificed what Agaisha regarded as the greatest advantage of being a Sahelian Nigerien.

The Nigerien experience of armed conflict incorporated class-specific agendas and interests. Women's vested class interests constrained their ability to arrive at a common vision of how to confront patriarchal authoritarianism, political manipulation of identity, and the international and local forces that profited from the conflict to the detriment of women and children. Nigerien women, in other words, did not reach the level of political consciousness that would have enabled them to overcome conceptual boundaries of "difference" during wartime. As a result, the strategies conceived by urban, middle-, and upper-class women failed the Tuareg women and other women victims of the conflict.

Even Agaisha, a product of *brassage sahélien*—the daughter of a Hausa-Ba'adare father and a Tuareg mother, married initially to a Zarma and later to a Tuareg—reinvented herself to deal with her entrapment in the war. She was entrapped by her physical Tuareg appearance, by her marital bond with a Tuareg who was apparently deeply involved as an arms trafficker on behalf of the rebellion, and by her internalization of patriarchal values. She reacted to the horrors of a war that women had no role in initiating. In the absence of organized support from other women and women groups that could incorporate her and women like her in antiwar efforts, Agaisha transformed herself from an innocent child of *brassage sahélien,* from a suffering victim, into a militant nationalist. She slid slowly into Tuareg ethnonationalism to serve as a spy for the rebellion, finally to emerge as a Tuareg political figure of national importance.

In the final analysis, therefore, *brassage sahélien* became a liability rather than an asset within a political dispensation that seeks to exploit difference for the advancement of individuals, groups, and class agendas. Members of the different ethnic groups—the very groups upon which her *brassage sahélien* identity came to be constructed—now viewed Agaisha with some degree of suspicion, wondering where her actual allegiance lay. The *brassage* that had once been the pride of Nigeriens had now been sacrificed at the altar of a national conflict rooted in material interests and distributive injustices. In fact, the conditions of regional exploitation and inequalities became the foundation for the systematic deconstruction of *brassage sahélien* and reversal to a colonially inscribed reductionist and "purist" understanding of ethnicity and belonging.

Conclusion

While most studies on Muslim women make it their main goal to investigate how Islam views women or to examine the oppression of Muslim women resulting from Islam, this book has explored the lives of women as agents in several ways. The overarching concern has been with how the statuses and roles of Muslim women in Niger have changed as a result of local and global processes. We have discussed here how the processes of French colonialism, the development agenda of the 1960s to late 1970s, the Structural Adjustment Programs of the 1980s, and the democratization and pluralism of the 1990s have made, in the presence of globalization and the rise of political Islam, an impact on traditional gender statuses and roles in a predominantly patriarchal society. This book also analyzes how the Muslim women of Niger have responded to the above forces.

Sections of the book have also been concerned with how Muslim women have inscribed feminine public meanings to Islam by participating in the production and enactment of legitimizing symbolic images of piety.

Their strategies have included Islamic literacy, Islamic dress discourse, involvement in religious rituals, and formation of Muslim women's networks that use Islam as an organizing principle. All this has taken place in a climate where extremist militant Islamist groups are engaged in violent aggression on Muslim women who do not fit their "prototypical model" of the "real Muslim woman."

Of equal concern has been the militarization of society resulting from the confrontation between the state's armed forces and the combatants of a disenfranchised citizenry and the confrontation between religious militant orthodoxies and their secularist counterparts, which has transformed Muslim women's consciousness of their statuses and roles during the conflicts and in their aftermath. Finally, the book has also demonstrated the mechanisms by which Muslim women project themselves and act as *agents* in various cultural, political, and economic fields such as in religion, performing arts, and government, contrary to the mainstream beliefs that persist in seeing Muslim women only as recipients of ideology and passive respondents to the consequences of ideology on their lives.

This exercise of Muslim women's agency has often taken place in an overlapping space between tradition and modernity, reinforced by the reemergence of the politics of pluralism since the early 1990s. Malama A'ishatu Hamani Zarmakoy Dancandu followed the trajectory of education for years within the domain associated with "tradition." However, in her late seventies, within the context of democratization and the rise of political Islam, she rose to public visibility as a female Qur'anic commentator. By drawing on her Qur'anic educational background, Malama A'ishatu inscribed a Qur'anic woman's face in Islamic exegesis through the national electronic media, a domain that had hitherto been the preserve of the Muslim male clergy.

In the meantime, education itself was transformed under colonial and postcolonial conditions. Though disproportionately represented, women had the opportunity to partake of this "modernist" education as a result of which some came to be highly placed in modern institutions of government, administration, economy, and politics. Yet when the chips were down and the country was confronted by crises in various sectors, particularly in education, some of the same successful secularist Muslim women came to rely and draw on the legacy of traditional and Islamic education in the quest for a new direction in their lives and of their children. Furthermore, they joined hands with some elite and nonelite women who have been using Islam to chart out an alternative modernity for the Muslim women's agenda.

Similar observations can be made in the areas of the performing arts. Habsu Garba essentially broke out of the "traditional confines" of culture and its caste foundations by choosing to become a public performer with an "activist"—even if not radical—orientation. Yet she has continued to justify her choices as a calling, rationalized on the basis of her Afro-Islamic heritage that shaped her life, even as she continues to function as a clerk within a postcolonial administration inherited from the French colonial legacy.

It is perhaps within the same understanding of agency between tradition and modernity that Habsu Garba preferred to select a particular version of a Hausa Cinderella tale to retell in the national media. The story itself appraises women's intelligence and agencies for transforming their conditions and those around them. These women's capacities to act upon their lives often involve transgression of boundaries—roles and statuses traditionally ascribed—set by the dominant social order without seeming to violate tradition. Just as Habsu Garba herself endeavors to be a bridge-builder across boundaries of caste, class, sexuality, and gender, her story projects Facima, the main character of the tale, as a healer who subverts gender boundaries through cross-gender dressing and other strategies.

The issue of women's agency has also been explored in this book in relation to the domains of religion (Islam) and politics. Within much of the Islamic world (as in Christianity and Judaism), religious authority in terms of leadership and interpretation of doctrinal texts has been invested in the male clergy. The emergence of *Izala* in Niger, with its appeal to some patriarchal fundamentals of religion, threatened to marginalize women even further in this authorial sphere. But the particular historical juncture of the politics of pluralism in Niger since the early 1990s made it expedient for the Izalaists and other Islamists to appear to promote the visibility of women within Islam. Often in reaction to what they see as the commodification of the woman's body in the West, they have crafted their own model of the "modern Muslim woman" within the new framework of the imported *hijab*.

Naturally, Islamist women of various persuasions seized this opportunity to advance their own understanding of Islamic doctrine and to begin inscribing themselves in the national space as authorities of Islam in their own right. In the process, Islamism in Niger itself became gendered, with women developing understandings and practices of Islam that are distinct from those of their male counterparts, even within the same denominations. Even more important is how women—as teachers, mothers, nurses, government employees, artists, homemakers—have come to invoke shared symbols of Islam in their attempts to reconfigure the space of civic and public life in the nation and their place within it.

Moreover, this development of Muslim women as *agentes religieuses* provided a context where privileged secularist women educated in the mainstream French-based institutions have begun to realize that even in addressing the women's agenda they have to contend with the new force of other Muslim women whose perspectives have been shaped by experiences in Islamic education. But the failure of the Western modernist paradigm led a great number of secularist women to develop a great empathy and eventually a coalition with the Islamist women, and some were even converted to it. But between the religious and the secular there is a whole range of overlapping identities that are performed constantly by women, especially in the urban landscapes, to different degrees in different cultural locations. Whether a woman is predominantly secularist or Islamist in orientation, and regardless of her class, she always draws from the other domain (whether traditional African spirituality, Islam, or secularism) at different times to fulfill different needs. Again, therefore, the idea of the Muslim woman irredeemably chained to some unchanging religious tradition is disputed by reality in the case of Niger.

If some degree of bridge building has been attainable between women across the religious/secular divide, women's coalition in the areas of politics and ethnicity has been more of a challenge. As the tide of political pluralism began to gain momentum in the late 1980s, at a moment of economic decline in the country, the politicization of ethnicity, especially by the elites, reared its ugly head with calamitous consequences. The fact of *brassage sahélien,* an identity construct that has been central in this study, was now put to serious test as the country itself was drawn into an ethnically defined civil war triggered by the so-called Tuareg rebellion. Tuareg women drew from their traditional *Tifinagh* literacy skills to communicate secretly with their male kin in the war front; others drew on traditional songs and recrafted a particular song genre, the *tende,* and used it as an instrument of mobilization; and still others became spokespersons in the international media for the Tuareg cause.

The Nigerien experience of armed conflict, however, incorporated class-specific agendas and interests, and its resolution led to different class-based healing strategies in the construction of a new social order in the aftermath of the conflict. Vested class interests among the women themselves became a constraint in their ability to arrive at a common vision of how to confront patriarchal authoritarianism, political manipulation of identities, and international as well as local forces that profited from the state of the conflicts to the detriment of women and children. Here again women's agencies were certainly in operation, but directed at different goals and interests. As a result, the urban, middle- and upper-class strategies of women's political activism undermined the reality of *brassage sahélien* that defines the nation and failed the Tuareg and non-Tuareg women in the conflict zones. Thus, the postconflict healing process was undertaken without any attempt to take full stock of the circumstances and conditions of crime under which women in the war were subjected. It becomes paramount, therefore, for the newly formed Nigerien chapter of the Coalition of African Women Against War to openly and truthfully address the injustices that were associated with the conflict. This needs to be part of the process of reconciliation and reembracing of *brassage sahélien*, which is again popularly invoked now in political speeches, popular songs and other national performances to promote national unity.

By the time of the National Conference in the early 1990s, whose outcome led to the country's return to the multiparty system of governance, interethnic political elite competition for executive authority was now in its full swing. The concrete manifestation of this competition was revealed by how some of these elite labored to recruit members for their parties on the basis of manipulating ethnoregional symbolisms. Often the behavior of interethnic political elites converges with that of their supporters and at other times diverges from them with unpredictable outcomes. This pattern in Niger is in line with the more general theoretical observations on the behavior of political elites made by Reilly (2001, 177) and Horowitz (1985, 573–74).

In the Nigerien experiences of multipartism, the following were the outcomes of interethnic political elite competition: (a) the awakening of old tensions between so-called *énergie de l'Est* (Eastern energy, in popular understanding known as AMAKA) and *énergie de l'Ouest* (Western energy), and (b) the armed conflict pitting Tuareg and Tubu advocates of regional federalism against the national armed forces in the northeastern regions. In both types of tensions, the political elites tried hard not to use the card of ethnic identity they had been manipulating because they recognized the significant fluidity of that ethnic symbol in the context of *brassage sahélien*. In Niger, it is very common for members of the same family to regard themselves as belonging to different ethnic groups or to belong to many ethnic groups all at once. Moreover, in spite of the divisive rhetoric they adopt in political campaigns, interethnic elite accommodation is quite common, and this is demonstrated by the kinds of political coalitions they form beyond party lines during elections or in parliament. However, the manipulation of such a sensitive symbol as ethnicity for political ends is such that it sometimes influences the rank-and-file followers to resort to more volatile measures than their leaders had intended, but within which they have now become inadvertently embroiled.

As would be expected, elite women—many of whom participated in political party formation from the very beginning—were also heavily implicated in the politics of ethnic manipulation within their respective parties. This can be observed by women's activism within the party and their embrace of the symbols and ideologies of given political parties. Furthermore, they expressed and continue to express heterogeneous responses to the types of tensions and armed conflicts resulting from such political orientations that need to be incorporated into a thorough analysis of women's identity in the nation.

While so far in this conclusion, I have tended to focus mainly on local factors that have influenced the agency of women in Niger, my discussion throughout this book has also revealed that globalization has been an important player. The face of globalization has ranged from the arm of *francophonie* in the postcolonial dispensation to the social and economic conditionalities of the World Bank and IMF and indeed the transnational connections of the Islamist networks. But what has been the actual impact of globalization on the Nigerien sociopolitical terrain? There is a school of thought that globalization is not destructive in its sociocultural effects, but merely transformative. Anthony Giddens seems to belong to this school of thought when he claims that "[globalization] is not just an 'out there' phenomenon, referring solely to the emergence of large-scale world systems, but to transformations in texture of everyday life. It is an 'in here' phenomenon, affecting even intimacies of personal identities. . . . Globalization invades local contexts of action but does not destroy them; on the contrary, new forms of local cultural identity and self expression, are causally bound up with globalizing processes" (Giddens 1990, 367–68). In this respect, the process tests the flexibility of local communities with modern trends and best reflects what Stewart Hall (1994, 299) describes as globalization's power to integrate and connect local and global communities through its force to compress time and space.

While in this book the analysis of the transformations affecting local communities fully supports Giddens's assertion that globalization produces multiple identities, it contests the second part of his definition, which claims that globalization "does not destroy local contexts of action." Take, for example, Niger's incorporation into the global market through the exploitation of uranium. Economic globalization forced an alliance among Western nuclear arms producing interests, the elite of the country, and the military forces. In the process, the average citizens of the country became the target of brutal forces deployed against them each time they resisted their integration into a paradigm of development that was destroying them for the benefit of mining companies and the French-educated and military elites. Uranium companies eventually precipitated the forced sedentarization of nomadic pastoralists such as the Tuareg, Tubu, and Woodabe peoples without providing them with the material means to support their transition into this new life. As indicated at various points in this book, the global politics of uranium eventually led to dramatic demographic, social, economic, and cultural dislocations for large segments of the population in the country. In the process, gender relations have sometimes been transformed in ways that have not been healthy for the social welfare of nomadic pastoralist women. Niger's new visibility in the arena of world politics as the result of a false claim by the United States and Britain that the country recently sold uranium to Iraq's Saddam Hussein has provided a new international context for the revisitation of the broader implications of uranium mining in Niger for the local populations.

Globalization is also inextricably linked to Structural Adjustment Programs (SAP), and their resulting economic disasters have widened sharply the economic gap between social classes. In the process, SAPs have pushed young women into the life of prostitution and trafficking to the Western metropolis. For example, in the summer of 2002, when I was on a fellowship at a German university, I took the opportunity to inquire about the status of African women trafficked into the country, among whom were Nigerien women, and what the laws were regarding this international crime. Some German social science colleagues working on the topic said that some government officials felt more sympathetic with the German men who exploited these foreign human commodities because they felt (and still feel) that, given the national economic problems the country was facing, these men could not afford to support a real family and therefore have real wives. Thus, these officers of the government did not feel that the country's male citizens should be subjected to any further punitive actions, given their prevailing economic conditions. This apologetic attitude toward the crimes of these German men has eventually created room for the victimization and abuse even of those women in the prostitution industry who are legally resident in Germany. Of course, Germany is not the only European metropolitan country that produces these tragic events affecting female African prostitutes.

Locally too, prostitution has become rampant, partly triggered by the state's failure to provide young women with adequate educational and employment opportunities as Structural Adjustment Programs continue to weigh heavily on its resources. Most often the clients of these young prostitutes are the "expatriate workers" from international organizations and local men. Ironically, even the new Islamism with its claimed "purity" also is implicated in the trafficking of women to Islamic countries or Islamic communities located within the West. This is the kind of prostitution that operates with a new discourse of understanding of the "permissible" marriages within Islam, and in particular the *mut'a*—the practice of temporary "contractual" marriages for a specified interval of time as short as a day (Haeri 1989). Thus, a good number of Nigerien Muslim women now travel to places like Nigeria, Dubai, Saudi Arabia, and Western countries to serve as "comfort" women for a very temporary period for the new Islamist men located or traveling abroad. All these developments are outcomes of globalization whose impacts on the very fabric of Nigerien society cannot be described as anything less than destructive.

It is perhaps true that many of these African women working in the prostitution industry especially abroad, have been able to support their parents and even finance the education of their siblings (most often brothers) either in Africa itself or in the West, even as they themselves live a life of hell in the sexual underground. But it would be a big mistake to romanticize the benefits of this kind of "choice" while ignoring its disastrous consequences for the women themselves and the society at large, ranging from being trapped in criminality in the drug underworld, to exposure to HIV-AIDS and a variety of sexually transmitted diseases, to the murder of violated young women.

An area of the impact of globalization in Niger that continues to unfold in complex ways, and which has been discussed in parts of this book, is that of fashion. Since the late 1980s there have been the violent clashes between Alphadi—a Nigerien who has become a celebrity in Western centers of high fashion and who is said to have brought the country out of anonymity in Western geographic consciousness in search of native erotic exoticism—and the militant *Izala* Islamists over the hosting of a beauty pageant accompanied by dress fashion shows. Contrary to popular perception, these clashes have little to do with religiosity. In this book I argue that they are rather conflicts between two capitalist orthodoxies that use Westernism and Islamism as networking principles to prey on young Muslim women's consumption of the products (from clothes to social values and styles to educational interests) they impose on them. Clashes over market interests produce casualties since each competitor will try to protect profits and in this case women are the most afflicted in this duel. While pro-Alphadi fashion and Western designer companies cater mainly to Western-oriented young women, Islamist merchants' trade involves the market of clothes and other products imported from Arab-Islamic and Islamic Asian countries intended to shape a new image of the Muslim woman, but for a commercial motive.

In reality, however, these two types of fashion (the Western and new Islamist) promote the same conception of the woman's body in relation to male desire. As Fouad Zakaria notes with regard to the duality of spirit and body in the Arab world: "A veiled body supposedly, attains a higher level of [spirituality] than one that is unveiled. . . . An unveiled woman vulgarly exposes her body with great skills for various purposes, not the least of which is to draw attention and admiration. But we may observe that a strong relation exists between wearing the thickest of veils and the most vulgar display of the body. They may be considered two sides of the same coin, a positive and a negative face. They both place great emphasis on the importance of the body and the insistence that is a perennial object of desire and constant source of temptation" (Zakaria 1998, 31). In short, then, both ideologies seek to force women to think of their existence and their reality only in terms of their bodies. But as shown in this book, women in Niger have become very aware of the patriarchal ideologies behind these contested capitalist fashions and often subvert their symbolisms for their own ends.

While the violence promoted by the Islamists in the country against Alphadi's fashion show must be condemned seriously for its violation of human rights, it is equally important not to ignore the nonextremist constituency in the population that does not welcome the Alphadi-Western beauty fashion industry, just as it is fought against by women and men in India and even by some women in the West. The latter clearly see the exploitative nature of this fashion trend above and beyond its effects on local cultures. Indeed, they see in it a fetishization and commodification of local symbols and motifs for Western and Westernized appetites for the exotic.

For those scholars and women's rights activists upset by the protest against the bikini-tight fashion dumped on Niger, the conflict in reality becomes a productive field of academic research while the real problems confronting the society become trivialized. Since the latter are concerned about violation of human rights, for example, is it possible that the understanding of African women's human rights could be extended to incorporate an understanding of the link between the trafficking of African (Muslim) women in Western brothels and the HIV-AIDS pandemic among the targeted communities? This is the young African women's right to proper health and conditions of existence. It would also be necessary to study the serial marriages and divorces and remarriages, as well as other serious violations of Muslim women's rights promoted by the Islamist paradigm under the pretext of combating Muslim women's attraction to Westernism. After all, Westernism and Islamism are two sides of the same coin of globalist capitalist convergence on the Nigerien local scene, both of which seek to exploit women. The findings of such studies would serve to empirically test Giddens's assumption about the malleability of local contexts of action by globalization.

It is probably undeniable that, for a minority, globalization does indeed transform the texture of their lives without destroying them. However, there are numerous others who are not only wounded, but are subjected to extinction—as is the case of young women caught up in the transnational drug subculture in Western metropolis. These realities confronting the powerless African women both locally and abroad make Giddens's and Stewart Hall's notion of healthy interconnection of world cultures a romantic kiss of death between neocolonial subjects and the subject of their domination.

What remains intact locally, then, is not determined by the positive effects of globalization, but rather by local cultures resisting annihilation by this new hegemonic force. This is partly why the new African Muslim modernists resist Western hegemonic modernity by refusing to absorb all its normative recipes. Furthermore, that local resistance persists in incorporating local idioms that are precisely judged as "undesirable" by the West. These processes of crafting local alternative modernities demonstrate awareness of the connection with "real" or "imagined" traditional heritage (with all its problematics) as fundamental to the struggle against Western neocolonial capitalist domination promoted under the promise of economic globalization. And for the Muslim women in Niger, the alternative modernities they are struggling to construct have to contend creatively with both local and global hegemonies of the patriarchal capitalist agenda.

Appendixes

Notes

References

Index

Appendix A

Abdoul Salam's Dance Song *Tigyedimma:* Transregional and Transethnic Sahelian Brassage

Armen buzuwa jidali ne	Marrying a Tuareg woman is such a tough business
Armen buzuwa da kai tsada	Marrying a Tuareg woman is quite expensive
Armen buzuwa jidali ne	Marrying a Tuareg woman is such a tough business
Armen buzuwa da kai tsada	Marrying a Tuareg woman is quite expensive
Da mai rak'umi dakana	Only those who own the noble camel
Sai mai turkud'I gwanin tsada	Or those with the most expensive [indigo] turban
Ko sarkin rawar *Tigyedimma*	Or the master dancer of *Tigyedimma* [drum] [can marry a Tuareg woman]

In an ka ce *Tigyedimma*	When people talk about *Tigyedimma*
In an ka ce *Tigyedimma*	When people talk about *Tigyedimma*
In an ka ce *Tigyedimma*	When people talk about *Tigyedimma*
Kama anka ce da Buzu	It is like calling upon a Tuareg person
Buzun da yake cikin daji	A Tuareg from the rural homestead
Ra nan za ya je *Tigyedimma*	That day to step in for *Tigyedimma*
Buzun da yake cikin birni	As for a Tuareg living in the city
Ra nan za ya je *Tigyedimma*	that day he or she will step in for *Tigyedimma*
Domin shi kid'in *Tigyedimma*	Because we inherited the *Tigyedimma* dance drum
Mun gado shi don ga kakanni	From our forebears
Ke nan ba mu yadda gadonmu	Therefore we won't throw away our heritage
Ke nan ba mu yadda gadonmu	Therefore we won't throw away our heritage
(Ya Allah)	Oh! God!
In an ka ce *Tigyedimma*	When people talk about *Tigyedimma*
Kaman an ka ce da Buzu	It is like calling upon a Tuareg person
Buzun da yake cikin daji	A Tuareg from the rural homestead
Ra nan za ya je *Tigyedimma*	That day to step in for *Tigyedimma*
Buzun da yake cikin birni	As for a Tuareg living in the city
Ra nan za ya je *Tigyedimma*	that day he or she will step in for *Tigyedimma*
Domin shi kid'in *Tigyedimma*	Because we inherited the *Tigyedimma* dance drum
Mun gado shi don ga kakanni	From our forebears
Ke nan ba mu yadda gadonmu	Therefore we won't throw away our heritage
(Gaskiya!)	Truthfully!
Ke nan ba mu yadda gadonmu	Therefore we won't throw away our heritage
Hausawa suna *Tigyedimma*	The Hausa people perform *Tigyedimma*
Zabarma suna *Tigyedimma*	The Zabarma people perform *Tigyedimma*
Hullani suna *Tigyedimma*	The Fulani people perform *Tigyedimma*

Barebari suna *Tigyedimma*	The Kanuri people perform *Tigyedimma*
Tubawa suna *Tigyedimma*	The Tubu people perform *Tigyedimma*
Larabawa suna *Tigyedimma*	The Arab people perform *Tigyedimma*
Balle mu abun mu gado ne	Let alone we the ones for whom it is a heritage
Agadaz na je wurin wasa	I traveled to Agadez to perform
Can na ga Buzuwa da kyawo	It is there that I saw a beautiful Tuareg woman
Gashin nata sai ga banta	Her hair falls to her back
. . . .	. . . .
Da tsananin tana da kyawonta	Because of her striking beauty
Suna 'yen gari suka sa mata	The people of the town gave her a nickname
Na so su ba in aura	I wanted them to give her to me
Na san ba su ba ni	I know they won't give [her] away to me
Na so su ba in aura	I wish they would let me marry her
Na san ba su ba ni	I know they won't give [her] away to me
(A'a, ba su ba ka)	(No! they won't let you [have her])
Ba ni da rak'umi da kala	I do not possess a noble camel
Ba ni da turkud'I gwanin tsada	I do not possess an expensive [indigo] turban
Ba ni da rak'umi da kala	I do not possess a noble camel
Ba ni da turkud'I gwanin tsada	I do not possess an expensive [indigo] turban
Sanan ba ni kid'in *Tigyedimma*	In addition, my drum is not *Tigyedimma* drum
Balle in yi rawar su aura min	For me to dance to it, for them to marry her to me
Ke nan ba su ba in aura	Therefore they won't give her away to me to marry
Ke nan ba su ba ni aura	Therefore they won't give her away to me to marry
. . .	. . .
Haba! Maryama. Haba! Maryama	Please! Maryama, Please! Maryama.
Tashi ki zo ki d'an taka	Stand up and help me out with some dance steps
Haba! Maryama. Haba! Maryama	Please! Maryama. Please! Maryama
Tashi ki zo ki d'an taka min	Stand up and help me out some dance steps
Ki tashi ki taka Maryama	Stand up and dance some steps, Maryama

Tunda dai kin gado	Since you inherited it
Ki tashi ki taka Maryama	Stand up and dance some steps, Maryama
Ba a kumyal gado	One cannot shy away from one's heritage
Gado abun bege ne	A heritage is to be celebrated
Kuma gado abun shawa	And a heritage is something to be proud of
Ki tashi ki taka Maryama	Stand up and dance Maryama
Tunda ke gado	Because you inherited it
Ki tashi ki taka Maryama	Stand up and dance Maryama
Ba a kumyal gado	One cannot shy away from one's heritage
Gado wuri in yak'I	A heritage is needed in wartime
Gado wuri takalmi	A heritage needs some shoes/steps
Ba'adare Buzu ne Marie	Ba'adare is a Tuareg, Marie
Haba Maryama	Please! Maryama
Ba'adare Buzu ne Marie	Ba'adare is a Tuareg, Maryama
Ki tashi ki taka	Stand up and dance some steps
Haba Maryama	Please, Maryama
Haba Maryama	Please, Maryama
Marie ki zo ki d'an taka nan	Marie, come on and dance some steps here
Haba Maryama	Please, Maryama
Haba Maryama	Please, Maryama
Marie ki zo ki d'an taka nan	Marie, come on and dance some steps here
Samarin Adar	Young men of Adar
Da ku samarin Abzin	And it is for you, young men of Abzin
Samarin Adar	Young men of Adar
Da ku samarin Abzin	And it is for you, young men of Abzin
Ga kid'inku na Adar	Here is your drumming of Adar
Na ce	I say
Ga kid'inku na Abzin	Here is your drumming from Abzin
Ga kid'inku na Adar	Here is your drumming of Adar
Na ce	I say
Ga kid'inku na gado	Here is your inherited drum
Ga kid'inku na Abzin	Here is your drumming from Abzin
Na ce	I say
Ga kid'inku na gado	Here is your inherited drum

Na ce	I say
Ga kid'inku na gado	Here is your inherited drum
(Ayiiii . . . Ayiiiiii!)	(Ayiiii . . . Ayiiiiii!)
Tigyedimma	*Tigyedimma*
Tigyedimma	*Tigyedimma*
Tigyedimma	*Tigyedimma*
Eheeeeeeeeeeeeeeeee	Eheeeeeeeeeeeeeeeee
Azaq wa Tigyedim mada	Here is your inherited drum
Azale wa Tigyedim mada	Here is your inherited drum
Azaq wa Tigyedim mada	Here is your inherited drum
Azale wa Tigyedim mada	Here is your inherited drum
Tigyedimma	*Tigyedimma*
Tigyedimma	*Tigyedimma*
Tigyedimma	*Tigyedimma*

Appendix B

Biographical Sketch of Dr. Malama Zeinab Sidi Baba Haidara

Malama Zeinab Haidara was the first woman to hold a doctorate degree in Islamic theology in Niger Republic.[1] She had distinguished herself in her media programs by openly challenging the patriarchal interpretation of Islam as promoted by a dominant male clergy who had enjoyed, prior to the democratization era, a monopoly of Islamic radio and television broadcasting programs. Malama Zeinab Haidara was a staunch voice against premature girl marriage, the exploitation of young Qur'anic students—*talib*—by their greedy *marabouts*, and the violation of women's rights through a misreading of Islam. Nonetheless, Dr. Malama Zeinab Haidara was not an intellectual that could at face value be described as "feminist" according to her biographers.

The ninth child of a big family, Malama was born in Nigeria. After the premature death of her father when she was young, she was adopted by one of her uncles who lived in Ghana where she attended Qur'anic school. As an adolescent, she moved to Burkina Faso where the majority of her family members live. There she enrolled in a formal modern Arabic and Islamic studies school up to the high school. After graduation, Malama Zeinab benefited from a scholarship that allowed her to attend the Islamic University of Kuwait where she specialized in both Classical Arabic and Islamic theology.

Upon her return to Burkina Faso, she taught both Arabic and Islamic studies. Dr. Malama Zeinab moved to Niger Republic where her husband, a graduate from China and the Tibet school of martial arts, opened a school to train Nigeriens in Niamey. Malama Zeinab herself was a dedicated practitioner of martial arts, Kung Fu, and Yoga. She was also a devoted mother to her two children and to the community children whom she trained in street theatre.

Till her premature death from a car accident in 1998, Dr. Malama Zeinab had been the target of violent attacks from misogynist Islamic male clergy and patriarchal secularist men of various shades opposed to her uncompromising rereading of Islam with regard to gender issues in Niger Republic. Following her legacy, many Nigerien women have become committed to speaking out publicly on women's and children's rights. While her tragic death was silently welcomed by extremist Islamist clergy, the majority of (Muslim) women and men committed to justice and equity in Islam and in the society at large continue to mourn her premature departure and consider the cynical extremists' reaction as an indication of her victorious impact to induce positive change in the Islamic psyche of the nation.

Notes

Introduction

1. The text of Abdoul Salam's song entitled "Tigyedimma," which celebrates the common ancestry of the Tuareg and Adarawa, is in appendix A.

2. For a more detailed discussion on European colonial reconfiguration of the African marriage structure and its implications for inheritance, see Quayson (2000, 119–31) and Oppong (1981). Even though Quayson and Oppong describe this colonial experience in the Anglophone region—Ghana and Nigeria—their observations are equally valid for the francophone region of West Africa under French colonialism.

3. *Madarasa* is the term for the modernized Islamic schools, whereas *makaranta* refers to the more traditional Qur'anic schools. However, the two are often employed interchangeably.

Chapter 1. When *Kuble* (Seclusion) Literacy Invades the Electronic Space

1. Of course, the *kuble* (*kulle* in Nigeria) or *purdha* tradition of seclusion of women in Islamic societies was not practiced during the life of the prophet Muhammad, nor of the four caliphs who succeeded him. And we know that writing in Arabic predated Islam. But within much of Islamic Africa, these two practices came with the spread of Islam in the region.

2. The works of Aliyu na Mangi and his famous poem "Imfiraji" are discussed in detail by Graham Furniss (1996, 208–9).

3. *Ilimi:* "knowledge/education/science/intelligence," recited by Malama A'ishatu's students (recording I collected from the Niger National Radio Broadcasting System, summer 1996).

4. Finally, Callaway and Creevey (1994) cite scholars who provide a definition of what Islamic learning is in comparison to Western understanding of learning, but do not include other researchers whose definitions of the same subject matter offer alternative understandings. These include scholars such as Brian V. Street (1993), Stefan Reichmuth (1993), or Fatima Mernissi (1987a, 1987b).

5. The Qur'an is divided into sixty equal-length sections to ease memorization and reading process.

Chapter 2. Women and the Political Economy of Education

1. See Masquelier (2001, 264) for an illustration of Bori leaders in Muslim attire in Mauri land of Dogondoutchi, Niger. And Echard (1991, 215) for a discussion of *Halima*, a female spirit with a Muslim name.

2. See S. Muhammad Umar (2001); for a discussion of similar Islamic education in Northern Nigeria, see pp. 129–30.

3. See Federici, Caffentzis, and Alidou (2000) and Olivier Meunier (2000) for a detailed analysis of the impacts of World Bank and International Monetary Funds' Structural Adjustment of education in Africa in general and in Niger more particularly.

4. The first *medersa Franco-Arab* in Say (near Niamey) was initiated by President Djibo Bakary in 1957 with the hope to rally electoral votes from the religious communities (Meunier 2000, 71).

5. See Robert Glew (1996) for a detailed description of Islamic associations in Niger.

Chapter 5. Islamisms, the Media, and Women's Public Discursive Practices

1. The 1998 U.S. Embassy census indicated that there are 80 percent Muslims, 15 percent Christians, and 5 percent traditionalists in Niger. Of course, most data about religious demographics must be read with a little caution, given the political undertone of the issue in most counties of the world and also given the political orientation of the census career.

2. *Tijaniyya* is one and the predominant mystical order of Sufi Islam in Niger. The order is the Gadiyya. For a more detailed discussion of Sufi orders in Niger, see Grégoire (1993, 106–15).

3. "Fundamentalism" when linked to Islam has conjured up so much negativity without offering any adequate explanatory account of its forms and substance in all its diversity. When used in this essay, it refers to the militant extremist expression of the Islamic revivalist movement experienced in the Muslim world.

4. This decree was first applied to any potential political opponent of the government. This included virtually all the key politicians from the Hamani Diori regime who were released from prison. It was later extended to *Malams* and their young disciples, potential opponents within the ranks in the military, and was reinforced by the State engineered xenophobia that created suspicion among and between social groups in the nation.

5. The Izala movement has been studied more extensively in Nigeria, and the range of works on it include, for example Umar (1993, 167–78), Kane (2003), Watts (1996), to cite a few.

6. Elowe Arlene MacLeod's (2001, 396) concept of "accommodating protest" as she applies it to the renewed veiling among low middle-class urban Egyptian women in Cairo is inspired by a new reading of Gramsci's account of the multifaceted aspects of the subordinate's resistance to hegemonic coercive attempts. (See Lila Abu-Lughod's [1998] discussion of how forms of resistance from subordinate groups, such as those adopted by Bedouin women in Egypt, can inform us about the forms of power operating within the culture.)

7. Comments taken from an interview done with a woman (whose name I am concealing), former minister in Niger Republic, winter of 1998.

8. Interview with Mamane Shitu Garanda (Nigerien immigrant) conducted April 6, 2001, New Brunswick, New Jersey.

9. Interviews conducted in Dakoro, winter 1998.

10. In Niger, both minority Christians and Arna (Hausa, Songhai) are culturally, if not religiously, assimilated into Muslim cultural identification which is visibly reflected in the adoption of some names such as Musa for "Moses," Yacouba for "Jacob," Mariama for "Marie," or through both linguistic and the other forms of interpersonal social interactions.

11. For an account of the political dynamism of the Association of Niger's Women in Maradi (eastern Niger), see Barbara Cooper (1995).

12. See Fatima Mernissi (1996).

13. Some of the women who are very active in the Islamicist movement in Niger are graduates from the bilingual French-Arabic schools known as Franco-Arab schools in most of the francophone Afro-Islamic countries. The training in these schools involves both the teaching of Islamic religious education, the use of Arabic as the main medium of instruction of the French curriculum, and the use of French as a subject rather than the main medium of instruction. The graduates from Niger's Franco-Arab schools have been marginalized for a long time and have suffered discrimination from all sectors of employment as well as from proper recognition in higher education in spite of their qualifications as a result of the francophile favoritism.

14. Malama Zeinab Haidara died in a car accident while on a UN family planning campaign touring the interior of the country in 2001.

Chapter 6. Through the Eyes of Agaisha

1. This chapter does not cover the transnational dimension of the Tuareg Armed Resistance in North Africa and West Africa. Its main focus is the impact of the conflict on women in Niger Republic. The place and role of women, especial Tuareg women, in the national conflict has not been the main focus in either Dayak (1992) or Salif (1993).

Appendix B. Biographical Sketch of Dr. Malama Zeinab Haidara

1. My biographical sketch of Dr. Malama Zeinab Haidara draws a great deal from essays written about her by various newspapers and Nigerien women's organizations both during her lifetime as well as from eulogies in her honor. I thank Mrs. Zeinabou Hadari for drawing my attention to these records.

References

Abu-Lughod, Lila, ed. 1998. *Remaking Women: Feminism and Modernity in the Middle East.* Princeton: Princeton University Press.

Abu Manga, Al-Amin. 1985. *Baajankaro: A Fulani Epic from Sudan.* Berlin: Dietrich Reimer.

———. 1986. *Fulfulde in the Sudan: Process of Adaptation to Arabic.* Berlin: Dietrich Reimer.

———. 1999. *Hausa in the Sudan: Process of Adaptation to Arabic.* Köln: R. Köppe.

Adamou, Aboubacar. 2002. *Agadez et sa région: Contribution à l'étude du Sahel et du Sahara Nigériens.* Etudes Nigériennes 44. Niamey, Niger: Institut de Recherche en Sciences Humaines (IRSH); (1979, Ph.D. dissertation, Université de Lyon).

Ahmed, Leila. 1992. *Women and Gender in Islam.* New Haven: Yale University Press.

———. 1999. *Border Passage: From Cairo to America—A Woman's Journey.* New York: Farrar, Straus and Giroux.

Alcoff, Linda. 1988. "Cultural Feminism versus Post-structuralism: The Identity Crisis in Feminist Theory." In *Reconstructing the Academy: Women's Education and Women's Studies,* ed. Elizabeth Minnich, Jean O'Barr, and Rachel Rosenfeld, p. 283–86. Chicago: University of Chicago Press.

Al-Ghazali, Zaynab. 1977/1986. *Ayyam min Hayati* (Days from my life). Cairo: Dar al-Shuruq.

———. 1994. *Nazarat fi Kitab Allah* (Views on the Book of God). Cairo: Dar al-Shuruq.

Ali, Abdullah Yusuf. 1993. *The Holy Qur'an: Translation and Commentary*. Beyrut: Dar al-fikr.

Alidou, Ousseina. 1988. "Esquisse linguistique d'une langue dite 'Mixte': Le Tasawaq d'Ingall." Master's thesis, University of Niamey.

———. 2002. "Gender, Narrative Space and Modern Hausa Literature." *Research in African Literatures* 33 (2): 137–53.

———. 2003. "The Emergence of Hausa Written Literature." In *History of African and Caribbean Literature,* ed. Abiola Irele and Simon Gikandi, 329–356. Cambridge: Cambridge University Press.

Al Zeera, Zahra. 2001. "Paradigm Shifts in the Social Sciences in the East and West." In *Knowledge across Cultures,* ed. Ruth Hayhoe and Julia Pan, 55–74. Hong Kong: The University of Hong Kong.

Amadiume, Ifi. 1998. *Re-Inventing Africa: Matriarchy, Religion and Culture*. London: Zed Books.

Appadurai, Arjun. 1990. "Disjuncture and Difference in the Global Cultural Economy." *Public Culture* 2: 1–24.

———. 1996. *Modernity at Large: Cultural Dimensions of Globalization*. Minneapolis: University of Minnesota Press.

Aschcroft, Bill, Gareth Griffiths, and Helen Tiffin. 1995. *The Postcolonial Studies Reader*. New York: Routledge.

Barreteau, Daniel, and Ali Daouda. 1997. *Systèmes éducatifs et multilinguisme au Niger: Résultats scolaires, double flux*. Niamey, Niger: ORSTOM-Université Abdou Moumouni.

Bayard, Mariama Gamatchié. 1999. Interview in Reuters. WebInfo.

Beik, Janet. 1987. *Hausa Theatre in Niger: A Contemporary Oral Art*. New York: Garland.

Ben Wahab, Aichatou. 1999. "Contribution à la Conférence tenue à Dakar (1998) sur les femmes dans période de reconstruction de l'après-guerre en Afrique." *Bulletin of Africa Concerned Scholars: Women and War* 55/56 (Spring/Summer): 55–57.

Bernal, Victoria. 1994. "Gender, Culture, and Capitalism: Women and the Remaking of Islamic 'Tradition' in a Sudanese Village." *Comparative Studies in Society and History* 36 (1): 36–37.

Boven, M. 1983. "Muslim Women in the Periphery: The West African Sahel." In *Women in Islamic Societies*, ed. B. Tuas, 66–103. London and Malmo: Scandinavian Institute of Asian Studies.

Boyd, Jean. 1989. *The Caliph's Sister: Nana Asma'u, 1793–1865, Teacher, Poet, and Islamic Leader*. London and Totowa, N.J.: Case.

———. 2001. "Distance Learning from Purdah in Nineteenth-Century Northern Nigeria: The Work of Asma'u Fodiyo." *Journal of African Cultural Studies* 14 (June): 7–22.

Boyd, Jean, and M. Last. 1985. "The Role of Women as 'Agents Religieux' in Sokoto." *Revue Canadienne d'Études Africaines* 29 (2): 283–300.

Boyd, Jean, and Beverly Mack. 1997. *Collected Works of Nana Asma'u*. East Lansing: Michigan State University Press.

Brenner, Louis, ed. 1993. *Muslim Identity and Social Change in Sub-Saharan Africa*. London: Hurst.

Brenner, Louis, and M. Last. 1985. "The Role of Language in West African Islam." *Africa* 55 (4): 443–46.

Brown, G. N., and M. Hiskett, eds. 1975. *Conflict and Harmony in Education in Tropical Africa*. London: George Allen and Unwin.

Busia, Abena. 2003. "In Search of Chains without Iron: On Sisterhood, History and the Politics of Location." In *African Women and Feminism: Reflecting on the Politics of Sisterhood*, ed. Oyèrónkẹ́ Oyewùmí, p. 256–67. Trenton, N.J.: Africa World Press.

Butler, Judith. 1987. "Variations on Sex and Gender: Beauvoir, Wittig and Foucault." In *Feminism as Critique: Essays on the Politics of Gender in Late-Capitalist Societies*, ed. Seyla Benhabib and Drucilla Cornell, 128–42. Cambridge: Polity Press and Blackwell.

Callaway, Barbara, and Lucy Creevey. 1994. *The Heritage of Islam: Women, Religion, and Politics in West Africa*. Boulder: Lynne Rienner.

Chafe, Wallace. 1982. "Integration and Involvement in Speaking, Writing and Oral Literature." In *Spoken and Writing Language: Exploring Orality and Literacy*, ed. Deborah Tannen, 35–53. Norwood, N.J.: Ablex.

———. 1994. *Discourse, Consciousness, and Time: The Flow and Displacement of Conscious Experience in Speaking and Writing*. Chicago: University of Chicago Press.

Charlick, Robert. 1991. *Niger Personal Rule and Survival in the Sahel*. Boulder: Westview Press.

Chittick, William C. 1995. "Mi'raj." In *The Oxford Encyclopedia of the Modern Islamic World*. ed. John L. Esposito, 3: 116–17. Oxford: Oxford University Press.

Chtatou, Mohamed. 1992. *Using Arabic Script in Writing the Languages of the People of Muslim Africa*. Rabat (Morocco): Mohamed V University, Publications of the Institute of African Studies.

Climo, Shirley. 1989. *The Egyptian Cinderella*. Illustrated by Ruth Heller. New York: HarperCollins.

Coles, Catherine, and Beverly Mack, eds. 1991. *Hausa Women in the Twentieth Century*. Madison: University of Wisconsin Press.

Comaroff, Jean, and John Comaroff. 1993. *Modernity and Its Malcontents: Rituals and Power in Postcolonial Africa*. Chicago: University of Chicago Press.

Conway, Jill Kerr, and Susan C. Bourque, eds. 1993. *The Politics of Women Education: Perspectives from Africa, Asia, Africa, and Latin America*. Ann Arbor: University of Michigan Press.

Cooper, Barbara M. 1995. "The Politics of Difference and Women's Associations in Niger: Of 'Prostitutes,' the Public, and the Politics." *Signs* 20 (4): 851–82.

———. 1997. *Marriage in Maradi: Gender and Culture in a Hausa Society in Niger, 1900–1989*. Portsmouth, N.H.: Heinemann; Oxford: J. Currey.

———. 1998. "Gender and Religion in Hausaland: Variations in Islamic Practice in Niger and Nigeria." In *Women in Muslim Societies: Diversity within Unity*, ed. L. Herbert Bodman and Nayereh Tohidi, 21–38. Boulder: Lynne Rienner.

Coulon, Christian. 1988. "Women, Islam and *Baraka*." In *Charisma and Brotherhood in African Islam*, ed. Donal Cruise O'Brien and Christian Coulon, 113–30. Oxford: Clarendon Press.

Cox, Marian Roalfe. 1967. *Cinderella: Three Hundred and Forty-Five Variants of Cinderella, Castskin, and Cap o'Rushes (with an Introduction by Andrew Lang)* (1893). New York: Kraus Reprint.

Crehan, Stewart. 2001. "Patronage, the State, and Ideology in Zambian Theatre." In *Politics and Performance: Theatre, Poetry and Songs in Southern Africa*, ed. Liz Gunner, 251–72. Johannesburg: Witwatersrand University Press.

Dalla Costa, Maria-Rosa. 1974. *The Power of Women and the Subversion of the Community*. Bristol: Falling Wall Press.

Dan Inna, Chaibou. 1978–79. "La théatrilité en pays hawsa." Master's thesis, Université Nationale de Côte d'Ivoire.

Dayak, Mano. 1992. *Touarègues: la tragédie*. Paris: Lattès.

de Foucald, Charles. 1920. *Poesie Touaregue de l'Ahaggar*. Paris.

Diarra, Fatouma Agnès. 1971. *Femmes africaines en devenir: Les Femmes Zarma du Niger*. Paris: Éditions Anthropos.

Diawara, Idrissa. 1988. "Cultures nigériennes et éducation: domaine Zarma-Songhay et Hawsa." Paris: *Présence Africaine* 148: 9–19.

Diawara, Manthia. 1995. *Rouch in Reverse* [video]. Formation Films. San Francisco: California Newsreel.

———. 1998. *In Search of Africa*. Cambridge, Mass.: Harvard University Press.

Djibo, Hadiza. 2001. *La participation des femmes africaines à la vie politique: Les exemples du Sénégal et du Niger*. Paris: L'Harmattan.

Djité, Paulin. 1987. "Francophonie in Africa; Some Obstacles." *Journal of the Washington Academy of Sciences* 77 (1): 40–46

———. 1990. "The Place of African Languages in the Revival of the Francophonie Movement." *International Journal of the Sociology of Language* 86: 87–102.

———. 1991. "Les langues africaines dans la nouvelles francophonie." *Language Problems and Language Planning* 14 (Spring): 20–32.

———. 1992. "The French Revolution and the French Language: A Paradox?" *Language Problems and Language Planning* 16 (Summer): 163–77.

———. 1993. "Francophonie: Gain d'Humanité ou Perte d'Identité." *Language Problems and Language Planning* 17 (3): 254–64.

Doumato, Abdella Eleanor. 2000. *Getting God's Ear: Women, Islam, and Healing in Saudi Arabia and the Gulf*. New York: Columbia University Press.

Dunbar, Roberta Ann. 1970. "Damagaram (Zinder, Niger) 1812–1906: The History of a Central Sudanic Kingdom." PhD diss., University of California at Los Angeles.

———. 1991. "Islamic Values, the State and 'the Development of Women': The Case of Niger." In *Hausa Women in the Twentieth Century*, ed. Catherine Coles and Beverly Mack, 69–89. Madison: University of Wisconsin Press.

———. 2002. "Comparative Reflections on Muslim Women, Religion, and the Shaping of Political Action." Paper presented at the African Studies Association Annual Meeting, Washington, D.C., December 5–8.

Dundes, Alan. 1982. *Cinderella, a Folklore Casebook*. New York: Garland.

Echard, Nicole. 1991. "Gender Relationships and Religion: Women in the Hausa Bori of Ader, Niger." In *Hausa Women in the Twentieth Century*, ed. Catherine Coles and Beverly Mack, 207–20. Madison: University of Wisconsin Press.

Egbo, Benedicta. 2000. *Gender, Literacy and Life Chances in Sub-Saharan Africa*. The Language and Education Library. Vol. 16. Clevedon: Multilingual Matters.

Eickelman, F. Dale. 1978. "The Art of Memory: Islamic Education and Its Social Reproduction." *Comparative Studies in Society and History* 20: 485–516.

———. 1985. *Knowledge and Power in Morocco: The Education of a Twentieth-Century Notable*. Princeton: Princeton University Press.

Eickelman, F. Dale, and James Piscatori. 1996. *Muslim Politics*. Princeton: Princeton University Press.

Ekkhard, Wolff, and Ousseina Alidou. 2001. "On the Non-Linear Ancestry of Tasawaq (Niger) or: How 'Mixed' Can a Language Be?" In special issue on Historical Language Contact in Africa edited by Derek Nurse, *Sprache und Geschichte in Afrika (SUGIA)* 16/17: 523–74.

El Saadawi, Nawal. 1991. *My Travels around the World*. London: Minerva.

———. 1997. *The Nawal El Saadawi Reader*. London: Zed.

———. 1999. *Daughter of Isis*. London: Zed.

Emeagwali, Gloria, ed. 1995. *Women Pay the Price: Structural Adjustment in Africa and the Caribbean*. Trenton, N.J.: Africa World Press.

Europa World Year Book. 2002. "Niger: Introductory Survey." Vol. 2. London: Europa Publisher Ltd.

Fairclough, N. 1989. *Language and Power*. New York: Longman.

Fanon, Frantz. 1967. *A Dying Colonialism*. New York: Grove.

Farman-Farmaian, Sattareh. 1992. *Daughters of Persia: A Woman's Journey from Her Father's Harem through the Islamic Revolution*. New York: Crown.

Federici, Silvia, George Caffentzis, and Ousseina Alidou, eds. 2000. *A Thousand Flowers: Social Struggles against Structural Adjustment in African Universities*. Trenton, N.J.: Africa World Press.

Fisher, H. J. 1961. "Early Muslim Western Education in West Africa." *The Muslim World* 2 (4): 288–98.

Foucault, Michel. 1980. *Knowledge/Power: Selected Interviews and Other Writings in 1972–1977*. Translated and edited by Gordon Colin. Brighton, Sussex: Harvester Press.

Furniss, Graham. 1996. *Poetry, Prose and Popular Culture in Hausa*. Washington, D.C.: Smithsonian Institution Press.

Gado, Boubé. 1980. *Le Zarmatarey: Contribution à l'histoire des populations d'entre Niger et Dallol Mawri*. Niamey, Niger: Institut de Recherche en Sciences Humaines (IRSH).

Gee, James Paul. 1996. *Social Linguistics and Literacies: Ideology in Discourses*. London and Bristol, Penn.: Taylor and Francis.

Gervais, Myriam. 1997. "Niger: Regime Change, Economic Crisis, Perpetuation of Privilege." In *Political Reform in Francophone Africa*, ed. F. John Clark and David E. Gardinier, p. 86–107. Boulder, Colo.: Westview Press.

Giddens, Anthony. 1990. *The Consequences of Modernity*. Cambridge: Polity.

Gilman, Lisa. 2001. "Purchasing Praise: Women, Dancing, and Patronage in Malawi Party Politics." *Africa Today* 48 (Winter): 42–64.

Gilroy, Paul. 1993. *The Black Atlantic: Modernity and Double Consciousness*. Cambridge, Mass.: Harvard University Press.

Gladwin, Christina, ed. 1991. *Structural Adjustment and African Women Farmers*. Gainesville: University of Florida Press, Center for African Studies.

Glew, Robert. 1996. "Islamic Associations in Niger." *Islam et Société au Sud du Sahara* 10: 187–204.

Goody, Jack. 1987. *The Interface between the Written and the Oral*. Cambridge: Cambridge University Press.

Gough, John. 1990. "Rivalry, Rejection, and Recovery." *Children's Literature in Education* 21 (June): 99–107.

Greenberg, Joseph. 1943. "The Impact of Islam on a Sudanese Religion in Hawsa Country." *American Ethnological Society, Mémoire* 10.

Grégoire, Emmanuel. 1991. "Accumulation marchande et propagation de l'Islam en milieu urbain: le cas de Maradi (Niger)." *Islam et Sociétés au Sud du Sahara* (Paris) 5: 43–55.

———. 1992. *The Alhazai of Maradi: Traditional Hausa Merchants in a Changing Sahelien City*. Edited and translated by Benjamin H. Hardy. Boulder, Colo.: L. Rienner.

———. 1993. "Islam and the Identity of Merchants in Maradi (Niger)." In *Muslim Identity and Social Change in Sub-Saharan Africa*, ed. Louis Brenner, 106–15. Bloomington: Indiana University Press.

Grossberg, Lawrence. 1989. "Pedagogy in the Present: Politics, Postmodernity, and the Popular." In *Popular Culture: Schooling and Everyday Life*, ed. Henry Giroux and Roger I. Simon, 91–116. Granby: Bergin and Garvey.

Gunner, Liz, ed. 2001. *Politics and Performance: Theatre, Poetry and Song in Southern Africa*. Johannesburg: Witwatersrand University Press.

Gyekye, Kwame. 1997. *Tradition and Modernity: Philosophical Reflections on the African Experience*. Oxford: Oxford University Press.

Haeri, Shahla. 1989. *Law of Desire: Temporary Marriage in Shi'I Iran*. Syracuse, N.Y.: Syracuse University Press.

Hale, Thomas. 1998. *Griots and Griottes: Masters of Words and Music*. Bloomington: Indiana University Press.

Hall, Stuart. 1980. "Encoding/Decoding." In *Culture, Media and Language*, ed. Stuart Hall, et al., 128–39. London: Hutchinson.

Hamani, Abdou. 2000. *Les femmes et la politique au Niger*. Niamey, Niger: Edition Démocratie.

Hamani, Djibo. 1989. *Au carrefour du Soudan et de la Berbérie: Le sultanat Toureg de l'Ayar*. Etudes Nigériennes 55. Niamey, Niger: Institut de Recherche en Sciences Humaines (IRSH).

Haviland, Virginia. 1966. *Favorite Fairy Tales Told in Czechoslovakia*. Boston: Little, Brown.

Heath, Shirley B. 1983. *Ways with Words: Language, Life, and Work in Communities and Classrooms*. Cambridge: Cambridge University Press.

Hirsch, Susan F. 1998. *Pronouncing and Preserving: Gender and the Discourses of Disputing in an African Islamic Court*. Chicago: University of Chicago Press.

Hiskett, Mervyn. 1984. *The Development of Islam in West Africa*. New York: Longman.

Holland, Dorothy, William Lachicotte Jr., Debra Skinner, and Carole Cain. 1998. *Identity and Agency in Cultural Worlds*. Cambridge, Mass.: Harvard University Press.

Horowitz, Donald. 1985. *Ethnic Groups in Conflict*. Berkeley: University of California Press.

Hunwick, John. 1985. "Songhay, Borno and the Hausa States, 1450–1600." In *History of West Africa*. ed. J. F. A. Ajayi and Michael Crowder, 1: 323–71. New York: Longman.

———. 1997. "Sub-Saharan Africa and the Wider World of Islam." In *African Islam and Islam in Africa: Encounters between Sufis and Islamists*, ed. David Westerlund and Eva Evers Rosander, 28–54. Athens: Ohio University Press.

Hunwick, John, and R. O'Fahey, eds. 1995. *The Arabic Literature of Africa: The Writings of Western Sudanic Africa*. Leiden: E. J. Brill.

Hunwick, John, and Troutt Powell, eds. 2002. *The African Diaspora in the Mediterranean Lands of Islam*. Princeton: Marcus Wienner Publisher.

Huston, Alaine S. 1997. "We Are Many: Sufis and Islamic Scholars in Twentieth Century Kano, Nigeria." PhD diss., Indiana University.

———. 1999. "The Development of Women's Authority in the Kano Tijaniyya, 1874–1963." *Africa Today* 46 (Summer-Autumn): 42–64.

Ibrahim, Jibril, and Abdoulaye Niandou Souley. 1996. "The Rise to Power of an Opposition Party the MNSD in Niger Republic" *POLITEIA* 15 (3): http://www.unisa.ac.za.

Imam, Ayesha. 1991. "Ideology, the Mass Media, and Women: A Study from Radio Kaduna, Nigeria." In *Hausa Women in the Twentieth Century*, ed. Catherine Coles and Beverly Mack, 244–52. Madison: University of Wisconsin Press.

Imam, Ayesha, Amina Mama, and Fatou Sow, eds. 1997. *Engendering African Social Sciences*. Dakar: CODESRIA.

Inden, B. Roland. 1993. *Imagining India*. Oxford: Blackwell.

Ivy, Marilyn. 1995. *Discourses of the Vanishing: Modernity, Phantasm, Japan*. Chicago: University of Chicago Press.

Kanafani, Fay Afaf. 1999. *Nadia, Captive of Hope: Memoir of an Arab Woman*. New York: Armonk, M. E. Sharpe.

Kanda, Siptey, and M. Abdou Galadima. 1992. "Les Nigériens chrétiens de l'Église Catholique et L'Eglise Évangelique de la République du Niger: 'Débat sur la laicité de l'Etat: les réactions de l'Église.'" *Le Démocrate* Sept. 28.

Kane, Ousmane. 2003. *Muslim Modernity in Postcolonial Nigeria: A Study of the Society for the Removal of Innovation and Reinstatement of Tradition*. Boston: Brill.

Kane, Sheikh Hamidou. 1963. *Ambiguous Adventure*. London: Heinneman.

Karimou, Mahamane. 1977. *Les Mawri zarmaphones*. Niamey, Niger: Institut de Recherche en Sciences Humaines.

Kaziende, Hélène. 1992. "Le déserteur" [The desertor]. In *Kilomètre 30. Afrique: 30 ans d'indépendance* [Kilometre 30. Africa: 30 years of independence], 81–86. Saint-Maur: SEPIA.

Kimba, Idrissa, 1997. "Ethnicité, politique et démocratie au Niger." *Sociétés Africaines et Diaspora* 5 (1): 45–71.

The Koran. 1994. Translation from Arabic by J. M. Rodwell. Rutland: Everyman Library.

Kress, Gunther R. 1997. *Before Writing: Rethinking the Paths to Literacy*. New York: Routledge.

Lal, Jayati. 1999. "Situating Locations: The Politics of Self, Identity and 'Other' in Living and Writing the Texts." In *Feminist Approaches to Theory and Methodology: An Interdisciplinary Reader*, ed. Sharlene Hesse-Biber, Christina Gilmartin, and Robin Lydenberg, 100–137. Oxford: Oxford University Press. This article also appeared in *Feminist Dilemmas in Fieldwork*, ed. Diane L. Wolf, 185–214 (Boulder, Colo.: Westview Press, 1996).

Lanehart, Sonja L. 2002. *Sista, Speak! Black Women Kinfolk Talk about Language and Literacy*. Austin: University of Texas Press. 2002.

Larrier, Renée. 2000. *Francophone Women Writers of Africa and the Caribbean*. Gainesville: University of Florida Press.

Larson, Charles R., ed. 1997. *Under African Skies: Modern African Stories*. New York: Noonday Press.

Lazreg, Marnia. 1994. *The Eloquence of Silence*. New York: Routledge.

———. 2001. "Feminism and Difference: The Perils of Writing as a Woman on Woman in Algeria." In *Theorizing Feminism: Parallel Trends in the Humanities and Social Sciences*, ed. Anne C. Herrmann and Abigail J. Stewart, 321–44. Boulder, Colo.: Westview Press.

LeBlanc, Marie Nathalie. 1999. "The Production of Islamic Identities through Knowledge Claims in Bouake, Côte D'Ivoire." *African Affairs* 98 (393): 485–508.

Levine, K. 1986. *The Social Context of Literacy*. New York: Routledge and Kegan Paul.

Lionnet, Francoise. 1996. "'Logiques métisses': Cultural Appropriation and Postcolonial Representations." In *Postcolonial Subjects: Francophone Women Writers*, ed. Mary Jean Green, et al., 321–43. Minneapolis: University of Minnesota Press.

Mack, Beverly. 2004. "Muslim Women's Educational Activities in the Maghreb: Investigating and Redefining Scholarship in Morocco and Northern Nigeria." *The Maghreb Review*.

Mack, Beverly B., and Jean Boyd. 2000. *One Woman's Jihad: Nana Asma'u, Scholar and Scribe*. Bloomington: Indiana University Press.

MacLeod, Elowe Arlene. 2001. "Hegemonic Relations and Gender Resistance: The New Veiling as Accommodating Protest in Cairo." In *Theorizing Feminism: Parallel Trends in the Humanities and Social Sciences*, ed. Anne C. Herrmann and Abigail J. Stewart, 387–412. Boulder, Colo.: Westview Press.

Mahamane, Azara. 1998. "Contribution à la conférence sur les femmes dans la période de reconstruction de l'après-guerre en Afrique de l'Ouest." *Bulletin of Africa Concerned Scholar: Women and War* 55: 52–56.

Mahmood, Saba. 2001. "Feminist Theory, Embodiment, and the Docile Agent: Some Reflection on the Egyptian Islamic Revival." *Cultural Anthropology* 16 (2): 202–36.

Maiga, Amsou. 2000. *Unveiling Traditions: Postcolonial Islam in a Polycentric World.* Durham, N.C.: Duke University Press.

———. 2001. *Analyse de la situation actuelle de la femme au Niger.* Niamey, Niger: Direction de la Promotion de la Femme, CEDID-ORSTOM. 11–29.

Majid, Anouar. 2000. *Unveiling Traditions: Postcolonial Islam in a Polycentric World.* Durham, N.C.: Duke University Press.

Malam Adji, Souley. 1991. "Logiques socio-communautaire et loyautés politiques en Afrique: essai d'analyse de la construction de l'Etat au Niger." Ph.D. thesis, Bordeaux II.

Manh Kah, Dang. 1979. *In the Land of Small Dragon: A Vietnamese Folktale.* Told by Dang Manh Kah Nolan Ann Clark, illustrated by Tony Chen. New York: Viking.

Masquelier, Adeline Marie. 2001. *Prayer Has Spoiled Everything: Possession, Power, and Identity in an Islamic Town of Niger (Body, Commodity, Text).* Durham, N.C.: Duke University Press.

Mbembe, Achille. 2001. *On the Postcolony.* Berkeley: University of California Press.

Mernissi, Fatima. 1987a. *Women's Daily Battle.* London: Zed Books.

———. 1987b. *Beyond the Veil: Male-Female Dynamics in Modern Muslim Society.* Bloomington: Indiana University Press.

———. 1994. *Dreams of Trespass: Tales of a Harem Girlhood.* New York: Addison-Wesley.

———. 1996. *Women's Rebellion and Islamic Memory.* London: Zed Books.

Meunier, Olivier. 1997. *Dynamique de l'enseignement Islamique au Niger: Le cas de la Ville de Maradi.* Paris: L'Harmattan.

———. 2000. *Bilan d'un siècle de politique éducative au Niger.* Paris: L'Harmattan.

Mies, Maria. 1989. *Patriarchy and Accumulation on a World Scale.* London: Zed Books.

Miles, William F. S. 1994. *Hausaland Divided: Colonialism and Independence in Nigeria and Niger.* The Wilder House Series in Politics, History, and Culture. Ithaca, N.Y.: Cornell University Press.

Mindaoudou, Aichatou. 1995. "Full Participation of Niger's Women (editorial)." In *Niger Women: Myth and Reality,* 9–10. Niamey, Niger: Ministry of Social Development, Population and Women Advancement.

Ministry of Education and Research. 1997a. *Atelier de Restitution du Projet de Politique Educative du Niger. (Report).* Niamey, 15–19 December 1997.

———. 1997b. *Report.*

———. 2001. *Report on Medersa in Niger.*

———. 2002. *Report on Medersa in Niger.*

Ministry of Social Development, Population and Women Advancement (NIGER). 1995. *Niger Women: Myth and Reality.* Niamey, Niger: Ministry of Social Development, Population and Women Advancement.

Mirza, Sarah, and Magaret Strobel. 1989. *Three Swahili Women.* Bloomington: Indiana University Press.

Mohanty, Chandra. 1991. "Catographies of Struggles: Third World Women and the Politics of Feminisms." In *Third World Women and the Politics of Feminism,* ed. Chandra Mohanty, 1–47. Bloomington: Indiana University Press.

Moore, Henrietta. 1994. *A Passion for Difference*. Bloomington: Indiana University Press.

Moumouni, Abdou. 1968. *Education in Africa*. New York: Praeger.

Moumouni, Seyni. 2002. "Actualité du Cheikh 'Uthman dan Fodiyo (1754–1817): un héritage Convoité." In *L' Afrique Politique 200: Islams d'Afrique entre le Local et le Global*, 111–20. Paris: Katharla.

Mounkaila, Fatouma. 1995. "Female Condition of Niger Women: Between Myth and Reality." In *Niger Women: Myth and Reality*, 23–26. Niamey, Niger: Ministry of Social Development, Population and Women Advancement.

Moussa-Aghali, Fatimane. 2000. *Yarintata*. Niamey, Niger: Edition Albasa/GTZ-2PEB/Ministère de l'éducation Nationale.

Mphande, Lupenga. 1996. "Dr. Hastings Kamuzu Banda and the Malawi Writers Group: The (un)Making of a Cultural Tradition." *Research in African Literatures* 27 (1): 80–101.

Ngugi Wa Thiong'o. 1998. *Penpoints, Gunpoints and Dreams: Towards a Critical Theory of the Arts and the State in Africa*. Oxford: Clarendon Press.

Nicolaisen, Johannes, and Ida Nicolaisen. *The Pastoral Tuareg: Ecology, Culture and Society*. New York: Rhodos International Science and Art Publishers.

Ong, Aihwa. 1990. "State versus Islam: Malay Families, Women's Bodies, and the Body Politic in Malaysia." *American Ethnologist* 17 (2): 258–76.

———. 1992. "Rethinking Modernity: Space and Factory Discipline in China." *Cultural Anthropology* 7 (1): 93–114.

———. 1997. "Chinese Modernities: Narratives of Nation and Capitalism." In *Ungrounded Empires: The Cultural Politics of Modern Chinese Transnationalism*, ed. Aihwa Ong and Donald Nonii, 171–202. New York: Routledge.

Onyefulu, Obi. 1994. *Chinye: A West African Tale*. New York: Viking.

Oppong, Christine. 1981. *Middle Class African Marriages: A Family Study of Ghanaian Senior Civil Servants*. Cambridge: Cambridge University Press.

Oyewùmí, Oyèrónké, ed. 2003. *African Women and Feminism: Reflecting on the Politics of Sisterhood*. Trenton, N.J.: Africa World Press.

Pigg, Stacy Leigh. 1996. "The Credible and the Credulous: The Question of Villagers' Beliefs in Nepal." *Cultural Anthropology* 11 (2): 160–201.

Quayson, Ato. 2000. *Postcolonialism: Theory, Practice or Process?* Cambridge: Polity Press.

Reichmuth, Stephan. 1993. "Islamic Learning and Its Interaction with 'Western' Education in Ilorin, Nigeria." In *Muslim Identity and Social Change in Sub-Saharan Africa*, ed. Louis Brenner, 179–97. Bloomington: Indiana University Press, 1993.

Reilly, Benjamin. 2001. *Democracy in Divided Societies: Electoral Engineering for Conflict Management*. Cambridge: Cambridge University Press.

Reynolds, Eileen M. 1997. "The Democratic Transition in Niger (1991–1996): Women Leaders Theories and Organizational Strategies for the Empowerment of Women." M.A. thesis, Clark University.

Rinehart, Jane. 1994. "Roaming in the Margins, Speaking with Broken Tongues." *Frontiers* 14 (3): 19–48.

Robinson, Pearl. 1994. "The National Conference Phenomenon in Francophone Africa." *Comparative Studies in Society and History* 36 (3): 575–610.

Rofel, Lisa. 1999. *Other Modernities: Gendered Yearnings in China after Socialism.* Berkeley: University of California Press.

Royster, Jacqueline Jones. 2000. *Traces of a Stream: Literacy and Social Change among African American Women.* Pittsburgh: University of Pittsburgh Press.

Rustin, J. D. 1995. *The Multicultural Cinderella.* Oakland, Calif.: Rusting Educational Services.

Sadiqi, Fatima. 2003. *Women, Gender and Language.* Boston: Brill.

Salifou, André. 1993. *La question Touarègue au Niger.* Paris: Karthala.

Schein, Louisa. 1999. "Performing Modernity." *Cultural Anthropology* 14 (3): 361–95.

Schön, J. F. [1886] 1971. *Maganar Hausa.* Nelden: Kraus.

Scribner, Sylvia, and Michael Cole. 1988. "Unpackaging Literacy." In *Perspectives in Literacy,* ed. Eugene R. Kintgen, Barry M. Knoll, and Mike Rose, 57–70. Carbondale: Southern Illinois University Press.

Sidikou, Aissata. 2001. *Recreating Words, Reshaping Worlds: The Verbal Art of Women from Niger, Mali and Senegal.* Trenton, N.J.: Africa World Press.

Simone, T. Abdou Maliqalim. 1994. *In Whose Image? Political Islam and Urban Practices in Sudan.* Chicago: University of Chicago Press.

Sittirak, Sinith. 1998. *Daughters of Development: Women and the Changing Environment.* London: Zed Books.

Skinner, Neil. 1968. *Hausa Readings: Selections from Edgar's Tatsuniyoyi.* Madison: University of Wisconsin Press.

———. 1969. *Hausa Tales and Traditions,* Vol. 1. London: Cass.

———. 1977. *Hausa Tales and Traditions.* Vols. 2–3. Madison: University of Wisconsin Press.

———. 1980. *An Anthology of Hausa Literature.* Zaria: Northern Nigeria Publishing Company.

Smith, Valerie. 1997. *Not Just Race, but Gender and Class.* New York: Routledge.

Smock, Audrey Chapman. 1981. *Women's Education in Developing Countries: Opportunities and Outcomes.* New York: Praeger.

Snipe, Tracy. 1998. *Arts and Politics in Senegal, 1960–1996.* Trenton, N.J.: Africa World Press.

Sow, Fatou. 1997. "The Social Sciences in Africa and Gender Analysis." In *Engendering African Social Sciences,* ed. Ayesha M. Imam, Amina Mama, and Fatou Sow, 31–60. Dakar: CODESRIA.

Sparr, Pamela, ed. 1994. *Mortgaging Women's Lives: Feminist Critique of Structural Adjustment.* London: Zed Books.

Spivak, Gayatri Chakravorty. 1995. "Can the Subaltern Speak?" In *The Post-colonial Studies Reader,* ed. Bill Aschcroft, Gareth Griffiths, and Helen Tiffin. New York: Routledge.

Starratt, Priscilla. 1993. "Oral History in Muslim Africa: Al-Maghili Legends in Kano." PhD diss., University of Michigan.

———. 1996. "Islamic Influences on Oral Traditions in Hausa Literature." *The Marabout and the Muse: New Approaches to Islam in African Literature,* ed. Kenneth W. Harrow, 159–75. Portsmouth: Heinemann.

Stephens, Connie. 1981. "The Relationship of Social Symbols and Narrative

Metaphor: A Study of Fantasy and Disguise in the Hausa Tatsuniya of Niger." PhD diss., University of Wisconsin.

———. 1991. "Marriage in the Hausa Tatsuniya Tradition: A Cultural and Cosmic Balance." In *Hausa Women in the Twentieth Century*, ed. Catherine Coles and Beverly Mack, 221–31. Madison: University of Wisconsin Press.

Street, Brian V. 1984. *Literacy in Theory and Practice*. Cambridge: Cambridge University Press.

———. 1993. *Cross-Cultural Approaches to Literacy*. Cambridge: Cambridge University Press.

———. 1995. *Social Literacies: Critical Approaches to Literacy in Development, Ethnography and Education*. New York: Longman.

———. 2001. *Literacy and Development: Ethnographic Perspectives*. New York: Routledge.

Strobel, Margaret.1979. *Muslim Women in Mombasa, 1890–1975*. New Haven: Yale University Press.

Sule, Balaraba B. M., and Priscilla E. Starratt. "Islamic Leadership Positions for Women in Contemporary Kano Society." In *Hausa Women in the Twentieth Century*, ed. Catherine Coles and Beverly Mack, 29 –49. Madison: University of Wisconsin Press.

Tamari, Tal. 1996. "Mali, l'Exégèse Coranique en Milieu Mandingue." *Islam and Sociétés au sud du Sahara* 10: 43 –79.

Tannen, Deborah, ed. 1982. *Spoken and Written Language: Exploring Orality and Literacy*. Norwood, N.J.: Ablex.

———. 1994. *Gender and Discourse*. Oxford: Oxford University Press.

Trevor, Jean. 1975. "Western Education and Muslim Fulani/Hausa Women in Sokoto, Northern Nigeria." In *Conflict and Harmony in Education in Tropical Africa*, ed. G. N. Brown and M. Hiskett, 247 –70. London: Geoge Allen and Unwin.

Umar, S. Muhammad. 1993. "Changing Islamic Identity in Nigeria from the 1960s to the 1980s: From Sufism to Anti-Sufism." In *Muslim Identity and Social Change in Sub-Saharan Africa*, ed. Louis Brenner, 154 –78. London: Hurst and Company.

———. 2001. "Education and Islamic Trends in Northern Nigeria: 1970–1990s." *Africa Today* 49: 127 –50.

———. 2004. "Profiles of New Islamic Schools in Northern Nigeria." UCLA Fellows Paper.

UNICEF-Niger. 1994. *Analyse de la situation des femmes et des enfants au Niger*. Niamey, Niger.

Villalon, Leonardo. 1994. "Democratization, Westernization, and Human Rights: The Debate over the Family Code in Niger's Transition to Democracy." Paper presented at the Canadian Association of African Studies, Toronto.

Watts, J. Michael. 1996. "Islamic Modernities? Citizenship, Civil Society and Islamism in a Nigerian City." *Public Culture* 8 (2): 251–90.

Weinstein, B. 1976. "Francophonie, a Language-Based Movement in World Politics." *Internationational Organization* 30 (3): 485 –507.

White-Kaba, Mary, and Hassana Alidou. 1994. *The Situation of Nigerian Women*. Niamey, Niger: GTZ and World Bank Unpublished Report.

Wilks, I. 1968. "The Transmission of Islamic Learning in the Western Sudan." In *Literacy in Traditional Societies,* ed. Jack Goody, 162–97. Cambridge: Cambridge University Press.

Yamba, Bawa. 1995. *Permanent Pilgrims: The Role of Pilgrimage in the Lives of West African Muslims in Sudan.* Edinburgh: Edinburgh University Press for International African Institute.

Yusif, Al Khalifa (AB). 1988. "The Development of Islamic Education in Africa." *Bulletin on Islam and Christian-Muslim Relations in Africa* 6 (Oct.): 12–18.

Zakaria, Fouad. 1988. "The Standpoint of Contemporary Muslim Fundamentalists." In *Women of the Arab World,* ed. Nadia Toubia, 27–35. London: Zed.

Index

WOMEN IN AFRICA AND THE DIASPORA

Engaging Modernity: Muslim Women and the Politics of Agency in Postcolonial Niger
Ousseina D. Alidou

Tired of Weeping: Mother Love, Child Death, and Poverty in Guinea-Bissau
Jónína Einarsdóttir

Surviving the Slaughter: The Ordeal of a Rwandan Refugee in Zaire
Marie Béatrice Umutesi
Translated by Julia Emerson